DREAM ON AND MAKE IT HAPPEN

CAROLINA LUIZA RIEDEL

Copyright © 2025 by Carolina Luiza Riedel

Originally published 2024.

All rights reserved. No part of this book may be reproduced in any form or by any electronic or mechanical means, including information storage and retrieval systems - other than "fair use" as brief quotations embodied in articles and reviews - without written permission from the author.

Any information given in this book is solely based on the author's experience. In the event you use any of it for yourself, the author assumes no responsibility for your actions.

For privacy reasons, some names, locations, and dates may have been changed.

Contact: carol@carolriedel.com

Book cover photography: Carolina Luiza Riedel (carolriedel.com)

Editing and formatting: Quinton Li (quintonli.com)

Paperback ISBN: 978-1-7638072-4-2

Ebook ISBN: 978-1-7638072-1-1

2nd edition, October 2025

*To all the people in my family
who forgot to dream.*

CONTENTS

1. Living is better than dreaming.   1
2. Little girl, big dreams.   3
3. The other side of the world.   6
4. It's a new day, it's a new life.   10
5. Just another new kid on a different block.   17
6. To be or to be-long? What a beautiful question!   22
7. Redefining Brazilian.   28
8. Chasing sunsets.   32
9. The Backstory. (Here it is)   41
10. I wanna rock and roll all night and work every day.   53
11. Satisfying my soul.   57
12. Making it happen.   64
13. An open road.   67
14. Living history.   82
15. What are we made of?   91
16. A clean slate.   100
17. Landing my first job.   106
18. Finally home.   112
19. Going with the flow.   117
20. You live, you learn.   126
21. Digging deeper.   134
22. Energy matters.   140
23. Welcome to the good life.   144
24. Feeling the energy.   155
25. Patterns?   164
26. Trusting the unknown.   170
27. What if it all works out?   183
28. Counting down.   190
29. A real-life adventure.   194
30. Day 1.   198
31. Day 2.   203

32. The world (really) is a small town.	206
33. Work hard, play hard.	208
34. A new state of mind.	217
35. You got me in love again.	231
36. A little crack in time.	237
37. Every end is a new beginning.	246
38. Girls don't just wanna have fun. They want (and deserve) respect.	255
39. The (im)permanence of things (and people).	265
40. Work hard(er), play hard(er).	275
41. When in Paris.	285
42. London calling.	300
43. Hola, Barcelona!	309
44. A little Brazilian surprise.	317
45. The nature of the unexplainable.	322
46. Back on the Aussie side.	327
47. Redefining love.	330
48. What are we living for?	335
49. Reality check.	342
50. Finding Mr. Right.	348
51. Big dreams, big moves.	352
52. You may say I'm a dreamer, but I'm not the only one.	356
Bibliography	361
Acknowledgements	365
About the author	369

1. LIVING IS BETTER THAN DREAMING.

I'm inspired by the human experience.

I love stories. I read people all the time — literally and intuitively. It fuels me. And it keeps me alive.

I'm in awe at the courage some individuals have to register their most vulnerable experiences in writing to help advance humanity even after they're gone.

In my dreams, I saw myself as one of them.

But my mind is so complex that I even have trouble navigating it. That's why I write. To make sense of myself in a more clear and articulate way. When I read my life, somehow it all fits together.

I was given a very wise piece of advice by poetry writer "butterflies rising" in her book "wild spirit, soft heart":

"Write it out until what hurt you heals."

That was powerful. I knew it was time to let my words bleed while celebrating my scars.

Acceptance is a gift. It is what it is. I take it. The good, the bad, and everything in between. It made me who I am.

Thank you, life. For giving me exactly what I needed for my growth.

Brené Brown once said: *"We own our story or it owns us."*

That really hit home. And I decided to own mine.

This is my first book. A very personal memoir about the young, brave and somewhat naive girl I used to be twenty years ago. A girl who believed in love over fear — and in herself above all else.

They may say I'm a dreamer, but I know I'm not the only one.

Experience has shown me: *dreams do come true.*

So, I urge you to keep dreaming. Big and bold. Then do something about it.

You may be the only person standing between you and your dream. Try getting out of your own way and watch what happens.

2. LITTLE GIRL, BIG DREAMS.

I'm an 80s kid. I played on the streets until late at night. Hide and seek, ball games, tree climbing, mountain climbing. You name it. I've had what can be called a very "wild" childhood. I literally danced like nobody was watching, because most of the time, let's be real here, they weren't. They were busy. Still, I entertained myself as much as I could — and I suspect this is how I turned out to be so independent.

I know it sounds old-fashioned, but I miss those times. Everything was so real. The joy, the pain, the freedom, the boredom. We felt it through our skin and bones. No escape. We just had to be. Whoever we were.

So, I grew out of that and into my teens. And let me tell you, that was an even wilder ride. From the countless parties I found myself in, all I remember is that I kept dancing. That's when people started to watch and, sometimes, they made me feel uncomfortable.

I don't know who I would be without music. I still sing from the top of my lungs all of the words that shaped my take on life — and probably inspired most of my writing. You'll notice that I quote a lot of songs in this book. I borrowed from Austin Kleon's book this interesting concept *"Steal like an artist"* — and credit where credit is due.

After all, we are an amalgamation of the things that inspire our lives. Each one of us compiles different references for different reasons to create different stories.

In my case, I was always inspired by music. It was the first art form that I truly got — and mostly danced to (way before the existence of TikTok).

I have this insatiable curiosity for what goes through everyone's minds. That's why I'm really into lyrics. I pay very close attention to them. It's poetry in motion.

I must admit that, as a Brazilian born and Portuguese native speaker, I was lucky to have a father who made me study English early in life. Having a second language opened up my world from the age of seven, which I highly recommend to anyone. It presented culture to me as this ever changing, underlying thread of combined behaviors from many places.

We are all one. In many different ways.

Dave Grohl, from the Foo Fighters, once brilliantly articulated this idea in an interview. He said:

> *"The luxury of my life is that I can sit down with an instrument and write a song and then go out and play in front of a bunch of people and they sing it with me."*

But the best part is this:

> *"It could be 50,000 people singing the same lyric, for 50,000 different reasons. Because that lyric means something specific to them. They are not singing it for my reasons, they are singing it for their reasons."*

This is so true of anything we create. People will interpret it for their reasons. We must do it for ours.

So, when it came to writing, I was a bit like Sinatra. I just wanted to do it "my way".

As a little girl with big dreams, I wanted to know more, see more, do more, be more. My dream was to get out of my own bubble and burst my most wild thoughts into solid vivid colors. I wanted to make life happen. Big, bold and beautiful.

And, in my early twenties, I finally did. After meeting a stranger on a random night, I learned about this country called Australia.

It was 2004. Daniel was the guy who told me everything I never knew about the land down under *"where women glow and men plunder"* as I learned through the Men at Work (an amazing Australian rock band from the late 70s, in case you didn't know).

Up until then, I never personally met anyone who lived on the other side of the world. Let alone for six years. Don't worry, the full backstory is in this book, just read on.

But, for now, all you need to know is this: I had a dream to live overseas and had no idea how to make it happen. Daniel was this person who literally helped me to paint a full picture of what that dream could look like. In Real Life (IRL as they say these days).

I don't know about you, but I learn through experience. So here are the memories I have from making that big dream come true.

I hope you enjoy reading it as much as I did writing it.

3. THE OTHER SIDE OF THE WORLD.

March 2005, Western Australia.

"Welcome to Perth," a middle-aged man greeted me, holding a small sign that read: Carolina Luiza Riedel.

Two oceans apart from everything I knew, it suddenly hit me: I made it.

I was on the other side of the world, completely alone. I didn't know if I was excited or terrified, but I chose to own my decision.

From that moment on, my life was in my hands. I was 22 years old.

The man showed me the way out of the airport. We arrived at a relatively empty car park. A van was waiting for us. I jumped in, greeted my fellow international students and sat by the window. All I could hear was my silence.

Outside, a completely foreign landscape overwhelmed my external senses and unveiled an entirely new world. Inside, an avalanche of thoughts threatened my idea of self and questioned how that next chapter of my life would unfold.

I had surrendered to the great unknown.

"Carolina, here we are," the driver announced, while I was still trying to fully land in the new country.

Maylands, my homestay neighborhood, was just a 10-minute drive from the airport. I was the first drop-off.

I quickly jumped out of the van and grabbed my luggage. Two suitcases and a backpack. I looked at them and the first thing that came to mind was "*can life really be that simple?*"

We entered this residential complex with identical townhouses. At one of those doors, I met my hosts.

"Welcome, Carolina," Yoko kindly greeted me while Flynn picked up my luggage.

"Thank you very much. I'm happy to be here."

"Come in, let me show you your room." She walked and talked at the same time.

I smiled, relieved, while I followed her in.

Flynn was from New Zealand. Yoko was Japanese. I soon realized there were no rules for "a typical Australian family". They could come from anywhere in the world.

I instantly felt at home.

My new room was perfectly designed to fit a single bed, a double-door wardrobe and a small desk. Sunlight streamed in through the floor-to-ceiling window, making it bright and peaceful. I had a private little heaven.

It took me almost 40 hours to get there. I was exhausted, in need of some grounding.

First things first: a shower. Under the water, I watched all my racing thoughts go down the drain, one by one. After just a few minutes, my body and soul were realigned.

"Everything is going to be alright," I kept telling myself. I knew it was just a matter of time.

Next, food. In my clean clothes, I joined my new family for our first dinner.

"How are you feeling, Carolina?" Flynn started a conversation.

"Much better now."

"You'll be alright," he said, almost as if reading my thoughts.

I started to observe my new family dynamics. Two little boys were playing on the floor. Kenji was five years old and Ben just two. I was amused by their natural ability to just be. Kids have so much to teach us if we let them.

Yoko, who was busy cooking, made an announcement in a delightful Japanese accent, "Dinner is served, guys."

"Wow, this is delicious, Yoko! What is it?" I asked, curious about the new dish.

"Yakimeshi. It's a Japanese fried rice that comes together in minutes from just a handful of simple ingredients. Nothing fancy."

"I love simple. Simple is beautiful."

Slowly, my body and mind met in the same place. I felt present.

"So, what are your plans for the weekend, Carolina?" Flynn curiously asked.

"Not sure, but I'd like to go to the beach. How far is it?"

"It's probably about 45 to 50 minutes. You'll need to take a bus and a train," he explained.

"I thought we were closer," I said, slightly surprised.

"We are very close to your school, Carolina. It's less than ten minutes by bus. The idea is to make it easy for you to commute every day."

"It makes sense."

"Remember that you will be studying full-time."

"I know. I'll keep that in mind."

As we finished dinner, I offered to help with the dishes. And I learned a new way of doing the job. Yoko showed me how to rinse them in a full tub, instead of using running water straight from the tap. I thought it was interesting.

"Thank you for dinner, Yoko. I wish I could stay longer but I really need to sleep," I said, struggling to keep my eyes open.

"Of course, you must be exhausted."

"I am. Goodnight, everyone. See you tomorrow."

I went to my room and as I laid in bed, my mind went wild.

I did my research. Perth has amazing beaches. Why am I not close to them?

I'm a beachside girl. I need to do something about this.

I tried to pay attention to my inner self-talk but, thankfully, my body quickly shut itself down and put me to sleep.

4. IT'S A NEW DAY, IT'S A NEW LIFE.

"Good morning Flynn! How are you?" I asked as I entered the kitchen.

"I'm great, Carolina. How are you?"

"I'm hungry."

"You must be. You slept for almost 30 hours straight. It's past dinner time. We checked on you a few times. You were breathing. You seemed fine so we didn't wake you up."

"Oh, really? How embarrassing! I didn't realise I slept for that long."

"Don't be, it's ok. The jet lag from Brazil must be brutal. We're 11 hours ahead and your body requires a bit of time to get used to the change. We left some food for you in the kitchen. Help yourself."

"Thank you, Flynn. That's so nice of you."

"You're lucky, tomorrow is a public holiday. You have some extra time to recover before school starts."

"True. What can I do to get out of the house?"

"You could go to the city. Shops will be closed but you can walk around and get familiar with the surroundings. It's probably a good idea. I can drop you off at the train station, you'll be there in less than five minutes."

"Oh, that sounds great! I'll do that then. Thank you, Flynn."

I ate the leftover dinner, had another shower and went back to my bedroom.

My mind started another little monologue:

Jet lag, what a trip! Never before, in my entire life, have I slept for 30 hours straight. Even my body is finding it hard to pick up the pace in this foreign land. I can't sleep for 30 hours again! It's not practical. I better adjust to this new life quickly or I'm screwed.

Flynn and Yoko were early birds, usually up at 6am. So, I set my alarm for 7am and slowly drifted into a peaceful sleep.

The next day, I woke up feeling a lot more like myself.

After the shower, I met everyone in the kitchen and we had a nice chat. I played with the kids for a while and sat with Flynn for a little induction.

He showed me how to get to the city and gave me some tips on places to visit. He also gave me timetables for buses and trains and highlighted a few things on the map to prevent me from getting lost.

After breakfast, Flynn drove me around the neighbourhood and stopped at the golf course to show me some beauty. Picture this: green grass meets a river and a modern skyline. All in one image. It was a breathtaking view. I realised how close we were to the city and a little smile took over my face.

He then drove to the train station and helped me to buy a public transport card.

"Here, you catch the 186 home. Ah, don't forget to look at the Sunday and public holidays timetable, okay? There are restricted times."

"Thank you, Flynn. I'll see you later."

"Stay safe."

The sound of the next train arriving created urgency. My little adventure was about to start and I was ready to jump in.

Everything moved so fast that I could hardly process it. The woman on the speakers kept us updated along the way. "This is Perth Station," she announced, followed by, "Doors open". Most people stepped off the train. Including myself.

I couldn't help but sing *"just a small town girl, livin' in a lonely world, she took the midnight train going anywhere"* from Journey's 1981 hit *"Don't stop believin'"*. Right on theme for a Brazilian Believer.

Coming from a small Brazilian town with less than 200,000 people, I literally stepped into a totally new world. Trains that ran all day, every day, every few minutes were not part of my life back home. I noticed the different train tracks, all meeting at Perth Station. It was amazing!

I started my walk towards the main streets, still getting used to how clean and organized everything was in this beautiful city made of modern and old buildings, large department stores and random parks and squares.

With a population of 1.5 million, Perth felt like a huge metropolis to me. It was overwhelming, but in a good way.

I kept walking. That simple action brought me closer to the world. I had no destination so I allowed my intuition to guide my steps. I paid close attention to where it was leading me.

After a while, my legs started to slow down. I looked around and noticed a public garden filled with benches and trees. The open gates felt like an invitation to a little empty haven where I could rest. It looked safe and peaceful.

I entered as if entering a sacred space and sat on one of the benches to pray. I acknowledged how blessed I was. I thanked God for that moment. It was the first time in a while that I was actually in my own company.

My quiet mind held space for clear reflections and divine intervention. Tears started rolling down my face. Not sure how one is able to feel so many emotions at once, but there I was. Processing joy, relief, anxiety, fear and happiness. All at the same time.

I didn't hold a single tear. I was crying my heart out.

As I opened my eyes, I noticed three girls coming my way. They looked familiar.

"Hey, are you Brazilian?" one of them asked.

"I am. Can you tell?"

"Yes, I guess we can recognise each other. My name is Fernanda. This is Mari and this is Cintia. Are you alone?"

"Yes."

"How long have you been here?"

"Two days. You?"

"Two years for me," said Fernanda.

"Wow, that's a very long time. Wanna sit?"

They sat down and started talking about their lives in Perth. I realized I was not alone. A lot of people were living their dreams too. For very different reasons.

Hearing their stories made me feel a lot better. They even mentioned this little Brazilian community in town who seemed to all know and support each other. I couldn't help but ask about the only person I knew: Daniel.

"Oh, do you know him?" Mari replied with a question.

"Yes, I met him last year while he was on holiday in Brazil. I was planning to go overseas for a year and he told me all about Perth. So, here I am. Following a stranger's advice," I said, laughing, while fully acknowledging my somewhat impulsive behavior.

A brief silence. They looked at each other, not knowing what to say. I knew something was coming.

"It was an accident. He hit a kangaroo. It happens here, it's like hitting a horse on a highway in Brazil. Those unpredictable things, you know?"

"What do you mean? I'm not following."

"Daniel didn't resist the crash. Everyone is devastated. It happened last week."

My heart skipped a beat. I couldn't process what I had just heard.

"Wait, this can't be happening. Can you tell me more about him?"

"Sure. He is from São Paulo and has been living here for many years..."

As they kept describing Daniel, I realised it was not the same person — they only had the same name. Still, I found it really hard to process that story. I never met this other Daniel who was no longer with us, but my heart felt deeply. I couldn't believe what happened to him.

It was impossible to imagine what his family would be going

through. Thinking about them reminded me of my own family and our distance.

I took a minute to breathe and think about everything. I wasn't sure I was equipped to handle all the emotions that were yet to come in this new phase of my life, but I didn't want to get ahead of myself either.

"Look, we know this is really sad. We're all grieving. But a lot of us are still heading to Margs in a couple of weeks. If you wanna go, this may be a good time. It's the Salomon Masters" Mari surprised me with her words.

"Yes, it's a surf competition. The qualifying series. WQS, you know? Neco Padaratz won last year so it's a big deal for us Brazilians" Cintia continued, excited.

"It's a three-hour drive. We already booked a little cottage. You can stay with us if you want. We have a spare bed," Fernanda casually extended me an invitation.

"Wow, it all sounds almost too good to be true. Were you God sent or something? Going to Margaret River is on my priority list. I just had no idea it could happen so soon. I literally got here yesterday."

"Right place, right time." — a cliché that never felt so right.

"Thank you for making me feel so welcome. You girls are really nice. Let me see how I can work this out. Can I get back to you during the week?"

"Sure, here's my number. You can call me if you need anything," Mari said smiling, handing me a little piece of paper.

I checked my watch. It was time to go.

"Wow, this was very special to me. Thank you again for everything, girls. I'll talk to you soon."

I gave them hugs and started my walk back to the city to catch the bus just outside the train station.

I sent my prayers to the young Brazilian I never had a chance to meet and his family. Then, I thanked God for giving me another chance to see Daniel again.

I jumped on an empty bus. I asked the driver if he could let me know when it was time for me to get off. I gave him my stop number. He pleasantly agreed and I sat nearby.

I let my mind flow freely. Brand new feelings started to emerge.

Stories give me hope. Somehow, they inspire me to believe in new things I never thought possible. Hearing a story about real people and their real experiences was like reality catching up with the million questions in my head and saying: *"There it is. Still doubt it?"*

Those girls were living in Perth for a while too. Meeting them felt like a sign. I couldn't explain exactly how much confidence I got from that simple moment, but I did. I was able to picture real opportunities for my life in this city after hearing their stories.

I truly believe *"chance encounters"* are blessings in disguise. They can profoundly impact our existence. Or, at the very least, give us a new perspective.

It suddenly hit me how interconnected we all are, and how *"magical"* things can actually happen if we surrender to trust.

As the bus approached the beautiful golf course, I knew I was almost home.

5. JUST ANOTHER NEW KID ON A DIFFERENT BLOCK.

First day of English school.

I felt exactly like a little child on the first day of kindergarten. Only without my mom to kiss me goodbye and say *"everything will be alright"*. It was hard.

The decision to live in Australia for a year was one-hundred-percent mine. I own it. Still, I felt my insecurities coming up. I had no choice but to embrace my inner-child and her special gift: curiosity.

I stepped into my childlike nature who had this intense desire to see, hear, learn and try new things. She had no awareness of fear. My inner-child loved to play too. And there we were, together, in this newly found playground we were about to explore.

Let's be honest: when you're 22, your whole life seems like an adventure. You don't have a lot of experience to assess your actions and how (il)logical they seem. It's a perfect place to be. You simply act on your desires, intuitively, from a place of pure love and faith — and hope for the best.

If you allow yourself to go with the flow, things tend to magically unfold. If you don't, you may have to live with the fact that you'll never go back to that place again and the possibilities you saw there may haunt you — sometimes, forever.

I didn't want to be haunted, so I took a chance. With both feet on the ground, I felt safe. I remembered why I was there. I wanted to grow. Just like this massive tree planted in the school yard where I was standing.

I heard the bell ringing. Introduction was about to start. We all headed towards the hall, right at the center of the school. The speech officially announced us as international students of English.

Coming from the most diverse countries and backgrounds, I soon realized that we all felt the same way. Each one of us was displaced from our own little worlds. Regardless of nationality, at this school, we were all equal. What united us was our interest in the "global" language and a desire to cross borders and open ourselves to new possibilities.

Learning English was a way to facilitate connections around the world and get rid of a lot of prejudices. Until that moment, I never realised how powerful a common language really was. And even though I had no idea what the next four months would do to me, I knew I was in the right place, at the right time. I just had to let things be.

As the speech ended and we started to move away from the hall, I saw this girl walking in front of me. Her long, dark hair, perfectly straight and shiny, combined with a cheerful and colourful outfit reminded me of home. I felt an instant connection. My internal voice whispered *"talk to her"*. And since I didn't know anyone, I decided to listen.

"Excuse me," I said, approaching the new girl.

"Hi." She smiled with her slightly Asian eyes, while everything else about her confirmed that she was also Brazilian.

"I'm Carolina, nice to meet you."

"Nice to meet you. I'm Paula."

Paula was from São Paulo and worked in advertising, just like me, but for very big agencies. She was only 24 and was already managing global clients. She explained the main reason for her being there: mandatory English. She needed to learn as quickly as possible to return to Brazil and work her way up the corporate ladder to even better positions. Her determination was contagious!

As I imagined her clear future, I started to reflect on my own. My plans were not so ambitious. In fact, I hadn't even made a concrete plan. I was there following my heart, remember?

I also had a pretty close relationship with English. My father always believed in a globalized world. His bet was a future where everyone would speak English, regardless of birth country. So, he enrolled me (and my brother) in English classes very early on (at the age of seven). As a result, I got along really well with the language.

Unlike hers, my clients were small, local businesses. They didn't have the English requirement. Most of them didn't speak the language themselves. The reality was: my father anticipated a very promising future for me and I still seemed to be a very long way from it.

The idea of moving to a big city like São Paulo to have the job opportunities she had sounded great on paper. I just wasn't sure that my beach girl nature could handle the pressure of a concrete jungle.

My dream was to live in a foreign country to immerse myself in a complete cultural experience. I was aware of the difference between functional and fluent. I wanted to be fluent. A fluency that could only be achieved by living and breathing the language, even if just for a short period of time.

Could my big dreams grow any bigger? Possibly.

The bell rang again and we all went to our classrooms. My brain made a quick switch. *"We're living in English now, Carolina. You got this."*

My previous knowledge didn't go unnoticed. At the end of my class, the teacher suggested that I retake the placement test so I could level up. I thanked him for being so kind.

On my way out, I bumped into Paula again and we exchanged phone numbers. Both of us had already managed to buy a little Nokia with an Australian SIM card. Prepaid, of course.

Without a full plan, I had taken a big step towards making one of my dreams come true.

On the bus back to my homestay, I opened my backpack and reached for my discman (yep, those were the times). I pressed play:

> *"In times like these*
>
> *And times like those*
>
> *What will be will be*
>
> *And so it goes*
>
> *And it always goes*
>
> *On and on and on and on and on*
>
> *On and on and on and on and on it goes"*

Jack Johnson, along with Ben Harper, Donavon Frankenreiter and Eagle Eye Cherry often kept me company. Their songs made me feel at home.

Santa Catarina is the state in Brazil where I come from. It's a very special place on Earth. A lot of people describe it as the *'Brazilian California'*, but I can't confirm. I still haven't been to California.

What I could tell was this: Australia was starting to feel a lot like home to me. Even Neco Padaratz (he's from Santa Catarina too) was making waves here, which reminded me of the surf competition down south.

I kept reflecting. *What if meeting those girls wasn't just a coincidence?*

I crossed the entire world to be here. I wanted to see Daniel again and he lived in Margaret River.

The WQS only happens once a year. I wasn't sure I'd be there for the next.

Yes, it was probably too soon for me to travel, and I had to be very wise with my budget. But, sometimes, not taking a risk is the riskier thing we can do.

I decided to trust my gut — and the Universe.

I was all in.

6. TO BE OR TO BELONG? WHAT A BEAUTIFUL QUESTION!

It felt like a lifetime, but it all happened in less than a week.

I was just starting to understand the real meaning of freedom and the intensity of my feelings. Away from family and everything familiar, I was the only responsible person for all my decisions. In my mind, anything was possible.

As optimistic as I may sound, there was another thing that undoubtedly lived inside me, something I'd rather leave unspoken: fear. There was this palpable fear of living in a different country. And even my fears were different.

In Brazil, I was afraid there was not enough room for my growth and evolution. In Australia, I feared not being able to manage this amount of possibility on my own.

While it was refreshing and exhilarating that, without the baggage of my past, I could be anyone I wanted to be, I also realised just how much of "me" was based on geographic location and what was known and familiar, and not necessarily my truth.

No matter where we come from, we all have webs of people, places and behaviours we keep going back to over and over again. Family, friends, jobs, habits — but, most of all, beliefs. And that does not necessarily have anything to do with the country you were born in.

It's very hard to leave those things behind, unless we get tired of the same answers, options and opinions. In that case, a great way to escape the program and wipe a clean slate is to go somewhere new.

Too many of us leave our home countries trying to escape ourselves, but we end up finding who we truly are. And that's exactly what I was doing.

I discovered that fear is actually courage making itself known. It doesn't disappear. We simply learn to live with it. So, the best way I found to overcome my fears was by being myself.

No matter where we come from, humans are natural storytellers. As I shared my story with whoever I met, I discovered that most people ended up feeling comfortable sharing theirs too. And I was fascinated by them.

It's comforting to have someone to share our personal experiences and to talk with about cultural differences, without judgement. This exchange helps us to learn from the experiences of others too. It may seem contradictory, but it's the difference that unites us.

I started to value differences more than ever. I realized that there was no single formula for living. Everyone *"made it"* in a different way.

If we are a reflection of our environment, when that changes, we change too. Different parts of our personalities come to life. We take on qualities, habits and opinions that reflect the new people surrounding our new life. Although scary, the unknown is a perfect place for our evolution. But there's a catch: the excess of possibilities can also have a paralyzing effect. *What to do next?*

That's when another undesired feeling emerged: *anxiety*. In the uncertainty of the future, I decided to surrender to the present. My focus was on making the necessary adjustments to feel somewhat safe and stable exactly where I was.

I don't know about you, but, for me, nothing beats a good old checklist. Here's the first one I made:

1. Master the nuances of the language (so I could call myself fluent)
2. Find a way to make a living (yes, I had bills to pay — and they came in local currency, so I had to earn that way too)
3. Make new friends (life is best shared anywhere in the world)

Now, let's be honest: when we're young, we have no idea when there's a serious transformation going on in our lives. All we know is that we're having fun. Or having a meltdown. There's nowhere in between.

And while all the shiny new things fascinate us, unconsciously, our minds keep asking this repeated question over and over: *"What am I missing back where I 'belong'?"*

That's why *"foreign"* bars are so popular. Just a few drinks and a warm, nostalgic chat can take us *"home"*. They are the perfect spots for releasing internal resistance.

Perth had a number of interesting bars and pubs for all nationalities. *"The Deen"* (a friendly nickname for The Aberdeen Hotel) was the place to be on Thursday nights. Guess why? They had a very famous Brazilian night.

It was only my first week, but I was known to never miss a little party. Everyone was talking about it at school and I was curious to check it out for myself, but unsure how to make it happen.

Angela, another Brazilian who was already living in Perth for a few months, was a big fan of the green and yellow party. She was in my class and we started talking:

"Come on, Carol. You should join us. It will be fun."

"I know. I want to. I'm just not sure how to make this work, Angela. My homestay parents are a little conservative. They have two kids and it's not ideal for me to arrive home late on a weeknight. Also, my last bus is at 10pm. There are no trains there. I don't think it's worth it. I'll miss the best part."

"Don't be silly, you can sleep at my place. I live very close. We can walk there."

"Really?"

"Really. We help each other here. That's how we roll, newbie."

"I can't say no to that, can I?"

"No. You're definitely coming with us."

As I got back to my homestay, I packed a backpack and told Flynn and Yoko that I was going to catch up with some friends in the city. I specifically told Yoko not to worry about my dinner or breakfast. I'd only come home the next day after school.

She understood and graciously gave me a couple of muesli bars to make sure I wouldn't starve. I guess that's what mums do.

Angela lived in a share-house in Northbridge with three other students. I caught the bus to her house and arrived there close to 7pm.

Unlike in Brazil, Australians go out early. Between 8 and 9pm. They do that because pretty much everything closes sharply at midnight. We had a couple of warm-up drinks and got going. It was literally a five-minute walk to the pub.

A line was forming as we arrived. Standing outside, I was struck by the architecture.

The Aberdeen Hotel was one of Perth's oldest hotels, built in 1884. Originally called the All Nations Hotel, it had a number of alterations over the years, eventually ending up as an amalgamation of three different buildings. The masonry arched colonnades from the ground to the first floor gave it an imponent look. It was a historical building. And it was huge!

As we entered, the atmosphere completely changed. Inside, funk beats, samba grooves and lots of people performing very cheesy dance moves gave me a whole new perspective of my new world. It was a wild party!

Until then, I wasn't much of a beer drinker. In the early 2000s, I was all about electronic music, vodka and energy drinks. That was *"the thing"* back home.

But, right there, I started changing.

The famous jugs were the cheapest option (even cheaper if you were Brazilian) so I surrendered. On a student budget, our main goal was to stretch every dollar and maximize our fun.

It didn't take us long until we hit the dance floor and unashamedly exposed our moves too. Literally *"dancing like nobody was watching"*. Or, if they were, we didn't know them. Or cared. It was so lame. And good.

It was the early years of a Brazilian band formed by three Australians (one, half Brazilian) and Léo, a full Brazilian who happened to be in the same school as me.

Super talented, they performed a fine selection of the best Brazilian music. Some real classics mixed with samba-rock, reggae and everything in between. They knew how to have fun and played whatever it took to get people dancing (and singing!) with them.

Like this all-time favorite, voted by the Brazilian edition of Rolling Stone as the fifth greatest Brazilian song:

"O ariá raió

Obá obá obá

*Mas que nada (*Yeah, right)

Sai da minha frente (Get out of my way)

Eu quero passar (I want to pass)

Pois o samba está animado (Because this samba is joyful)

O que eu quero é sambar (And I want to dance)"

"Mas, que nada!" (Portuguese pronunciation: [mas ki ˈnadɐ]) was written and originally performed in 1963 by Jorge Ben on his debut album "Samba Esquema Novo" (Samba's New Scheme), but became Sérgio Mendes' signature song in his 1966 cover version.

In 2005, it was still going strong — almost as this unofficial Brazilian anthem. Whenever and wherever it came on, crowds went wild. That night, I sang every word from the top of my lungs while shaking my fears off.

To my surprise, they pulled together this huge percussion set of loud, tight, Brazilian Carnival Drumming. It left me speechless! It was this authentic Brazilian experience I never had in my home country.

Ironically, I had to cross the whole world to reconnect with my Brazilian roots. Another side of my *"Brazilianess"* began to emerge. I liked it.

7. REDEFINING BRAZILIAN.

I had always lived in Brazil, but I was just learning about what was considered stereotypically Brazilian. Up until then, it never occurred to me that stereotypes could be so deceiving even for the ones facing them.

New parts of my culture were being revealed to me through my international experience and that was eye-opening.

I consciously put myself in this somewhat uncomfortable new situation to force me into a new phase of my life. I was ready for adulthood. I wanted to evolve, to change, to grow up. But, my first task was to tame the wild, spoilt creature that lived inside of me. That stubborn, self-entitled childish beast my parents both loved and resented.

What no one tells us is that freedom comes with a huge amount of responsibility. And change involves a surprising amount of loss.

Was I ready for all that? Absolutely NOT.

But I had an inherent belief within myself: we all have the ability to create space for new things to come into our lives. As long as we're open to engaging in a new life current.

Very few things are more profound than starting over with just the basics, relying only on yourself to build a life again. Having to start from zero fundamentally alters us.

The new country and its people have their own effect on who we are and how we feel. We have to re-learn how to live and carry out everyday activities just like a child. At school, at work, and even when having fun.

As with anything in life, it all starts with survival. With very few exceptions, most international students had to work to pay rent and food. Our working rights allowed us to work 20 hours a week.

With classes running from 8:30am to 3pm (and a quick lunch break from 12 to 1pm), we had to learn how to organize our routines to make space for those part-time jobs in the time we had left, without forgetting to have a little fun.

As a 22-year-old I had to basically make my own life happen 24/7. Was it easy? Nope. But that was the most important part of the whole experience.

My new friend Paula and I were waiting in line to use the computer lab to check our e-mails (those were the days — no phone internet, my friends). We engaged in a little chat to kill some time and workshop new ideas about our futures in the new land.

"I think it's time to move out of my homestay, Paula."

"Why?"

"It's not in the right area. It's also expensive. But the main thing: I need freedom."

"I hear you. That's why I never went to a homestay. I have a friend who lived here before. She helped me to rent an apartment."

"That's what I want. Where do you live?"

"Cottesloe."

"Are you serious? That's the place that came up on my Google search. The beach with the most incredible sunset."

"You're right. I love it there!"

"Do you think it would be easy to find a job around the area?"

"I think so. There are lots of restaurants and cafés. You speak English, you can be a waitress."

"That's exactly what I want. But I prefer to work close to home."

"Do you wanna share my place?"

"What do you mean?"

"We could share a room. It's cheaper for everyone. I want to save money to travel."

"Sounds great. I want to save money too. How can we make that happen?"

"Why don't you come and stay with me this weekend? You can see the place, the area, and then make up your mind."

"Wow, that was easy. Thank you. I'm in. Can't wait!"

During our conversation, this hot Brazilian guy walked past us. I noticed the way he looked at Paula. Very intentional. I couldn't help myself.

"Hey, did you see the way that guy looked at you," I whispered to her.

"Who?"

"Rodrigo", I slightly tilted my head towards him so he wouldn't notice my move.

"Come on, are you crazy? He's hot!"

"I know. So are you! You make a very hot couple. He likes you. Trust me. I can see your future together."

She laughed. The kind of laugh that secretly said: *I hope so.*

I did too. I was a sucker for a great love story and something told me I was about to witness one unfolding.

After school, I went home and spent some time chatting with Flynn and Yoko about the week. We had dinner together and I went to bed early.

They say *"a little party never killed nobody"*, but my body was still adjusting. Going out drinking slightly stretched my limits.

Thank God I was young! The old glory days.

I miss the ability to get a full recovery on a single night's sleep.

8. CHASING SUNSETS.

Saturday morning.

I woke up bright and early and had breakfast with my Aussie family. Despite my little to no experience with kids, I enjoyed playing with Kenji and Ben. They were adorable and fun. They made me feel like a kid again.

Flynn started talking to me as usual.

"What are your plans for the weekend, Carolina?" he asked.

"I'm finally heading to Cottesloe. I'll stay with my friend Paula."

"You guys are fascinating in the way you make friends. It seems so easy for you."

"I agree," Yoko added. "And you sleep at each other's places."

"I never thought about this, but you're right. I think it's because we're all alone here. We're just happy to help each other. It's part of our experience, I guess."

"I think it's nice," Yoko said smiling. "We are not like that in Japan."

"We're all different, aren't we? And that's the beauty of it. We learn from each other."

"You're right, Carolina. We sure do."

Flynn watched us talk but didn't say much. We finished breakfast and as I was about to leave he said:

"Wait, I'll drop you off at the station. It will save you time."

"Oh, really? Thanks, you're the best! I won't be a minute. I'll just grab my backpack."

He quickly drove me there. Before I left the car, he carefully instructed me:

"Midland and Fremantle are basically the same line. You won't need to change trains. Just stay on this one until you get to Cottesloe, okay?"

"Sounds perfect, I will. Thank you, Flynn! I'll see you on Monday."

Flynn had a serious and reserved nature, but he was extremely caring and helpful. He made sure I was safe and knew what I was doing all the time. Pretty much like a real dad, always taking care of me.

As I boarded the train, I felt my entire body come to life in anticipation for a long awaited moment. I was finally going to see the image that sold me the entire Australian experience: the Cottesloe sunset. This time, for real.

Sitting by the window, I noticed how things kept changing at every station. I couldn't help but feel like I was in a movie.

My mind kept trying to make sense of it all. It demanded some kind of control. I wanted to know what I never knew, but it was impossible. So, I just surrendered to the new experience and allowed myself to be taken by this moment.

Is this all really happening or am I still dreaming?

Minds have a life of their own. They keep questioning, no matter what.

About 40 minutes later, the woman finally announced: "This is Cottesloe Station."

That was me. The doors opened and I got off the train only to be taken by an almost unbelievable neighbourhood. I walked through green grass and let the large shady Norfolk pines stretching along the streets guide my way.

It was the most beautiful scenery my eyes had ever seen. I couldn't imagine that such a place even existed. But it did. And I was about to live there.

"Dreams do come true." My mind loved to be right. "This is better than I imagined."

I kept walking until I found Paula's address. A three-story apartment complex. No fence, no security cameras, nothing. It was a block away from the beach and less than 10 minutes' walk from the station. She scored a great location.

I entered the building through the courtyard. It felt like the Melrose Place set, with an old fountain instead of a swimming pool. It was a ground floor unit. I knocked on her door.

"Welcome, my friend!" Paula and her big warm smile hugged me. "Come in, check this out."

"Wow, I love it! It doesn't feel like an apartment. It's kind of a house."

"Yep, nothing fancy, but it's cosy. Two-bedroom, one bathroom, kitchen, laundry and a little living room. It's all we need. We'll get another flatmate for the smaller room."

"It's perfect!"

"Come outside, let's sit here." She pulled a couple of chairs and lit a cigarette.

"Don't you feel like this is Melrose Place?" I asked while lighting one too.

"You're funny!" she said, laughing. "I don't know, do you?"

"I kind of do. I feel like we're just a bunch of young adults with big hopes and dreams trying to make life happen in this little apartment complex. Pretty much like them."

"You may be right. Come on, let's go to the beach."

We changed into our bikinis and headed down.

"Wow, how do you describe this?" my jaw dropped the second I saw the view.

"Cottesloe."

"Santa Catarina is a beautiful place on Earth. We both know. But this... this is something. Look at that water. It's actually blue. And the sand..."

"Yep, we got pretty lucky."

"Lucky? We hit the jackpot here, my friend. Thank you."

"You're welcome."

A long, shining stretch of soft white sand and crystal-clear blue waters weren't the only impressive features Cottesloe had to offer. Marine Parade was developed as a commercial precinct with several hotels, guesthouses and tearooms.

I read that the early British settlers created the Swan River colony and were inspired by the idea of going to a beach and experiencing the luxury of a seaside. Their goal was to turn the area into Western Australia's prime recreational resort. Well, I'd say their job was successfully accomplished.

"Paula, did you know that Perth is one of the most isolated cities on the planet?"

"Yeah, I read that too. Apparently, we're in the middle of nowhere. But, with this beach, what else do we need?"

"Sun. And that's why Perth is even more special. It's officially the sunniest capital city in the world."

"You did your research."

"Yep. It averages eight hours of sun per day, year-round. Trust me, I usually follow the sun. This is *the* place to be."

Perth, in general, seemed to do an amazing job at balancing both historic and contemporary buildings, and I loved that.

"Cott", as affectionately known among locals, is Perth's oldest beach and has a very nostalgic feel to it. Possibly because it played a very important role both during the Gold Boom in the early 1900s and also in the late 1930s, when great economic prosperity followed the Great Depression.

As a foreigner, I could only say that such significance and beauty really hit me. I was struck by its incredible architecture. Right there, on the central beachfront, was the most iconic example.

"Oh my God! This is the photo I saw on the internet. But even that photo doesn't bring it justice. It's much better in real life!"

"Ah, this place is cool. Everything seems to happen around here." Paula was clearly already familiar with the building I had only discovered.

It was the Indiana Tea House. Originally built as a humble ice cream parlour in 1910, a pit-stop for the playground that was Cottesloe Beach. It was not hard to imagine folks dressed in modest bathing suits, caps and trunks being served from a small shack-like composite. Or young couples dancing cheek to cheek in the 1920s. This place was born to be a hub.

Times change. Culture changes. Everything will always keep changing. But, deep down, we are all still after the same timeless things: *fun, joy, love*. We all live for those precious moments that remain in our memories and make it worthwhile for us to stay alive.

History has a funny way of recreating itself throughout time. Just like people, cultural icons also die. But their souls remain.

And that's what I found out when I did a little research on the history of this place. Apparently, due to council's policy, they cleared the beach of all buildings and, at some point, Indiana had to go. All that remained was the Centenary Bathing Pavilion.

Only in 1996, they redeveloped Indiana into the building I was lucky to know now.

The current version was partly inspired by the Pavilion itself. It combined elements from the late 20th century postmodern with the Australian nostalgic architectural style. Rising effortlessly from the snow-white beach sand, the building was intended to appear as if it had been there for 40 or 50 years.

Despite this practice being frowned upon, the gamble paid off as it became the most recognizable building on the WA coastline, managing to look as though it had perched there for a century.

For me, it was something beyond its physical structure. Indiana had a soul. It was still a real landmark for locals and visitors simply because it made us feel something special.

We never know how long things or people are going to last. That's why we must experience life with close attention and always enjoy every moment. Or we may miss it.

Paula and I threw our sarongs on the glistening sand and stayed there for hours, just relaxing and basking in the sun. Around us, pretty much everyone else was doing the exact same.

It was a classic summer day. Not a cloud in the sky. The sun was very hot. Dry hot. Unlike anything I've ever experienced before.

"Hey, I'm almost cooking and not sweating. How weird!" I shared my experience with Paula.

"The climate is different here," she said, laughing. "We're close to the desert. The air is super dry. The opposite of our tropical Brazilian humidity."

"Of course, that makes so much sense. I guess I must swim for some humidity then."

"Yep, I'll join you."

The water was freezing, but so refreshing. A clear example of life's little contrasts. And a good reminder to stay cool when things get really hot. On a sunny summer day, or just in life.

"I think I need something to drink. Do you?" I asked Paula.

"Oh yeah, but they don't sell it on the beach. We have to walk up there and get it."

"I don't mind going for a walk. You can stay. I'll be back soon. Are you hungry?"

"Not really. But I could have a snack. See what you can find."

As I got to the street, I saw another icon: Hotel Cottesloe, renamed to Cottesloe Beach Hotel. For most, simply *"The Cott"*. Built in 1905, the two-story building with a "Moderne" facade was one of the first beachside hotels in Perth's metropolitan area.

The hotel was a fine example of innovative design that also demonstrated considerable achievement in converting the original 1905 hotel building using Art Deco style in 1937. It had further significance because it was almost all that remained of the pre-war foreshore architecture along the entire coast.

Sometimes we forget how important architecture really is. Not only for its aesthetics or history, but for the social and spiritual value those symbols inspire in past, present and future generations. Spaces have souls. We can build and destroy physical structures, but the feelings always remain.

I acknowledge that I get carried away by history, but it's not every day that we are moved by these kinds of feelings that arise when we are curious and actually paying attention.

We get so used to people and places around us that we end up living almost on autopilot and miss all the depth and beauty. Unfortunately, we're not always present.

Any change of scenery awakens our curiosity and gives us an opportunity to experience the world with wide open eyes all over again. That's why people travel, so they can experience new places with fresh eyes.

I was completely in love with the idyllic beachy west-coast lifestyle. No matter where I looked, everything was inspiring.

But I was on a mission: to get drinks and snacks. I found a little café and got water, some freshly squeezed orange juice, and a raspberry and white chocolate muffin for us to share.

On my way back, I noticed my internal self-talk. I had way too much going on in my head. I needed to let it out. Paula made me feel very comfortable. She was funny, caring, and honest. Everything you could ask for in a friend. Maybe she would listen to me.

Back in the sand, she had fallen asleep.

"Your order is ready, miss," I said pretending to be a waitress.

"Thank you. What do we have?" she said, half just waking up and half smiling.

"Water, orange juice and a raspberry muffin."

"Perfect. I feel healthy already."

We laughed together. My thoughts were still racing.

"So, why Perth?" she asked almost as a cue for me to open up.

"Oh, it's a long story. Wanna hear?"

"Of course, go on. We have time, food, drinks. I'm all ears."

"Okay, this may sound very cliché but, believe me, it actually happened…"

9. THE BACKSTORY.
(HERE IT IS)

Ever since I was a child studying English, I had this dream of living in another country where I could actually speak my new language.

Growing up watching Beverly Hills 90210 and Melrose Place, while also listening to Ben Harper and Jack Johnson, made me think of California as the best place on Earth. The idea of being around Hollywood really appealed to me. I loved watching movies.

I had just graduated from a Bachelor of Communications, with a major in Advertising. I was very young and green, but I felt it was the perfect time to live my dream.

I had some limited experience in TV production that could eventually help. With time, I could try to transfer some of my skills to screenwriting. I would obviously need to study and work very hard, but a girl can dream.

So, I started looking at some options, often torn between American and British accents. Yes, we become who we hang out with.

After some research, I found Santa Barbara, near LA. A small enough town with strong cultural and historical heritage. It seemed a great fit for me. And the fact that it wasn't yet crowded with Brazilians like San Diego and other larger cities also appealed to me, since my goal was to actually speak English.

There was only one little problem: the US didn't allow work permits for international students. And I needed to support myself financially.

That's how my second option came into play: London. I knew a few friends who had gone there. Some loved it, others not so much. A classic case of mixed reviews.

The pros were culture, diversity and fun. What really triggered a negative bias was the weather. Let's just say that cold and grey is not appealing for most Brazilians. However, summertime was brilliant! I could picture myself traveling around Europe, enjoying music festivals while paying for everything in local currency.

In terms of Advertising, they were a lot more sophisticated. It felt challenging to me. But the one thing that was making me consider compromising on the weather was this: in London, I could legally work. Still, my heart was "California dreaming".

Meanwhile, as most 21-year olds from that era, I was out and about in our wild and open social network: the world around us. It was Easter long weekend. Me and a bunch of single friends went to a beach getaway. In the absence of devices and apps, we always trusted our feelings to establish new connections. Literally anywhere.

On the first night, I saw this guy, the shy type, talking with his friend. I could almost hear their conversation. It sounded like that classic line from the Counting Crows' *Mr. Jones* song: *"She's looking at you"* — *"No, she's looking at me"*. We often confused people with our looks, but that was part of the real life game.

As a result, the friend, who didn't seem so shy, came up to me and gave his best shot:

"It was impossible to ignore the way you looked at me," he said in a very seductive tone.

"I admire your initiative, but I was looking at your friend," I replied in my brutal honesty.

He laughed, and kept going, "You know what, we weren't sure. I'll be fair, he liked you too, but he's shy."

"I noticed. And I must confess: it's exactly what I liked about him."

We laughed together, fully bonded already. I have a soft spot for truth.

"Nice to meet you, I'm Cupid." The guy had a sense of humor. "Come on, girl. Let me introduce you two then. Someone must make a move here. I'm a good friend."

That's how I met Daniel. His friend made the first move and introduced me to him that night.

Daniel and I started talking, laughing at the awkwardness of it all.

"Where do you live?" I asked unpretentiously.

"In Australia."

I instantly felt the distance. It took me a few seconds to actually process the fact that a gorgeous man, as Brazilian as I was, inhabited what I perceived as a remote part of the Earth.

"On the other side of the world?" I asked, trying to pretend that information was not a big deal.

"Yes. I know, it's far."

A million thoughts raced through my mind. I took a deep breath and kept going, at my own risk.

"Are you just on holiday here?"

"Yes, I came to visit my family."

"And that arm?" I asked, referring to the cast that he couldn't hide under his red shirt.

"I broke surfing. Now, tell me about you. Where do you live?"

"Floripa."

"Nice, do you like it?"

"I've just moved there earlier this year. So far so good."

Interrupted by Cupid, we were asked to change our location to the next club. We walked together until we got to these two huge lines.

"We'll meet inside" — that was our deal as we went our separate ways.

In those times they had some weird rules. The male line was on one side, the female on the other. And, unlike bathroom lines, women were faster. For a simple reason: men paid to enter, we didn't.

I went in with the girls straight to the bar and waited for Daniel to arrive. After a while, there was no sign of him. I was physically tired after a long week of work and just couldn't be bothered staying any longer.

"Where is the Australian?" one of my friends asked, in a very cheeky tone.

"He must have gone back to Australia," I replied, balancing humor and frustration.

"There are lots of beautiful faces here, Carolina Luiza. You don't need to obsess over him. He's not the only one."

She was right, but I couldn't be any other way. My mind was set on him.

I respect those who don't believe in Astrology, but this personality trait may be related to my Scorpio moon. I love people, but I prioritize deep relationships. Shallow interactions just don't suit me. Yes, I'm all or nothing. And my intuition is like a torch, always lighting my way.

To balance it out, I have a Taurus sun with an Aries rising. That means I'm resilient, with plenty of initiative to go after what I want. But when I get tired, I prefer to sleep. And that's what I was determined to do.

That night, I only wanted Daniel. In his absence, I decided to go back to the hotel for my beauty sleep.

As I was about to cross the door, I felt a light tap on my shoulder. I turned back only to be overwhelmed by this surge of energy that felt like thunder. It was Daniel.

"Where are you going?" he asked.

"To the hotel."

"Now that I finally got in?"

I looked at my watch. 3am.

"Do you have a better idea?" I asked, hoping for a good answer.

"Sure. We'll watch the sunrise on the beach."

And looking at his shy smile, I felt safe. We both wanted the same thing. He grabbed two beers and we left together.

"Was it the surf that took you to Australia?"

"Surf is a big part of it, but living there is a dream come true."

"How long have you been gone?"

"Six years."

"For real? So, it's not just an exchange..."

"No, I live there."

"No plans to come back?"

"Not really."

"And your family?"

"They live in Curitiba."

"How can you stay away from them for so long?"

"You get used to it."

A small reflective pause. I looked into his eyes and felt my heart open like very few times in my life.

"Can I confess something?"

"Of course, whatever you like."

"I have this dream to live overseas."

"Really? And why were you so shocked when I told you that I do?"

"Because you made it real. And I never imagined it was possible to live away for so long."

"Time is relative, Carol. When we go, we have no idea what will happen. It's almost like an alter world that takes you in and changes everything."

"It's just hard for me to imagine."

"I get it. That's why you have to live it."

"Can I ask you something?"

"Go on."

"Do you mind if we speak English tonight? I have been studying since I was seven, but I can hardly practice in real life. Do you mind being a *gringo*?"

"Nobody has ever asked me that, but why not? It will be fun."

And that night, we experienced our own alter world. Just the two of us. Between one kiss and another, he told me about life in Australia. And I told him my dreams and fears that I hardly shared with anyone.

"I really want to have this international experience while I'm still young, but I'm afraid I'll miss all my opportunities here. I just graduated and my career is kind of taking off."

"There are many opportunities out there too, Carol. Don't limit yourself. Where do you think about going?"

"I did some research and I have two options: the first is California. The second, London."

"Wow, they are quite opposites. What are you actually looking for? I'm confused."

"California seems like the best place in the world. I'm thinking about taking a film course and the idea of being in Hollywood really attracts me, but I don't want a city full of Brazilians. So, at first, I thought about going to Santa Barbara to study English and then risk LA for the film course and to explore professional opportunities."

"And where did London come from?"

"When I discovered that, in the US, they don't give work visas to international students. I need to support myself. In London I can legally work. The culture attracts me a lot, but the climate terrifies me. On the bright side, I could travel around Europe and enjoy lots of cool things, earning and spending in the same currency.

When it comes to Advertising, Europeans are also more sophisticated than Americans. I would focus on that."

"And have you ever considered Australia?"

"No."

"Why?"

"It didn't even cross my mind. I don't think I know anyone who went there."

"Now you do. Please consider. You may be surprised."

Our conversation went a lot deeper. Daniel shared a number of specificities about the country he had chosen, which went far beyond kangaroos and surf. The more he told me these great things about Australia, the more excited I became. It was as if London and California had a baby and named Australia. At least in the parts he described.

My heart sang a little and I made a quick mental note: *maybe this is it.*

I suspected that our meeting was not just a coincidence. It felt more like a sign. Even if I wasn't sure I fully believed in those things back then.

Remember, I'm a Taurus. An Earth person. Grounded. I need to see it to believe it. And, right there, in front of me, was living proof of a Brazilian making a life in another country. A country called Australia.

It was "the dreamer" meeting the "dream come true".

And, as the night turned into day, the rising sun uncovered an emerging new feeling (at least for me). It felt like that Eagle-Eye Cherry song that was timely playing on the CD back in my hotel room:

"I'm falling in love again

Ain't nothing I can do

Falling in love again

And this time it's with you"

Daniel and I spent the next few days together. At the height of our connection, Daniel told me something that I never forgot: *"If you ever decide to go to Australia, look for me. I live in a small town, with very few Brazilians. People know me by name. You will find me."*

Hope is a beautiful thing.

The whole experience was so surreal that my mind could only interpret his words in one way: *if I was crazy enough to cross the world, I would have everything I needed to find him again*. I made another mental note: *Carolina, you're not that crazy*.

Even though that wasn't the ideal scenario for me to fall in love, that feeling was a path of no return. And I was left to deal with the consequences of not having what I wanted.

So, Eagle-Eye Cherry had another track that fit just perfectly for our last night together:

> *"Save tonight*
> *And fight the break of dawn*
> *Come tomorrow*
> *Tomorrow I'll be gone"*

Let me get something straight here: times were different.

In the early 2000s, it was very unlikely for us to keep a long-distance relationship. You couldn't just get a quick flight to the other side of the world (it's hard enough today, imagine then). International calls were a fortune and we only had dial-up internet. Would an email thread help or just worsen the pain of wanting what is out of reach? For me, I know the answer.

Our *"love story"* was fleeting. So, in the following week, Daniel went back to Australia, and I went back to my life. But that story never got out of my head. And I kept replaying his words *"you will find me"* like a broken record.

Hope can also be a stubborn thing.

Later that year, I was at work when a thought got stuck in my mind: *I can't postpone my dream any longer. I am ready to make it happen. What is it gonna take?*

I remembered Daniel talking about Perth. I decided to look into that. I *"googled"* it and this beautiful photo came up. I instantly fell in love with that image. I could totally see myself there. I started to read about the city and everything sounded exactly as he described. To be honest, even better.

I checked the currency and Australian dollars were a little cheaper than American. It was perfect! And, I could legally work.

The wise voice in my head whispered very softly, but surely: *"This is it, just go."*

End of back story — back to the beach with Paula.

"Well, that was November last year. The image I saw was exactly where we are right now. With the Indiana Teahouse and everything. I guess I made it. I'm here."

"Wow! You ARE crazy after all, my friend. But that is a great story. So, where's the guy?"

"I don't know yet, but he told me where to look."

"I hope you find him."

"Me too."

I am not fond of *"what ifs"*. I'm more of a *"screw it, let's do it"* kind of girl. I guess our greatest protection usually lies in being vulnerable and allowing the world to work its magic on us.

I always believe that whoever has the greatest capacity for discomfort and rejection rises the fastest in any situation. The quicker we learn to get things out of our system, the better. Otherwise, the same things will end up eating us alive later in life.

Deep inside, even for me, that move felt a little too crazy. And the expression on Paula's face confirmed my feelings. But one thing that I had learned was to trust that sweet voice in my head. The wise one. Somehow, it always knew where I had to go.

I was ready to live my dream. I also wanted to get the fantasy of Daniel out of my head and into reality. Why not do both? It just felt natural to me.

My future was uncertain, but also full of hope and possibility. I was no longer alone in my story. My little secret was out. I trusted Paula. And, against all odds, I felt safe.

From the sand, we looked up at the tall Norfolk Island pines. They were stunning.

Under them, flocks of people were enjoying the natural shade that still allowed for just a few sweet rays of sunshine. Some had organized little picnics while others saved time by getting takeaway food from the various places along the foreshore.

My silent reflections were suddenly interrupted by this very loud bird symphony. We noticed these lorikeet roosts flocking around the pines, producing this almost deafening noise.

"What is that?" I asked Paula, almost yelling at her.

"The birds?"

"Yeah. They are the loudest I've heard!"

"I know. Apparently, it's a daily ritual."

"You mean a sacred bird tradition?" I said, joking.

"Pretty much. People actually love it here. It's hard to imagine Cottesloe without it. It's part of this place."

"I love it, it's incredible. They are beautiful! It's actually a pretty powerful sound."

"I know. And it also means it's time to get some food. I'm starving!"

"I'm starving too!"

We spent pretty much the entire day on the beach. It was time to try another very Aussie tradition: fish and chips.

Next to Indiana, and opposite The Cott, there was this very unique set of grass terraces where people seemed to pile up towards the end of every day.

We sat on the lush green grass with our take away and spent the rest of our lazy summer day mesmerised by what I will forever call a "life changing ocean sunset".

"I could totally get used to this, my friend." I told Paula how I felt.

"Oh, don't worry. You will."

10. I WANNA ROCK AND ROLL ALL NIGHT AND WORK EVERY DAY.

Cottesloe was very popular, especially on weekends. People from all over Perth went there to enjoy a perfect day at the beach. It was also a must-see for anyone just visiting the city.

On Sunday morning, I went for a walk on Marine Parade looking for a place to dedicate my working hours to. I left my resume both at The Cott and the OBH, which was short for the Ocean Beach Hotel.

A little further down the road, the OBH was another Cottesloe icon. Originally designed in 1907 as a grand Federation Filigree style building, the hotel was renovated and altered beyond recognition during the 1930s. With numerous modifications, there wasn't a lot of history left for anyone to see there, other than its importance and popularity as a meeting point, especially for young people.

The Cott and the OBH were the two most popular spots in the area and obviously pretty busy. I just assumed they always needed staff. The managers said they'd get back to me during the week if there was anything available. They also apologised for not having time to speak to me properly. They were genuinely nice.

It quickly hit me that weekends were not the best time to get anyone's attention. It was insanely busy. So, I kept looking around but didn't leave my resume anywhere else that day. Instead, I just observed everything while getting a real feel for what I could do to land the right job.

It was my second weekend there. I wasn't desperate, so I decided to relax and enjoy some free time. I'd look for work again soon.

"Aussies" (short form for Australians) love to party. And I happened to have that in common with them. Cottesloe Sunday Sessions were a big hit. Something everyone should experience at least once. The place to go for drinks and fun with friends.

I obviously couldn't wait to experience that. I also thought it was a great idea to feel the vibe in case I got a job in one of those popular places. Every Sunday afternoon, people gathered either at The Cott or the OBH, normally both, starting early in the afternoon until about 10pm. After that, Club Bayview in Claremont was the option for extra drinks and dance floor action until the midnight curfew.

Paula wasn't a big fan of crowds. She preferred to stay back, chatting to our kiwi neighbour who seemed really cool. I joined Angela and a few other friends from school there.

I'll never forget that Sunday. It was a whole new experience for me. Daylight, relaxed vibes, no fancy clothes. A bunch of young folks wearing our famous thongs "Havaianas" to go out. I had never seen so many of those together, not even in Brazil (except on the beach). All the action and flirting happened very unpretentiously. In the beer garden or just in front of the band.

"I wanna rock and roll all night and party every day" met *"It's a long way to the top if you wanna rock 'n' roll"*.

The power of great music. Those classic rock tunes. Kiss, ADCD, Oasis and everything in between kept the crowd pumped and singing along. They actually knew the lyrics and sang all the words. Obviously. Oh, and their carefree dance moves! They were gold!

Aussies know how to have fun. They don't just walk; they truly live on the wild side. I wondered why we didn't have places like that in Brazil (at least where I was from). Maybe because we don't have a pub culture. Or possibly because our fun was mainly attached to late nights and dress-ups. I wasn't sure, but I instantly loved their way of being.

In my hometown, we mainly kept the action within our circles. We had warm-ups and after parties. Things were not so spontaneous. We had to know each other to hang out.

But the main difference was the time of day. We were all-nighters. Our rituals included watching the sunrise while listening to electronic music. It wasn't unusual for us to get home just in time for breakfast. Sometimes lunch.

My mind was comparing things when a slow nostalgic tune suddenly changed the entire mood of The Cott.

> "*How many special people change? How many lives are living strange?*
>
> *Where were you while we were getting high?*"

Oasis. It was the first time I truly understood those lyrics. Those words, the melody. I felt them deeply in my soul. I thought of all my friends back home, wishing we could be sharing that incredible moment together. I was on a high.

The entire bar, full of strangers, started to sing in perfect unison:

> "*Someday you will find me*
>
> *Caught beneath the landslide*

In a champagne supernova in the sky"

That was beyond powerful. I had to go outside to catch my breath and let my emotions come out. Everyone seemed to follow me. Apparently, it was the thing to do around that time.

Like flocking birds on tree branches, all of us went out searching for sitting spots on the grass terraces across the road. It was the sacred human tradition of Cottesloe beach.

Even though it happened almost every day, Australians never took sunsets for granted. Instead, they worshipped it. Everyone literally sat there receiving the brightest blessings of natural sunlight.

Straight ahead, the giant, yellow ball started to go orange while the entire sky adjusted to this dreamy color palette. Infinite shades of pink dancing in the blue. A picture-perfect moment a photograph could never translate in real resolution.

It was a completely new reality. Somehow, I felt part of it. I didn't even have to try. I fitted in effortlessly.

I was in love with absolutely everything about Australian culture. That part of the world seemed to have been made for me.

11. SATISFYING MY SOUL.

A new week had started and I kept my party mode on. Is there anything more interesting than discovering all the different ways one can have fun in an unknown city?

At 22, I doubt it.

A few people were talking about this amazing reggae band that played every Wednesday. It sounded really cool. Paula wasn't much of a party girl, but she was into reggae. We decided to check it out.

Totally immersed in our routines, we hardly felt time passing by. Suddenly, Wednesday hit us. I went to school with my backpack ready to stay another night in Cottesloe.

Life was so exciting. Every day was different. Every day, I was a little bit different too.

"We still have time to go to the beach," Paula said as we met after class.

"I know, let's do it!"

We caught the train together, quickly got changed and headed to the beach. It was another Perth-like hot sunny day. To save money on takeaway, we packed a few snacks to eat in case we got hungry.

"I can't keep up with you, Carol. Did you go out like this in Brazil too?"

"Yes, always. I can't help it, I'm a party girl. I used to produce this lifestyle TV show — mostly about nightlife. I know São Paulo is 24/7, but Balneário Camboriú earned its fame. There's always something on. At some point I used to go out almost Monday to Monday — all while studying and working."

"For real? How could you do it?"

"Not sure. Autopilot, maybe," I said, laughing. "I know it sounds crazy, but it was natural to me. I guess I just never stopped."

"I can't imagine that. Well, I had a boyfriend for years so you kind of settle. Did you have boyfriends?"

"Not long term. I've always dated party boys."

"Classic. You know what? I'm excited for tonight! I think Rodrigo will be there. I'm still thinking about what you said."

"You're totally going to hook up. You know that."

"Do you think?"

"No, I am sure. You tell me later."

After a couple of hours, we went home, cooked dinner and got ready for our reggae night. As we arrived at a large parking lot, surrounded by commercial real estate, I asked Paula.

"Where's this place? It doesn't seem right."

"I know, they said it wasn't the most obvious bar."

"Clearly. But is it hidden?"

In the middle of those odd shops we saw a regular commercial door open. A guy came out and we heard the music.

"Oh, it's there. Let's go in," she said, excited.

That door opened to a small room, full of people. On the other side, a long sliding glass door led us into an outside smoking area. It felt almost like a house party, full of strangers. The atmosphere was incredible.

"Do you wanna get a beer?" Paula asked me.

"Sure."

"Pint or glass?"

"Jug? Isn't that cheaper?"

"Yeah, we can do that."

"Perfect. It will last all night."

Reggae always felt like a B-side kind of territory to me, but I love it. Some pretty good bands came out of Santa Catarina, but the real Brazilian reggae was mainly from Brasilia. Also, there was a direct link between reggae and a spliff, which was somewhat real, but also overstated. You can still like the music, without the smoke.

Now, in terms of cultural impact, Bob Marley undeniably was the "Soul Rebel". His incredible lyrics were so easy to sing to, and relate.

But reggae kind of got into electronic music too. The Prodigy's "Out of Space" was a classic example. It sampled Max Romeo's 1976 anthem "Chase The Devil". Oh, that slow start. A mind-blowing, timeless hit that will forever and ever take us into another dimension.

How about Beats International's "Dub Be Good To Me"? Another incredible mix of house and reggae that is so easy to dance to. Even The Rolling Stones recognised a rootsy parallel with the blues that had originally inspired the band, covering Eric Donaldson's classic "Cherry Oh Baby".

Let's not forget UB40. They were the biggest-selling reggae group of the 80s, and grew out of the punk and folk scenes in Britain's Midlands. I guess we couldn't help but fall in love with them.

Truth be told, even fairly mainstream genres of music fail to translate across the oceans like reggae does. It's survived over the years in one form or another. Maybe because it's informing, energising and beautifying. It remains powerful, despite being infinitely diluted, like a homeopathic remedy we can dance to.

On stage, a four-piece band put together the ultimate modern-reggae jam. All those classics I mentioned above and more.

Great vocals, high quality musicians and a house music infusion resembling bassline roots. They had it all there. A really progressive vibe that sounded so fresh. It was brilliant. Different from everything we'd heard before. I was instantly carried away to my carefree days and good vibes.

"Everyone's feeling pretty

It's hotter than July

Though the world's full of problems

They couldn't touch us even if they tried

From the park I hear rhythms

Marley's hot on the box

Tonight there will be a party

On the corner at the end of the block

Didn't know you

Would be jammin' until the break of dawn

I bet nobody ever told you that you

Would be jammin' until the break of dawn

You would be jammin' and jammin' and jammin', jam on"

Oh, yeah! When they dropped Stevie Wonder's smash hit "Master Blaster", we all got jammin'! 'Cause *"When you're moving in the positive, your destination is the brightest star"*.

Again, those lyrics. Things never made so much sense to me. Singing along was a natural thing to do. We lost ourselves dancing. I almost forgot I had a drink. A semi-warm beer I never managed to finish. I was finally living in English and truly *"satisfying my soul"*.

I saw Rodrigo walking towards us. There was no doubt in my mind that he was going straight after Paula.

"Hi girls, how are you doing?"

"Good," Paula answered.

"I'm good too," I said, looking for my way out in order to leave the two alone to engage in a real conversation.

As they started chatting, another guy approached me.

"Hi, I'm André." He introduced himself while kissing my cheeks three times and still moving his feet to the beats. Amazing.

"Nice to meet you, André. I'm Carolina."

"I hear you're from the South. Santa Catarina, right?"

I was curious to know how this unknown guy already knew something about me, but Rodrigo must have told him. We had a few casual chats at school.

"Yes, that's right. How about you?"

"Curitiba, but I've been here for a while."

It suddenly hit me that living in Australia for "a while" wasn't a rare thing. In the very short period I was there, I met quite a few examples. André was from Curitiba. And so was Daniel. I wondered if they knew each other.

"How long have you been here, André?" I asked, trying to figure out how long 'a while' was.

"3 years."

"Oh, that's quite a long while. Do you like it?"

"Love it. Life is great, surf is great."

"Oh, a surfer from Curitiba." That was the cue I'd been looking for to ask further questions.

"That's right."

"You might know a few guys from Margaret River then." I naturally assumed trying not to sound too investigative, but he confirmed.

"Of course, heading there on the weekend for the WQS."

That was all I needed to feel comfortable and get into more specifics.

"Cool, do you happen to know Daniel? He's also from Curitiba."

"Sure, he's a legend. Been here longer than me. Do you know him?"

"Briefly. We met last year in Brazil. He seemed really nice and gave me some great tips about Perth. It would be good to catch up again."

"If you can, you should go down on the weekend. It's a big event. Lots of people, lots of fun. Great way to experience Margs."

"Yes, I heard. I'm actually going with some other girls I met here a couple of weeks ago"

"Perfect, you'll love it! Do you have his number?"

"No, I don't."

"Here. You can call him. He'll show you around."

"Oh, thank you. I will."

And that's how it happened. In the middle of a fun night, I got what I was after. Daniel was real. I remembered him saying I could easily find him if I ever decided to go there. I just didn't expect it to be THAT easy. It was literally in my hands to make the call.

I saw Paula and Rodrigo coming together in our direction. It felt like a happy beginning.

I couldn't believe just how much had happened on a regular midweek night out.

It was getting late and we all had to get up early for school the next day, so we got going. On our way home, I told Paula what happened. She was excited for me. And I was excited for her. Both of us were very happy for each other.

Those beautiful reggae vibes were still working their magic on us.

12. MAKING IT HAPPEN.

The next day, after school, I went to the city. I needed to buy a few things for the weekend in Margs. I sat at a random city bench to eat a sandwich. With Daniel's number in my hand, I decided to call him. As we did in those days.

"Hello, Daniel speaking," he answered, having no idea who was on the line.

"Hi Daniel," I tried to sound cool but I bet my voice was shaky. "I don't know if you remember me, and I know this will sound a bit crazy but..."

"Carol, you really surprised me," he interrupted as soon as he recognised my voice. We had spoken a couple of times on the phone when he was still in Brazil.

"André called me this morning to say he met you last night and gave you my number. So, you came?"

"I did," I answered, not knowing if that was a good or a bad thing.

"How are you?" he asked.

"I'm fine. You?" I almost automatically answered, still a bit short for words.

"I'm fine too. When are you coming down south?"

I took a deep breath and replied. I didn't want to freak him out.

"Tomorrow actually."

"That's awesome! Best weekend ever. It's the WQS. I bet you know."

"Yes, that's why I'm going. A few girls I met here had a spare bed in their cottage. I couldn't say no."

"Lucky you, you'll love it down here."

"I'm sure I will. It's nice to hear a familiar voice," I said, trying to extend the conversation.

"It's nice to hear your voice too. I was surprised, but I'm glad you came. Can't wait to hear how it all happened."

"Sure, I'll see you tomorrow then."

"You will. Now you have my number. Just call me when you get here and I'll come and meet you."

"Sounds good. Will do. Thank you."

"See you tomorrow. Drive safe."

It was a very quick conversation, but it felt good.

My mind started to put things together.

A dream is never just a dream. Possibility is what drives us forward to make things happen. We can dream ourselves into becoming whatever we want.

Most of our reality today was once just "someone's dream". If we let go of fear, we open space for any dream to come true.

Somehow, a stranger had inspired me to look beyond the outer edges of what I had considered my fixed identity. He helped me to see possibilities. His story and words of encouragement were everything I needed to make what I once called "a dream" my very own reality.

Daniel was real. Our story was real. We were meant to meet for a reason.

When our paths crossed, I knew I was onto something. These so-called "chance encounters" are orchestrated by higher intelligence to help us correct the course of our lives.

Sometimes, we're lucky to meet people who not only believe our dreams can come true, but also support us in the pursuit of them. Daniel did that for me.

I won't lie: I was terrified by the idea of seeing him again. But the whole point of my experience was to learn how to overcome my fears and live my dreams, right?

13. AN OPEN ROAD.

Everyone wanted to be part of the surf's action. A lot of Brazilians were also heading "down south" to watch the best surfers in the world battle on the big waves. It was a big deal!

Our little adventure was about to start. Four girls and one guy. All Brazilian. I had only briefly met Mari, but everyone seemed very friendly and excited. For them, it was another weekend away. Great surf and real fun. For me, the stakes were a little higher.

As we got to the car hire company, we obviously picked the most affordable option: a white Corolla hatchback.

Before setting off, the guy made sure we were well prepared for the Australian driving experience.

"First time driving here?" he asked me.

"Yes."

"Where are you from?"

"Brazil."

"Are you familiar with our rules?"

"I think so. I know you guys drive on the left side of the road."

"You're right. But, as you can see, our cars have the steering wheel on the right. It's the opposite from Brazil."

"I see."

"So, just be very careful with turn-signals and windscreen wiper stalks. They are on opposite sides and people often confuse them. It can get messy, but you'll get used to it."

"Of course. I'll make sure to pay extra attention."

"Pedals are standard worldwide. Also, this is automatic. Thankfully, one less thing to think about."

"I guess it helps."

"Distances are measured in metres and kilometres, speed in kilometres per hour. You guys are the same, right?"

"Right. Anything else?"

"Drive safe and pay attention to street signs. You'll be right!"

"Thank you very much, will do. Have a nice day!"

As we hit the open road, I felt the real meaning of this expression coming to life.

I grew up with road trips. Both my mum and dad enjoyed family getaways. But these wide-open spaces surrounded by magnificent natural scenery were something else. The 280km stretch between WA's capital and the world-famous wine, food and surfing mecca of Margaret River were a real treat.

"So, am I the only one who's never been to Margaret River?" I asked everyone in the car.

"Yep, we have all been there. But, except for me, it's everyone's first time at the WQS," Mari answered for the group.

"It's a big deal! I can't wait to see those guys in the water," I heard

Edu, the guy I had just met, say in a very energetic tone. He was also a surfer.

Obviously, he had no idea how big of a deal that was for me and I wasn't ready to share. We drove for a while with hardly any other cars passing by and nothing but trees along the perfect long road. Except, some "keep left" signs every so often.

"Do they really put these up to remind people to stay on the left?" I asked with genuine curiosity.

"Well, they have to. There are too many tourist drivers with licenses issued from countries that drive on the right. It's just a gentle reminder that makes a real difference in helping us to stay safe." Mari was very familiar with the country, culture and rules.

"It's very thoughtful and caring," I said, acknowledging how nice it felt.

"You're right. Australians really do care about people."

"I can feel that."

Some destinations are meant to be experienced by car. This was definitely one of them. We put some Donavon on and just enjoyed the drive for a while.

"We could let this love be the fading sky

We could drift all night until the new sun rise

Pass me a drink or maybe two

One for me and one for you

And we'll be free

Free

Free

Free"

The song was getting to my head. My mind was this unpredictable beast and she got unsettled. For some strange reason, we're wired to always rehearse worst-case scenarios in most situations. Instead of allowing space for all the things that could go right, we often mess it up by focusing on what could go wrong. It's hard to escape the program.

I managed to stay positive until that moment, but I was too close now. Opposing forces decided to hit me hard. Very hard.

You're an idiot, Carolina! What were you thinking? This was a fling a year ago. Things change a lot in a year. Shame on you! You'll be so embarrassed by this. Everyone will laugh at you!

My mind was on a roll. I was unable to stop the uninvited avalanche of negative thoughts. It was cruel. I felt like the most stupid person in the whole world. And I just kept everything to myself. I had literally gone too far.

> *"On a lifeboat sailing home*
>
> *With our drunken hearts and our tired bones*
>
> *Well I just take one last look around*
>
> *Yeah and every place feels like a familiar town"*

I was back in my familiar town of doubts and fears.

Can we ever be truly free? That was the million-dollar question I was trying to answer.

"Hey guys, welcome to Bunbury!" Mari happily announced. "Let's stop here. We need to stretch our legs and get a drink or something."

Fresh air. That was all I needed.

As I got out of the car, and looked around, this small town feeling took over me. It felt even smaller than where I came from.

"Carol, do you know Bunbury is WA's third-largest city after Perth and Mandurah?" Mari curiously asked me.

"Really? I was just thinking the opposite. It feels quite small."

"I know, you'll soon start to get some perspective on the low-density population here. Geographically, Australia is the sixth largest country in the world, but it basically has only 10% of Brazil's population. It's a huge difference. WA is even lower. In fact, the state features amongst the lowest population density in the world."

"Wow, it feels like a breath of fresh air. I might be just in the right place."

Mari had no idea what was going through my head, but breathing space was the most desirable thing for those moments when my anxiety took over.

Coming from Brazil, I instantly felt the difference. Bunbury was not huge, but I liked the welcoming vibe and friendly locals. There were not a lot of people and that felt liberating.

We got back in the car and followed the Bussell Highway southwest until we got to the charming holiday town of Busselton.

"Can we go to the Busselton Jetty?" I asked Mari who was already planning the same stopover.

"Of course, everyone has to see that."

The Busselton Jetty is a heritage-listed wooden jetty dated from the 1800s. It is the longest of its kind in the Southern Hemisphere and second longest in the world, stretching 1.8 kilometres out to sea. A really powerful piece of live history. Its grandiosity really blew my mind.

"Shame it's not open for public visitors now," Mari said, disappointed.

"Well, I guess we just have to admire it from here," I said, while sitting at the amazing beach and taking all that beauty in.

From this angle, all of us were in complete awe. An image so stunning I still have it photographed in my mind.

From Busselton, we took Caves Road. Mari, our official guide, said our next destination would be Dunsborough.

"Guys, this is a longer stop. We must go to the Cape Naturaliste Lighthouse."

"Cool, let's do it," everyone agreed.

Cape Naturaliste Lighthouse is one of the few operational lighthouses the public can access. An easy climb of 59 steps led us to the most incredible panoramic views of the Indian Ocean and surrounding areas.

"Wow, this is just beautiful!" I reflected out loud and Edu overheard me.

"It is, but it goes beyond beauty, Carol. This place reveals the fascinating maritime history of the Cape region. It's very, very special."

"I can certainly feel it."

The entire region was absolutely stunning. Pretty much everywhere I looked was worth a shot. We could've spent a lot longer immersed in all the beauty and incredible history of WA, but it was getting late. We needed to get to Margaret River before the end of day.

Once we left the lighthouse, we drove straight to our final destination.

As we got to this long high street, filled with interesting restaurants and very nice shops, I knew we had arrived. "Margs" was exactly as I pictured: a small town with a contemporary twist.

The streets were bustling with people from everywhere. We all wanted to join them. The main supermarket car park seemed to be the meeting point for everyone arriving in town. We left the car there and went for a walk.

I made a quick stop at the tourist centre which was almost like a mini-museum with lots of information about the local vineyards and history of winemaking in the region.

"Art galleries? Where can I find those here?" I asked the nice lady sitting there while reading a poster.

"Oh, we have a few. You can find artisan studios all over Margaret River."

"Really?"

"Absolutely. Where are you from?"

"Brazil."

"Oh, that's nice. If you like art, this is a fascinating little town."

"I love art! How can I find out more?"

"Well, here's a little guide. Painters, photographers, jewellers, furniture makers..."

"How come so many artists live in such a little town?"

"I guess it's the inspiration, darling. They all need it. I'm sure it will inspire you too."

"You're right. Thank you very much for reminding me."

The town was incredible, but mobile coverage back then didn't follow. I decided to call Daniel as soon as I found a signal. I told him we were headed to our accommodation and that our plan was to leave everything there, have a shower and hit the pub. It was Friday, after all.

The pub was where most of the action happened. He said he'd meet us there around 8pm.

In just a few minutes, we drove into this green area and found a calm and peaceful holiday cottage, perfectly blending with its immediate surroundings. As we stepped outside, dried leaves crackled under our feet.

"Guys, can you feel it?" Mari was having a moment, inhaling the cooler air from under the trees.

"This is awesome, Mari. How did you manage to get this place?" I asked.

"I have my contacts. You'll meet one of them tonight," she said laughing with a very cheeky smile.

She briefly spoke about this guy she was kind of dating. I had no idea who he was but I was impressed with the place he found right in the middle of nature, and just a few minutes from all the action. It was the best of both worlds.

I was also about to see Daniel and catch up on the entire year that we hadn't spoken.

I had a little checklist for the night:

1. Stay sober. This way I couldn't mess things up. I wanted to remember everything I said, heard or did that night.
2. Make myself comfortable. That meant feeling good about the way I looked and felt before seeing him.

Since I wasn't drinking, I took the designated driver role for the night. I felt good to be of service to others. It was a nice responsibility to hold. And it would keep me on my toes.

Around 8pm, we arrived at Settlers Tavern, or just "The Tav". Australians tend to shorten everything. It's just what they do. The

Tav was built as a haven for Margs' emerging surf culture of the 1970s. As most Aussie pubs, it was a hub for the town.

Mari and the others knew a lot of people and everyone started to catch up. I was excited about it all but I had one person in mind: Daniel. I wondered where he was. I waited for almost a year to see him again.

I felt a gentle tap on my shoulder. Exactly like the first time we met.

I turned around and there he was. Just as I remembered. We hugged for a while and my eyes became slightly teary. I made every possible effort not to show it, but I was clearly emotional. I had come a long way for this.

"I'm so happy to see you here," Daniel started the conversation smiling while slowly moving away to look into my eyes.

"I am happy to be here."

"Who are you with?"

"Those people there," I pointed to Mari and some of her friends so he could see them.

"Ah, in five minutes everyone knows everyone, right?"

"The world really is a small town."

"Do you like The Tav?"

"I actually do. It's nice."

"This is a classic pub. Family-friendly, live music, sports bar, beers on tap and an all-day menu. But, because it's Margs, it also has a premium wine list. It's all very low-key here as you probably already noticed."

"I have, and I like it."

"Margaret River is well known for Sauvignon Blanc and Cab Sav. You can't leave without tasting them."

"I can't tonight, but I sure will."

"Not drinking?"

"No, I'm driving."

"Impressive. It's funny to see The Tav like this. On a regular night, it's all about locals and families. Tonight is different. You'll find all types of people here, including surf stars. It's a big wild party."

"It definitely feels like 'the place to be'."

"Yes, especially tonight," he said, making a point, and continued, "Surprisingly, surf hasn't been great. We've had some pretty flat days here which is unusual. Everyone's a little frustrated."

"Does that mean they're all out drinking?"

"I'd say so. But I wanna know about you. Tell me everything. How did you get here?"

"Oh, I wouldn't know where to start," I said, laughing.

"How about you tell me what happened after I left Brazil."

"Well, I thought a lot about you. But life went on. Work, family, friends. The usual suspects."

"I thought about you too. It just never crossed my mind that you'd actually come."

"To be honest, I can't explain how it happened. But, one day, everything just clicked."

"You woke up and thought: 'I'm going to Australia?'"

"Pretty much," I said, laughing.

"It's loud here, isn't it? Do you wanna go for a walk? I can show you around."

"Sure, sounds good."

We left the pub and started to walk on those gorgeous streets. All the noise faded and I could clearly hear Daniel's voice.

"Let's sit somewhere we can actually talk. Tonight The Tav is a bit too crazy" he said, while walking to another place. "This is the Corner Bar. I think you'll like it here."

We sat down and he introduced me to the waiter. They knew each other. It felt very familiar. He ordered a beer and I got some Lemon, Lime & Bitters. I honestly could be anywhere with him but this place was beautiful.

My mind went straight back to when we met in Brazil.

"When you tapped on my shoulder earlier, I had a bit of a déjà vu," I said, reminiscing about our first encounter.

"Yes, you were about to leave. Lucky I found you."

"It was a funny story. I was literally hopeless."

"Come on, don't be so dramatic. We still made it."

"You sound like my brother now. But you're right: I can be a little dramatic."

"Just a little?"

"Don't make me feel bad. Life is complex. And things seem to work out in very mysterious ways."

"Sometimes, but not always. I have to say: I'm very proud of you. You are actually the first person who made it."

"What do you mean?"

"I love this place so much that I always tell people about it. I think everyone should experience Australia once. But the others never took my word for it. You did."

Right there, I felt my fears showing up. What I heard was that "I wasn't that special". It hurt, but I had to take it in. At least he was honest.

"I've been here for seven years now. Can you believe it?"

"Is this home for you?"

"Yes, I can see my future here. What are your plans?" he asked me while I was still trying to make peace with my own delusion.

"Honestly, no idea. I have four months of school and then I'll see. I really like Perth, I hope I can stay there for at least a year. But I'm not a real planner. I'll take one step after the other and see what happens."

"From my experience, people always start like that, but end up staying a lot longer. A lot of Brazilians never go back to Brazil."

"I've noticed. It's interesting what happens to people here. I guess I just have to wait and see."

"You've only been here for two weeks and you've managed to come down to the WQS. How did that happen?"

"It's a funny story," I said, trying to hide my embarrassment.

"Come on, tell me."

I told him about the chance encounter in the city. He acknowledged his friend's loss. We kept chatting and laughing for a while. I was happy to be there, but something inside me had changed during our conversation. I couldn't tell what it was. It simply felt off.

The Daniel I met in Brazil was not the same sitting across from me that night. He was different. I was different too. I was just trying to get my head around the fact that we were going nowhere. And it was a little challenging for a romantic like me.

We left the bar and went for a walk. Daniel knew every place, the background stories, the owners. He was basically a local in this small town across the world. He lived there for a lifetime.

Surf was a huge part of him. Most of those surf legends were his personal friends. It became evident that our lives were going in completely different directions.

Reality was catching up on me. I was overwhelmed. It wasn't the perfect love story I imagined, but the one question in my mind was this: *why did I come all the way here?*

I couldn't deny things were going wrong between us. Still, everything else felt right.

When I made that decision, I was ready to deal with the consequences. I knew it was risky. And I also knew life worked in mysterious ways.

That's what they call plot twist.

Back at The Tav, I joined the dance floor and the fun times with the drunks of the world. We all sang along to the usual songs. I slowly started coming back to myself.

I also lost sight of Daniel. After spending a couple of hours with him, I understood that the connection we felt in Brazil was indeed fleeting. There was no intention of repeating what happened the year before. My head and my heart were battling. All I wanted was for them to make peace.

I kept repeating to myself: *I am exactly where I am meant to be. I just have to wait and see.*

That's when I saw André coming in my direction. The guy from the reggae night who gave me Daniel's number. We started talking and he asked me about Daniel. I was elusive — actually, embarrassed. The last thing I wanted was to show him my real feelings. But he was smart. He could tell something was going on. He clearly had a lot more information about everything, including Daniel's life.

"So, how long have you known Daniel for?"

"About a year. We met during his last trip to Brazil."

"Interesting. Is that how you ended up here?" he asked bluntly.

"Yes and no. I guess it was just one of those coincidences."

I realised I could use someone's ear, but Paula wasn't there. She was the only person I could really talk to about this. Instead of overthinking, I decided to talk through some of my thoughts out loud to André. He seemed all ears.

"You know, last year, after I graduated, all I could think about was living overseas. I had a good life, a good job, but something was missing. I knew I wanted to have an international experience while I was still young. If I waited for too long, my career was going to take off and I was never gonna make it. So, I researched a few places. Between London and California, I couldn't pick a side. Australia wasn't even an option. To be honest, it didn't even cross my mind. Until I met Daniel. He told me about Australia, Perth, Margaret River, everything. It sounded so incredible that I decided to do some real research. It turns out it was the perfect place for me. It ticked all the boxes. So, here I am. A long story short."

"Carol, I have never met anyone who doesn't love it here. You made the right choice." His words were somewhat comforting.

"That's how I feel."

"So, you and Daniel? Is there a thing?" He was clearly interested in figuring out my romantic endeavours.

"Not sure. I thought there was, but now I don't."

"Well, you'll probably understand why if you turn around."

As I turned around, I saw Daniel kissing a gorgeous girl. I couldn't say I was surprised. This thought crossed my mind a number of times. It was always a possibility and I knew it.

I suddenly realised what he was trying to tell me in the short time we spent together. Not with words. But energy doesn't lie. He was no longer available. It all made sense. I admired him for it. I liked him even more. He was loyal too.

Once I was over the initial shock, I felt relief. I couldn't help but think of Alanis:

> *"It's meeting the man of my dreams*
>
> *And then meeting his beautiful wife*
>
> *And isn't it ironic... don't you think"*

Yes, it was a little too ironic, but I chose to trust that life had a funny way of helping us out. I was hurt, but I was also free. And that was exactly what I had been looking for all along.

Love is courage. Sometimes you do for others what you wouldn't do just for yourself.

I needed an impulse to get me out of my comfort zone. Daniel played that role in my life.

Hope can be a revolutionary thing too.

That was not the end of my story. In fact, it was just the beginning.

14. LIVING HISTORY.

The next morning, we all headed to Surfers Point Prevelly. We left the car in one of the car parks and walked to the site.

A huge sign read "6th Annual Salomon Masters" and right below "Bico Classic 2005".

We were entering Margaret River's Pro. Following the highest standards, the six-star WQS event was impeccably organized.

It's one of eleven WCT events globally. WCT stands for World Championship Tour. It's part of the World Surf League (WSL). All events occur at iconic destinations like Australia, Indonesia, Brazil, South Africa, North America, French Polynesia, Europe and Hawaii. Top ranked male and female surfers compete over a 12-day period. It's the elite league for surfers.

Margaret River is world renowned for consistent swell and size. It's probably part of the reason why this tiny coastal town has become a surfing mecca, attracting some of the world's best surfers and a world-class contest.

We were at the "Main Break". The number one surfing location in Margaret River. The laid-back atmosphere was very welcoming.

"Wow, is this place even real? It's so beautiful!" I started talking to Edu as we were approaching the picturesque beach while overlooking the whole area from this incredible vantage point, only a few surfers in action.

"It's iconic, Carol. This place consistently delivers big waves and solid swells. It's thousands of kilometres of uninterrupted Indian Ocean between Africa and Australia. Can you imagine that? It's nature's masterpiece."

"Well, I'm not a surfer but the waves look pretty big to me."

"Today is nothing. This year hasn't been great. Everyone's a little disappointed."

As Daniel had briefly mentioned, apparently, for the first time in 20 years of history, the wave-rich Margaret River didn't deliver. Flat days and small waves made for a bunch of very frustrated surfers and event organizers.

Nineteen Brazilians entered the contest but only eight managed to move ahead. Our Brazilian surf army didn't perform as expected and we couldn't blame them in such unfavorable conditions.

Some heats even had to be postponed due to tiny surf. It was hard to believe, but it happened. I suddenly realised that things don't always go as planned, even for real planners on a much greater scale.

Life is unpredictable. We must learn to make the best out of all situations.

Although the surf wasn't great, everyone still managed to have a great time. A sunny day at the beach, beautiful people, good music and cold beers. I really enjoyed being amongst all the action. For me, it was a perfect way to recover from what happened the night before. Daniel may not have been "the one" but I was finally living my dream.

Surfers Point wasn't just a place for surfers. It was also a perfect spot for anyone who loved to watch the sun go down. We all stayed around and sat comfortably, noticing the changes in the sky. All the different colors ended in an incredible orange.

If you live in the west, you never miss a sunset!

"West is the best!" I heard someone next to us saying it and I had to agree. I was in west-heaven and didn't want to leave.

"Are you guys going to the festival? Gomez is playing," someone asked Edu.

"We didn't get tickets," he answered, hesitantly.

"Forget it then, it's sold out."

"Really? Is it gonna be that good?" I could feel disappointment in his voice.

"It's Gomez, man. What do you think?"

Well, I didn't think anything. I had just arrived from Brazil and I never heard of Gomez in my life. They were an English indie rock band who seemed like a big deal and were headlining that night's music festival. Obviously, if you know the band (and like it), you'd be a little disappointed. In my case, I had no idea what I was missing out on. The town was still buzzing and I was quite happy to just hit the pub and have a few too many drinks. No driving for me that night.

The Tav was again "the place to be". Between the beer garden and the band, I felt a great energy. People were having real fun.

"Hi, this is Carolina," Mari introduced me to a random Aussie.

"Brazilian, of course. I'm Michael. Nice to meet you."

"Nice to meet you too, Michael."

"Come on, people. Let's do shots!" He invited everyone to the bar.

We all drank together, cheering to everything!

> *To the terrible surf of 2005!*
>
> *To the winners!*
>
> *To the losers!*
>
> *To all the surfers of this year!*
>
> *To the Aussies!*
>
> *To the Brazilians!*
>
> *To Margaret River!*

I added my own cheers.

> *To another heartbreak!*
>
> *To dreams that do come true!*

Drinking is just one of those things that works both ways. We drink to celebrate, or to commiserate. I wasn't sure if I was celebrating or commiserating. I was already too wasted to figure that out.

I guess we all just secretly danced to our own feelings until we were told to leave. It wasn't even that late, but Australians had their own set of rules and small towns followed them to a tee.

Mari drove us back to our little cottage where we kept the party going for a while. I was starting to connect with some of the new people. They were fun. It didn't take long until all of us drifted off to sleep.

It was the last day of the contest. We woke up slightly hungover, but after a full breakfast, we all headed back to Surfers Point for the finals.

> *"This is a miracle! Margaret River's famous swell finally picked up. It's the finals and the surfers are on fire to catch those giant waves out there. You better be ready."*

The MC's warm-up speech was getting everyone excited.

"What's going on?" I asked one of the guys who was there earlier.

"Look at those waves, girl! It's Margs again! These finals are gonna be insane!"

"Of course," I said, not knowing any of the technicalities but acknowledging the size of the waves. They were wild!

> *"Everyone here today, you came for a great show. For the first time in the contest, it's man-on-man. The elite surf will show us why they made it all the way here."*

The MC kept going.

> *"Look, even the dolphins came to join us. Check out those unmatchable wave riding skills. Natural performers stealing the show! That's a good luck sign for all the surfers about to enter those waters. Magical moment here at the Margaret River Salomon Masters 2005. After a week of average conditions, Margs today is full of surprises. Guys, your tickets just gained a whole new value with that sideshow right there."*

He was so pumped! And absolutely right. It was priceless! Some things were simply impossible to predict. That moment was one of them.

"There is Neco Padaratz coming out of the water after a great performance. The Brazilian, our last year's winner, finished third this time. His fellow Brazilians Pedro Henrique and Armando Daltro finished equal fifth together. Brazilians are always solid here in Margaret River."

The quarter finals were already a great show.

"Now, here comes the final. The lone Aussie to reach quarter finals this year, Troy Brooks. He made it to the final up against one of the favorites: Hawaiian Roy Powers. Brooks carries the hopes of our nation today."

It was the final heat. We could hear the crowds going wild for Brooks. The competitive atmosphere of the man-on-man upped the stakes for everyone, but it was the final battle. Powers seemed to have the money in the bag. He had been ripping all day, dropping eights and nines every heat.

"It's Brooks vs. Powers. We're getting to the end of this water battle between them, the dying minutes. Wait, look at that huge wave coming up. It's Brooks. He is launching a massive aerial, his famous superman rodeo. He lands it and continues with critical forehand snaps. What an epic moment here in Margaret River today, guys! He might have just brought it home at the last minute. Absolutely incredible! Solid confidence from Brooks. He deserves to win."

Brooks had just turned 26 that week, and the win would mean a real reason for him to celebrate.

"It's done. A dramatic victory for Brooks on this incredible Sunday. Here he comes, carried from the water's edge all the way up. With a near-perfect 9.67 score, he's definitely a winner today!"

Brook's 2005 season was up to a perfect start. He not only got the prize money but also crucial ratings points. The media was there, we watched his interview:

> "Oh my God, this is unbelievable! It was so nerve-racking out there, and I knew I only had one shot at it. I sat and waited, and finally the wave came at the end. I saw a punt section and just went for it, and nailed it. I was just hoping it would go flat and he wouldn't be able to catch anything else," he laughed and said referring to Powers who was literally killing it. "How awesome is this? My first WQS of the year, and to win is a dream start."

Brooks was the winner, but there is a reason why surfing is such a strong sport. While it may have real competition, it is also about brotherhood. Powers was the next to be interviewed and he proudly acknowledged Brooks' victory in his own words:

> "I've had a great contest, but at the end of the final I was basically a spectator. There was nothing I could have done, and I'm so stoked to have gotten second. He definitely deserved to win with that aerial. He put it on the line, and that's what surfing should be about now. I was clapping from behind as he did it. It was a sick air. I'm just stoked to have such a strong start at the beginning of the year."

Victory or defeat, it didn't really matter. Everyone had fun in the water and the result was just a reflection of that fantastic Sunday for each one of those talented surf pros.

On the podium, three of the best surfers in the world shared champagne showers and joyful tears.

1. Troy Brooks (AUS)
2. Roy Powers (HAW)
3. Neco Padaratz (BRA)

A very emotional Neco was also being interviewed. He showed his love and respect for the amazing town of Margaret River.

> "Oh, man. Margaret River is a place that lives in my heart. I have so much passion about it, and feel like a man over here in this nature. There are so many sharks around, the waves are powerful, rocks everywhere. I feel like I did a good job and am so hungry to be back here again soon."

"*Thank you very much, man. You're a legend!*" — even the interviewer got emotional with him.

I finally understood how much that corner of the world meant to surfers. They all had a love-affair with Margaret River and its wild waves. No wonder there was a growing Brazilian community making their homes here. For them, there was no better place to be.

I felt the Aussie spirit cheering in my soul.

We never know the real value of a moment until all we've got are memories of it. But that's how history is made. Some people pay attention and document the times so others can access it. Storytelling is one of the most human things in the world.

Deep in my heart, I knew I would be telling stories one day. I also knew real lives were the richest material for creative inspiration. To me, reality is a beautiful thing. I love to see real human beings facing life and overcoming personal challenges.

I'll never forget how Brooks, Powers and Padaratz made me feel that day. And they may never know this, but I found the strength I needed to keep surfing my own waves.

I had no idea what was going to happen next. All I knew was that I had already crossed two oceans and I wasn't going to waste that amazing opportunity to finally exist on my own terms.

Right there, I learned my first lesson: in order to tell great stories, first we must live them.

So, I went back to Perth to live my 4-month prepaid plan and wait for the next wave to come.

15. WHAT ARE WE MADE OF?

People are water. Fluid, adaptable, open, wild. I was feeling like an ocean, ready to un-fix my identity and enjoy the waves outside my small-town safety.

I had travelled a long way and given myself a *"get out of jail free"* card. I was still a dreamer, but my soul was no longer a prisoner of my lack of further imagination.

As I entered a new world of possibilities, the seeds of my multiple identities were already growing inside of me.

People are also like trees. We're natural beings. And healthy growth comes from strong roots.

So, before moving forward, it was important to do a quick review to understand who I was and where I came from.

Back home, I was a young girl with a pretty good, comfortable, safe life. I always had a roof over my head, food on my plate and quality education. None of that was ever my responsibility. I didn't have to fight for survival. I'm aware this is called privilege.

But, like most families, we had our twists and turns. The first I experienced was my parent's divorce. I was six.

As I kept growing up, I noticed that my entire family had gone through divorces (even my grandparents, from both sides). As a result, I installed this unconscious belief: *marriage doesn't work.*

From my one-sided view, my dad was to blame. He left us. My spoiled, immature, childish nature never allowed me to see beyond my own needs. It was easier to fall into the victim role.

My dad was a somewhat successful businessman. His love language was money. Our relationship was heavily based on financial support and very little presence. He was too busy to deal with my emotional instability so he chose to overcompensate on material things. His intentions were good. The results? Not so much.

My mum was left with the job to "handle" me. God knows it wasn't easy. I may have screwed her entire life up with my teenage anger, but I was always very open about my feelings and she knew my reasons. Looking back, she might even have felt the same about him. Or me. She just never allowed her feelings to show.

From a positive standpoint, we all knew the problem. My anger was a secondary emotion to my fear. I was terrified just by the thought of ever repeating what I perceived as a nightmare. A broken family life.

I saw my mum as a vulnerable woman who had to silence her feelings in order to support herself and her kids. The whole idea of family was screwed up in my mind.

So, my goal in life was to be an independent woman and support myself. I honestly never even thought about having kids.

It's true: we get what we give. I was angry and disappointed. I blamed my parents for my misery. And the more I blamed them, the more I pushed them away. I wasn't giving them any of my love. The frustration and confusion made me blind to those feelings.

I had no idea what I was doing, but I wanted to be a better person. I just didn't know how. At some point, it was all too much and I wanted to run away. Some days, I didn't want to exist at all.

In order to recreate my life, I needed to find new inspiring references. Otherwise, the nightmare would go on.

I don't want to make it a general rule, but my impression is this: for parents, their kids will always be their responsibility — no matter how grown up and independent they become.

It's a beautiful thing. That's what parents should do. But that's not how humans grow.

I knew that "under my parent's watch", I'd always have to follow their rules. I felt trapped in their not-so-safe safety net.

I was obviously highly motivated to go overseas as a way to find my independence. In my mind, that was the only way I could start processing my feelings on my own.

But, having a university degree was important for my family. I wanted that for myself too. So, before I could leave Brazil, I decided to go to university.

1999 was the year that everything changed for me. To be fair, it changed for a lot of people.

Brazilian currency had depreciated over 60% against the U.S. dollar, making it harder for anyone to travel overseas. A devalued currency also initiated a financial crisis with a lot of business declining and the highest unemployment rate in over a decade.

My dad's business wasn't immune to the crisis and it got hit. Heavily.

Having your financial stability shaken is never an easy thing to go through, but it can be a real blessing in disguise. With money out of the equation, we had to renegotiate our love language.

It was challenging and painful. But, for the first time in my life, I remember having real conversations about my feelings with my father. We talked about things that had been buried for over a decade under a pile of cash. It felt so good.

In August of that year, I entered university.

Unlike most people I knew up to that point, I didn't have a single life destination. I loved communications because it would allow me to explore multiple avenues. I was gifted with enough curiosity to do just that.

In my view, we come into this world to be ever evolving, ever expanding. I never had a goal to get X job and X amount of money. My goal has never been to retire.

I am a big believer in growth as a way of life. I don't think we're here just for final achievements. For me, there is no finish line. As long as I'm breathing, I'll do my best to learn and develop all the important qualities for real growth: patience, resilience, compassion, joy and, ultimately, love. The kind that spreads all around.

But I had always been overprotected. I wasn't sure I had the strength to face life on my own. With the way my life was going, I'd probably end up settling for comfort over all those things my heart wanted. I was fully aware of the trap.

It turns out that, with great loss, comes even greater experience. And that's when I learned one of the most important lessons of my life: *do not allow success or failure to ever define you — because it doesn't.*

I knew I was not meant to be just one thing. I never wanted to be labelled as someone's daughter. Or wife. I wanted to be my own person. And if I was ever going to experience that, I'd need to allow myself real growth.

During my university years, I experimented with jobs and life. I still lived with my mum and my older brother, who helped to keep a roof over my head, but I worked part-time for the entire four and a half years of my degree and put some money towards the fees.

I had four different jobs. I started with an internship with the city council, moved to client services in a small advertising agency (very briefly), then managed to produce a local lifestyle TV show, until I finally went back to client services in a bigger agency.

That TV show experience was priceless — and probably the highlight of those years. It taught me so many things. It was the first time that I got paid to do something that I truly enjoyed. It felt amazing!

Picture this: a little town known for fun. I wish all of you could have experienced the party scene in the late 90's and early 2000's where I grew up. It was wild — and surprisingly diverse. Good old times!

Our show was all about that. A small, but very productive team. The presenter (who became my lifelong friend), the videographer (my boyfriend at the time, who got me the gig), an editor and me. It was hard work with endless late nights, but we were in our element.

That's when I got my first insight about balance: even when you enjoy what you do, you still have to take the bad with the good.

I honestly believe it was the best head-start I could get in life. Resourcefulness became my super power. I had no option but to develop multiple abilities. From there, anything was possible.

After I graduated, I decided to move in with my dad in an attempt to make up for too many years of disconnection. He was in Florianópolis at the time. And, as 'the Universe' would have it, I was offered a great position there that I decided to take.

My experience of living with him lasted an entire period of three months and needless to say, it was a little frustrating.

I didn't fully understand the extent of his loss, but I knew it was messy. He was still trying to figure his own way out of a pretty major breakdown that lasted years. He didn't just lose his business. His second marriage also ended. And both my little brother and sister were thrown into the mix. It wasn't easy for anyone.

In summary, my dad had four kids and two "failed" marriages. He was only 46.

Everyone deserves a clean slate. And he got it. He was offered an interstate sales position and decided to go for it.

Intellectually, I knew it was the right thing for him to do. Emotionally, I just couldn't believe he was leaving me again. I knew it wasn't all about me, but as a 21-year-old, I didn't know any better.

In the short time we lived together, he taught me some tough lessons about responsibility. Initially I hated it, but later I understood he was trying to do the right thing. He wanted to be the real parent he never was.

When he left, I had two options: stay there alone or go back to my mum's. I decided to stay. I already had a job. This time, I was going to make it on my own.

My real challenge was to cut the cords with my mum. She got so used to over-protecting her poor daughter that she would come on weekends to help at the first sign of an imminent crisis. It was only an hour's drive, and my brother was living away that year.

My mother's love language is service. How could I tell her that the over-protection was killing my own ability to survive and thrive?

I was uncomfortable with my dad pushing me so hard, but how was I supposed to learn anything if I didn't get a chance to make my own mistakes?

My mum was a fixer. She would fix everything. Nothing I ever did was good enough. So, I started to silence my feelings and turned into an unhealthy perfectionist who was a real nightmare to myself and everyone around.

I knew I had something to give and feared putting everything to waste because of my emotional instability and constant need to escape. I was also trying to balance my alcoholic tendencies with an incredible desire to be of service to the world.

I had to be very deliberate to stay on top of my game, in whatever I was doing. My 'big black hole' was too dark and deep for me to fall into. I wouldn't survive if I did.

And exactly around the time my dad left me, I met Daniel. A perfect moment of joy right in the middle of another breakdown. I craved human connection. I found it. Physically and mentally.

My urge for real freedom was undeniable. Months later, I felt stronger and ready to make my own decisions. That's when I pulled myself together and decided to finally do what was best for me: *go away*.

It's hard to imagine someone, with that background, crossing two oceans inspired by the prospect of a happy ending. But, as paradoxical as it sounds, that's how I found my own way to escape fate.

I knew I wanted a bigger life that wouldn't be available to me if I had stayed in my hometown. I just had to find the courage to face the world on my own.

My parents were both fine with my decision. In a way, I guess it was a relief for them. Obviously, they wanted me to grow. They just had no idea how to help. Going away was probably the best option for everyone.

My older brother knew me better (probably better than anyone else). He was a bit skeptical about my move. He wasn't sure that I was equipped to be on my own in the world. He knew the kinds of jobs I'd be required to do and was worried I wouldn't be able to handle them.

He trusted my potential and had envisioned a different future for me: an MBA followed by a big corporate job or something along those lines. Safety is what they called it. He was doing his best to protect his little sister, but I knew I wasn't meant for that.

I had to find my edge and grow up without a safety net. It was my turn to have a clean slate. A year away was exactly what I needed. I knew it in my heart.

I can almost hear him singing those 1970's lyrics from Cat Stevens (Yusuf Islam) that I heard from Emmerson Nogueira's cover album in the late nineties:

> *"Oh, baby, baby, it's a wild world*
>
> *It's hard to get by just upon a smile*
>
> *Oh, baby, baby, it's a wild world*
>
> *I'll always remember you like a child girl"*

My brother is only two-and-a-half years older than me, but he became "the man" in our family when he was nine years old. I know, it was so unfair.

Being a male firstborn, he was taught to follow my father's and grandfather's footsteps in life and business. They introduced him to work at the early age of 11. He surely knew the world better than I did. Maybe he knew too much.

He was my role model. I always admired and respected him for his achievements, but his life was the opposite of mine. He was safe. I was wild.

So, I decided to jump and be fully responsible for my actions. With no one close enough to come to my rescue, I would have no other option than to grow the hell up.

If I was the only person responsible for providing a life for myself, I would have no choice but to make it happen.

16. A CLEAN SLATE.

It was only my third week at school. After practicing my English, and feeling more comfortable, I decided to follow my teacher's guidance and retook the placement test.

He was right. They transferred me to the Advanced Level, where I would stay until the end of my four-month course and hopefully become fluent.

My routine was starting to become familiar and I seemed to have my life almost under control. My challenge was to balance study, work and fun.

I knew Cottesloe was my place and it was time for me to make some real moves. I decided to live with Paula and find a job close to home. My next step was to have a conversation with my host family and let them know I would leave soon.

"How was your day, Carolina?" Flynn asked me while we were setting the dinner table.

"Very good, Flynn. Thank you. In fact, there's something I need to talk to you about."

"Sure, what's up?"

"Remember my friend Paula?"

"The Brazilian who lives in Cottesloe?"

"That's right. She has this really nice apartment there and offered to share it with me."

"That sounds great. You planned on living there anyway, didn't you?"

"Yes, I did."

"Perfect. When are you planning on leaving?"

"This Saturday."

"That soon? But you still have another week here with us."

"I know, but I need to find a job and I guess it will be much easier if I already have something around there."

"Sure, you're right. It's a long way for you to commute and we know night transport around here is not ideal."

"Exactly. Are you okay with that?"

"Sure, no problem. In that case, we can give your money back for the week you have left. We can easily get another student here. This way you have some extra cash for bond and rent. You'll probably need it."

"Oh, really? That's so nice of you. Thank you very much. That will help me a lot."

"You're welcome, Carolina. It's the least we can do. You hardly spent any time here."

"That is true," I said laughing, while recollecting my last two weeks of little adventures.

Flynn was right. I wasn't spending a great deal of time at home. I was going out a lot and often staying overnight with friends or travelling on weekends. I wasn't expecting a full refund, but that money came in very handy.

I was paying AU$200 a week for homestay and the new apartment was AU$320 a month (it was a shared bed and a great deal). It covered over half of my first month's rent. It was perfect. The Universe seemed to be working in my favor.

The next day I had lunch with Caio. He was a DJ, also from the South of Brazil. We went to a nice pub close to our school.

"So, where exactly did you live before coming here?" I asked him to start our conversation.

"I was born in Blumenau, but later I moved to Balneário Camboriú where I met my girlfriend. She's in London now, coming here in a couple of months. You?"

"Funny enough I was also born in Blumenau, but my family moved to Itajaí when I was three. My grandmother is the only one left in Blu. I lived with her for almost a year when I worked at an ad agency there while still at uni. She is amazing. I miss her a lot."

"I hear you. My parents live there too. It's a nice city. I just couldn't handle the traditions. I like new things."

"I think it's the German heritage. They are conservative and like to keep things as they are. It works for them. So, what made you come all the way here?"

"I wanted to try something new. I was a DJ, then model, went into this industry and things got a little out of hand. I don't like to be exposed. I'm a very private person. I guess sometimes we just need a change, you know? I wanted to be unknown. Maybe I can find out who I really am, what I really wanna be. I love cooking, for example. Here, I can make pizza and nobody judges me. These things are just a little more complicated over there, if you know what I mean."

"Totally. And you're absolutely right. Being unknown is very liberating. I guess I'm after that too. Small town issues, right?"

"Spot on," he answered with a smile.

"Well, at least no one knows us here."

"Not yet," he said, laughing.

I felt comfortable talking to Caio. We weren't close or anything, but somehow, he understood where I came from. He was familiar with the culture I grew up in. In some ways, he was also familiar with my struggles. I wasn't surprised to hear his story. Suddenly, the world really seemed just like a small town.

It's interesting how connections are made in the most unexpected ways. You could spend your entire life in the same place as someone else, without ever meeting this person. And then, in a foreign country, on the other side of the globe, you almost instantly become friends.

Why do we tend to open up and bond with strangers a lot easier when out in the world?

I suppose this is just how life works. Think about it: we all start as strangers. It's a never-ending cycle of random encounters and coincidences. Out there, we're just more aware of it. But in the safety nets of life as we know it, we never dare to look beyond the safe option.

After lunch, we went back to school for another few hours and I caught up with Paula on my way out.

"It's done, my friend. I'm moving on Saturday. Yay!" I said, giving her a big hug.

"Perfect! Do you need help?"

"Not really. I'll just catch a cab with my suitcases. I don't have much."

"Oh, how exciting! The Cott girls! If you need anything, just call me, ok?" she said, smiling as usual.

"Of course. I'll see you tomorrow! Thank you."

I was starting to connect with some really incredible people I'd probably never have met unless I went to Australia. I would be lying if I said I wasn't scared at first. Of course, I was. But I guess we must find the courage to take the first steps in the dark, not knowing exactly where we'll end up if we ever want to do something new.

We might not have all the answers right away, but we should never give up on the questions.

All of us had very different reasons to be there. Some people were doing it for education. Others, for money. Some were there just for fun.

Why was I doing that? For freedom and growth.

What about love? I was still not sure I deserved that, to be honest.

And while we all had our own personal goals, there was one thing we shared in common: *change*.

I'm yet to meet a single person who wasn't somehow transformed by the whole experience of living in a foreign country.

There is a certain comfort and confidence that you gain with yourself when you go to a new place and start all over again. A knowledge that, whatever comes your way for the rest of your life, you'll always remember that you were capable of taking that leap and landing softly, at least once. And if you did then, you can do it again.

Self-confidence. Maybe that was the real thing I was after.

Every time I met someone I felt had "made it", I got more comfortable. If they could, I could too. In my heart I knew that, somewhere in the past, they were standing right where I was. And, just like them, I took the first step.

Things were not fully formed yet, but I could feel my path perfectly unfolding right in front of my eyes. I accepted that things didn't turn out in the way I imagined, but I trusted that they would happen exactly in the way I needed. Maybe even better.

I was ready to surrender and let myself be amazed by my very own experience.

17. LANDING MY FIRST JOB.

Thanks to Paula, my life in Cottesloe was already sorted. With a roof over my head, it was time to find my first job in Australia.

Our options were somewhat limited with full-time study. We could wait tables, clean offices, wash dishes and maybe do a few other odd jobs in services or hospitality. Most Brazilians I met did one of those things.

Wednesday afternoon, after school, I caught the train to Cottesloe and went for a walk on Marine Parade. I saw a few cafés and restaurants, until one stood out.

A small, modern, glass-walled café and restaurant. An absolute beachfront location with a balcony perched directly above the beach sand. I could only imagine working there while being totally amazed by an uninterrupted ocean view.

I walked in and asked for the manager. It was him. Juan. A very welcoming Chilean guy who hardly had an accent.

"Hi Juan, my name is Carolina. How are you today?"

"Nice to meet you, Carolina. I'm fine, how can I help you?"

"Well, I was wondering if you guys need any staff. I'm actually looking for work. Here's my resume," I asked while handing him my papers.

"Oh, it must be your lucky day. We actually are. South American?" he asked, curious.

"Yes, Brazilian. Can you tell?"

"The accent. It's beautiful. We never hired any Brazilians here so you'd be the first."

"Really? Why is that?" I asked, wondering if there was something wrong with us.

"I guess you guys are just hard to come by around here. Do you want a trial?"

"Sure. When?"

"Is tonight too soon?"

"Oh, I can make that work. What time and what do I need to wear?"

"Black pants, black shoes and yourself. We'll give you a t-shirt. How about seven o'clock?"

"Sounds great. See you then."

I left the restaurant with an overwhelming mix of happiness and surprise. I never thought things could be that easy. I felt so grateful, until it hit me: I didn't have either black pants or black shoes. At least not the kind people wore for work.

For a split second, I panicked. And then I went into solution mode.

First, I checked the time. 4pm. I knew I had an hour to find what I needed. I was about 15 minutes from Claremont. There was this department store just off the train station. I ran to the train and by 4:30pm I was inside the store.

I bought a pair of black pants and some black working shoes. I called Paula and told her the news. I went straight home for a quick shower and got ready for my first trial.

7pm sharp, I showed up. As I walked in, the most extraordinary sunset overtook the sky and caught my full attention. I stood in awe as words escaped my mouth, "Oh, I could get used to this." Juan approached me from the back and said, smiling, "I'm sure you will".

I had a good feeling about the trial, even though I had absolutely zero experience as a waitress. My real work experience in advertising was worthless to get that job, but I was resourceful, remember?

Juan showed me around, introduced me to the staff and told me what to do. That night, my only responsibility was to run food from the pass to the tables. I was anxious, but I knew I could handle the pressure. In just a few minutes, people started to arrive and the restaurant was pretty much full, which wasn't hard since the place was small.

I wasn't used to being on that side of a restaurant, so I just kept following Juan's instructions. I was also responsible for serving tap water to all the customers, making sure their glasses were always full. I loved that.

Basically, my job entailed walking around all night doing whatever was needed. I don't remember stopping for a second up until Juan called me to the side. I was nervous that I had done something wrong.

"Are you okay?" he asked, pointing to my shoes.

"Yes, why?"

"Your heels are bleeding."

"Oh, I am so sorry." I said, looking at the blood spilt on the floor. "I didn't even feel it. Let me clean this straight away."

"That's not what I meant, Carol. Is it hurting?"

"No, I'm not even feeling it. It must be the new shoes. Blisters, you know?"

"True, that happens sometimes. Here, get a band-aid. Go clean up and come back."

"Sure. I won't be a minute."

I felt so embarrassed. As I entered the bathroom, I saw the blood on my heels. It was actually pretty bad, but I didn't feel the pain. I washed up and put a band-aid on. Just like grown-ups do. I also checked myself in the mirror and realised I was a bit of a sweaty mess. I fixed what I could and went back outside. There was only one table left.

Everyone was more relaxed, at a slower pace. Juan asked me to sit with him at a table on the balcony. He gave me a glass of wine.

"So, what did you think?" he asked while sipping from his own glass.

"I loved it." I was sure my smile confirmed my feelings.

"You haven't done this before, have you?"

"Can you tell?" I said, really embarrassed.

"I knew it, but you did great! I was impressed."

"Really?"

"Yeah. I mean, you smiled a lot, you were very nice and polite to everyone. Plus, you didn't even feel your hurting heels. You must have been on a high!" he said, joking.

"That was pretty funny! And yeah, it was intense."

"I thought you were pretty focused. Do you want the job?"

"Of course I do."

"Well, then welcome to our team. You're officially the first Brazilian waitress here."

"Oh my God, thank you so much. It means the world to me."

"Here's your form. Bring it back with all your details tomorrow and we'll finish the paperwork, okay?"

"Sure."

"Ah, where do you live?"

"From Saturday, I'll be living just down the road. Five minutes' walk."

"Come on, you're lucky! I'll organize your schedule then. Do you wanna start on the weekend or do you need some time for the move?"

"I can do Saturday night or Sunday. I'm moving in the morning. I only have two suitcases. It will be a quick one."

"Perfect, I'll have your schedule ready for tomorrow."

"Thank you again. I'm so excited!" I gave him a hug and left.

On my walk back to my future home, relief started taking over my body. I got it! And it wasn't just any job. Given my circumstances, I won the job lotto.

An amazing restaurant with ocean views, really nice people and within a five-minute walk from home. I had to pinch myself to make sure it was real. It was.

I was definitely on a high. Everything I'd been dreaming of was starting to come true.

Paula was still awake when I got there to crash the night. I told her about the job and she was very happy for me.

With a little faith in myself, things were all starting to fall into place. I knew I could trust life. It was me that I had to learn how to trust.

18. FINALLY HOME.

Saturday morning.

I said my final goodbyes to my host family and left.

On my way to Cottesloe, I had time for some reflection.

Up until that point in my life, I never acknowledged my capacity for discomfort. While I could easily be called a "quitter", I was willing to try different things to see how they felt.

"Keep going" was my personal mantra (it still is). I usually keep going at one thing until I have nothing left to give. Then I move forward, trusting that better things are on their way to me.

I only quit things that I feel are not working. I believe that's healthy.

Unfortunately, not everyone feels this way. Some people overstay. For far too long. In a place, a job or a relationship. Until it kills them (metaphorically or literally). I wasn't willing to trade my life for any of these things. Ever. So, I *kept going*.

"Welcome home." Paula was waiting for me with her trademark smile.

"I am so happy to be here. Thank you, my friend! It's another dream come true."

"Come in, there's juice and some fruit here. Help yourself!"

"Oh, you're such a good friend. I wish I could stay longer and enjoy some time with you, but I have to go out soon."

"Where are you going?"

"Freo. I need to find proper shoes for work. I have my first real shift tonight."

"That's great! I'm very proud of you. But didn't you just buy new shoes?"

"I did, but you've seen what happened. I can't take that risk again. I'm gonna need to walk from five to eight hours a day, three to four times a week. I can't bleed every time."

"You're probably right."

"Do you wanna come?"

"I can't. I have a few things to do too."

"That's cool. We'll catch up later."

I had a clear goal: to find the perfect shoes. I didn't care so much if they were beautiful; comfort was my non-negotiable.

I spent almost an entire afternoon looking at all the shops and nothing felt right. I was about to give up when I saw this boutique that had some pretty fine Italian leather shoes in the window. One specific pair seemed to be exactly what I was after so I decided to go in. A very nice lady greeted me.

"Hi, how can I help you?"

"I'd like to try this one on," I said, pointing to the pair by the window.

"What size?"

"Six."

"Sure, I won't be a minute."

While she was gone, I started to look around. They had some amazing shoes, but they were all expensive (at least for my student budget).

"Here," she said, handing me the black shoes.

"Thank you."

As I put them on, I realised I was trying a totally different shoe category. I had literally gone to shoe heaven!

"Wow, they are amazing! I feel like I'm walking on clouds. So smooth."

"Yes, they are pretty amazing! We sell a lot of them here."

"I bet. How much are they?"

"90 dollars."

"Ouch. I was looking for something a little cheaper."

"You might find some at other shops around here. They won't be Italian leather but they'll do the job."

"Well, I have actually gone around the block and tried pretty much everything. I even bought a cheap pair on Wednesday for 40 bucks and they gave me these blisters." I showed her the damage.

"Shoes can be tricky like that."

"I know. That's why I need good solid ones. I'll take these. It's an investment."

"Shoes are always an investment, darling," she said in a very cheeky tone.

"They are. But these ones are even more. They are for work. I'm gonna spend a lot of time walking around in them."

"I'm sure you won't regret it."

"Me too. Thank you."

I left the shop feeling like I could conquer the world in those shoes. They were the first investment in my newfound Australian career that I took very seriously. I may have never been a waitress in my life, but with the right shoes, I was ready to do my very best.

On my way back, I heard Ben Harper putting my heart at ease.

"I knew a girl

Her name was truth

She was a horrible liar

She couldn't spend one day alone

But she couldn't be satisfied

When you have everything,

You have everything to lose

She made herself

A bed of nails

And she's plannin' on puttin' it to use

'Cause she had diamonds on the inside"

I love how life speaks to us through music. That song translated my feelings better than I ever could. I just listened to those words and felt the magic working all around me.

My heart was still broken. Things didn't go as I planned. But I found the courage to do something I always wanted to do. I was literally living my dream.

I was both hurting and healing — at the same time.

Deep inside, I knew everything was going to be alright. I just had to trust and be patient.

19. GOING WITH THE FLOW.

Love doesn't always last forever. Sometimes, it just comes to us in order to change our direction and lead us to a new place where we are meant to be. A lot of times, love is as simple as that.

I was only 22, but heartbreaks were somehow familiar to me. I had a fair share of those back in Brazil.

The foreign part was being in a new place fully on my own. Which was the whole point of my experience.

Daniel had done a great job at making me want to learn more about Australia: a unique and diverse country in every way.

History, geography, climate, population. All these elements made up for an amazing culture and an incredible place to be. I was very curious about it all.

One day, after class, I found myself sitting across from my teacher. He was an interesting character, but so busy that we rarely had time for real-life conversations. That day we did have time.

"Hey teacher, what can you tell me about Australia's history?" I asked him quite randomly to see what he would come up with.

"What do you mean, Carolina?"

"Well, let's take Brazil, for example. They officially credited Pedro Álvares Cabral for our country's discovery in the 1500s. He and his crew found our land on their way to India. Hard to imagine, but apparently it happened to Christopher Columbus as well. The thing is: people already lived there. Native indigenous people made their lives in Brazil long before the European arrival. And, ironically, the original Brazilians are known as Indians because of their little mistake. Sometimes I wonder what Brazil would be like if it wasn't a Portuguese colony."

"Wow, that's interesting. I had no idea."

"It's a lot more complex than that, of course. And we may never know the truth. But that's a tiny bit of history we can read from the books."

"Sure. We might have something in common then."

"Really? Tell me more."

"Aboriginals, you probably have seen a few here. The indigenous Australians inhabited our continent for over 60,000 years. They had their own unique stories and beliefs. It was called 'Dreamtime'."

"60,000 years? How's that even possible? Dreamtime. I like it already."

"You see, geologically, Australia is the most ancient part of the entire earth."

"Wow, I had no idea."

"Yep. But, in our case, Captain James Cook was credited with Australia's discovery, although a Dutch explorer is known to have found it first. Who knows?"

"Interesting."

"But the funny part is this: Australia was originally established as a penal colony. One in five Australians is the descendant of a convict."

"Convicts as in criminals?"

"Something like that," he said, laughing. "Well, serious crimes like murder and rape were punishable by death, but petty offences — such as stealing anything worth more than the average day's wage — were deemed worthy of a one-way ticket to an isolated corner of the globe."

"So, did they send them here?"

"That's correct. British convicts were a source of labor to build roads, bridges, courthouses, hospitals and other public buildings. They also worked on government farms. The educated ones may have been given jobs such as record-keeping for the government administration or something like that."

"Were there women too?"

"Yes, a lot less. They were mainly employed in domestic services or in government farms."

"Nothing new there. Does it feel a little embarrassing to come from this kind of background?"

"It's not an easy past to have as a country, and we can't change what has happened. For what indigenous Australians had to go through and what the convicts experienced, we can educate ourselves on their history and teach our young ones to do better. In a way, it is a story of second chances. While not ideal, our history is what shaped the country we live in today and we can learn from these lessons, to find freedom for ourselves, and for those still advocating for theirs."

"Absolutely. That is some interesting history there. I love it! It's all about resilience and adaptability, isn't it? Also overcoming obstacles to find freedom. Sounds a lot like me. How long ago was that?"

"Late 1700s. But Australia was only federated in 1901. It's kind of a young country with ancestral history."

"Fascinating. Politically wise, how does it work?"

"Well, the country was grounded in British culture and political traditions. We follow the Westminster system of Parliamentary Government and Elizabeth II is also Queen of Australia."

"Wow, there's so much more to learn outside the language here in Australia, right?"

"That is very true, Carol."

"Thanks for the chat, teacher! It was very insightful. I have to go now. See ya tomorrow."

"See ya!"

That conversation got me thinking about this country I was living in and the opportunities it had to offer.

My idea of success was to make a living, grow up, be responsible, while still keeping a young spirit and a fresh perspective to life.

With love out of the equation, my goal was to balance the other two areas of my life that were thriving: study and work.

Outside my necessary routine, I had to find ways to keep my creative juices flowing. Music, movies and books always helped me to do that.

I'd noticed a number of second-hand bookstores every time I made my way to the train station after school. Until I felt the urge to go in. When you step into one of them, a distinctive, dusty, old-fashioned smell instantly overwhelms you. It's hard to know exactly what creates the nostalgic aroma that lingers in those spaces, but somehow it inspires me.

The best way I could describe it is that second-hand bookstores smelled the opposite of new.

I had so much newness in my life that entering that bookstore brought back some memories of my own. A real rush of feelings that triggered my most basic instincts and led me to one single thought: *how could past stories inspire me into my new future?*

I thought that reading a book in English would be a perfect way to practice the language, while enjoying a nice little story. Since I was a student on a tight budget, second-hand was just what I needed. I was in the right place, at the right time.

I started wandering through the shelves until a particular and intriguing blue cover popped to my eyes: *The Celestine Prophecy — an adventure*, by James Redfield.

Still on the cover, I read:

> *In the rain forests of Peru, an ancient manuscript has been discovered. Within its pages are 9 key insights to life itself — insights each human being is predicted to grasp sequentially, one insight then another, as we move toward a completely spiritual culture on Earth.*

And right below Redfield's name, a powerful review by Elisabeth Kübler-Ross:

> *"A fabulous book about experiencing life — I couldn't put it down."*

I had no idea who Elisabeth or James were, but those words were exactly what I needed to read at that time in my life. Although, I had to admit that "spiritual" was almost a foreign word to my vocabulary.

On the other hand, adventure was a staple. The thought of reading a novel about the discovery of an ancient manuscript found in the Peruvian jungle seemed like an amazing idea to me. Not to mention, the possibility of finding out nine essential insights for human life and spiritual growth. That would be a real-life adventure. I had found my new read.

On my way home, I sat on the train and opened the book. Very quickly, I understood Elisabeth's cover review. She was right. It was hard to put it down.

> *"The transformation is beginning with the First Insight, and according to the priest, this insight always surfaces unconsciously at first, as a profound sense of restlessness."*
>
> *"Restlessness?"*
>
> *"Yes."*
>
> *"What are we looking for?"*
>
> *"That's just it! At first, we aren't sure. According to the Manuscript, we're beginning to glimpse an alternative kind of experience... moments in our lives that feel different somehow, more intense and inspiring."*

That dialogue clearly resonated with me. I wasn't sure what I was looking for, but I felt those kinds of moments happening in my life. Meeting Daniel in Brazil was exactly like that: intense and inspiring. So much, that it inspired me to go all the way to Australia.

> *"But we don't know what this experience is or how to make it last, and when it ends, we're left feeling dissatisfied and restless with a life that seems ordinary again."*

Oh-oh. The reality check. And the endless search for something extraordinary.

That initial dialogue stirred something inside me. As restless as I was, I had other things to do. That night I went to work and got home past midnight. I just showered and went straight into a very deep sleep. I was exhausted.

It doesn't take very long for anyone to fall into a basic routine. Mine, for example, entailed waking up, having breakfast, going to school, a quick lunch, back to school and catching the train home.

On alternate days, I would either go to work or enjoy the beach. Some days, I was able to do both. Those last ones were my favorite kind of days.

I also took the train ride as an opportunity to continue reading my newfound spiritual novel.

> *"We're all looking for more fulfillment in our lives, and we won't put up with anything that seems to bring us down. This restless searching is what's behind the 'me first' attitude that has characterized recent decades, and it's affecting everyone, from Wall Street to street gangs."*

"Me first" attitude. I started reflecting on that and it appeared to also be affecting me. I felt a little "entitled" sometimes. Not in a bad way, but it just seemed the way things were meant to be. Everybody was out for themselves; it was only natural to try to look after myself first. Could this be the reason why I was finding a little trouble in balancing my relationships?

> *"And when it comes to relationships, we're so demanding that we're making them near impossible."*

There it was. Relationship problems were not a privilege of mine. It wasn't exactly what I wanted to hear, but it felt comforting to know that I was not alone. Deep in my heart, I knew relationships were meant not only to be possible, but also good. I was hopeful this book would teach me something about that.

I wasn't even thinking about Daniel or any other specific person, all I wanted was to become the kind of person who is not just out for myself.

> "The First Insight occurs when we become conscious of the coincidences in our lives."

Oh, I had that one down. I could totally see the coincidences in my life. But how could that lead to a cultural transformation?

> "It's in the numbers. Once we reach the 'critical mass', the entire culture will begin to take these coincidental experiences seriously."

Is that right? How many are we talking about?

> "When a sufficient number of individuals seriously question what's going on in life, we will begin to find out. The other insights will be revealed ... one after the other."

That was obviously very exciting. Who didn't want to know all the insights?

I started to relate to the main character, especially in this part:

> "The next morning, I awoke suddenly with a dream still fresh in my mind. For a minute or two I stared at the bedroom ceiling, remembering it fully. I had been making my way through a forest searching for something. The forest was large and exceptionally beautiful.

In my quest I found myself in a number of situations in which I felt totally lost and bewildered, unable to decide how to proceed. Incredibly, at each one of these moments, a person would appear out of nowhere as though by design to clarify where I needed to go next. I never became aware of the object of my search but the dream had left me incredibly upbeat and confident."

The main character was about to embark on a trip to Peru to search for the manuscript. I had literally just arrived in Australia. And just like he described in the dream, I was experiencing something very similar.

It all started with Daniel. We randomly met and he showed me a new direction. I followed that insight and, ever since I arrived in Australia, people came out of nowhere to help me out. Mari, Paula, Juan. All of them were fundamental to keep me on track.

My questions were not so clear. All I knew was that my life needed some answers. I started to reflect on what all those coincidences could really mean and how they could lead me in the right direction.

I was looking forward to the second insight. I wanted to keep reading, but I had to go to work.

First things first. That's how life goes.

20. YOU LIVE, YOU LEARN.

Survival was my initial drive to take up a part-time job as a waitress. I needed the money to keep me going. What I had no idea of was how many invaluable skills I'd pick up on that job that I'd not only put to great use in my future career, but also in life.

First, let me get this straight: working as a waitress is not a piece of cake. It's managing people's expectations the whole time. Be them your customers or your team. It's crisis management, with a clear head, all day long — and with a big smile on your face.

Imagine it's a busy Saturday night. You, as a waitress, need to seat customers, take orders, serve tables, handle dietary requirements with the kitchen, and make sure everything is running on time. Not to mention, entertain the waiting lines during rush hours so they can stay. Yes, we need their business.

All of which happens simultaneously and at a real fast pace. It seems humanly impossible to even comprehend how it all works. It can become overwhelming at times, so we must develop patience and resilience to thrive in this heated environment.

The service industry has certainly taught me how to effectively multitask while handling things more elegantly. In order to hustle under so much pressure, it's inevitable to develop an observer's eye. Panicking is never an option. Our job is to be the solution and keep things rolling smoothly for the collective. Everyone is there for a good time.

Teamwork and cooperation are vital for success. Roles and responsibilities are important, but we quickly learn to put differences aside to get our jobs done efficiently. It's true: we work better together. When you lend a hand to a fellow co-worker, they'll often do the same for you.

If you want to succeed in hospitality, you must master three things: people, respect and responsibility.

You can't escape the odd unpleasant customer. What you can do is treat them with utmost respect, always with a smile on your face and a good sense of humour. Oftentimes, it's just a bad day for them. And, like us, they are only human.

In whatever we do, ultimately, we'll be dealing with people. All sorts of them. Some we might like, others possibly not. Our job is to put personal opinions aside and communicate nicely and honestly with everyone.

"Do not take things personally" was probably my most valuable lesson out of this experience. It's not always about us.

It doesn't mean that we have to agree or suck it up to people. No, not even customers. All we have to do is increase our adaptation energy and understand it's all just opinions and not everything is worth an argument.

"Build good relationships with everyone" was the second lesson. Life is about relationships. Once the meal (or the deal) is over, all people will remember is how they felt around us.

That's why honest kind gestures (big or small) can go a long way. People relate to people. Being genuinely human is very relatable. You can never go wrong that way.

Always remember: mistakes happen, whether we like it or not. In those cases, we do our best to fix them. Sometimes they may seem unfixable, but we must trust they happen for a reason. Here's a little story for you about that.

One night, four lovely ladies entered the restaurant. It was about 6.30pm. They were regular locals who reminded me of my own grandmas and their friends.

"Hello ladies, welcome! How are you doing?"

"We're fine, thank you. How are you holding up?"

"Fine, thank you. Here's your table."

"Oh, lovely. Thank you, darling!"

"You're welcome."

"Ah, we brought our wine. It's a nice red."

"Perfect, I'll bring the glasses over. Make yourselves comfortable."

"Thank you."

I had seen those ladies a few times at the restaurant. I loved to watch them chatting and laughing. They seemed to have reached that stage in life where you allow yourself to have less expectations and more fun. Their joy gave me hope for the future and lifted my spirit every time.

We were starting to get to know each other. Every time I served them, they seemed curious about my background. I was not only the new girl; I was a foreigner. They were not used to seeing people like me around there. They always treated me equally and were genuinely nice ladies.

"Hey Juan, are you busy? Could you help me to open the wine for the ladies over there?"

"I'd love to, but I'm a little caught up here. You know what? I think you can do it. You've been practicing, haven't you? Just do your best. You'll be fine."

"Are you sure?"

"Positive."

"Okay."

Juan knew I had zero experience as a waitress when he hired me. And when it came to the technicalities of serving wine, it was even worse. I was just getting used to carrying more than one plate on my arms. I still couldn't carry three coffees without spilling them. It was my adjustment phase. I knew I'd get through, but those early days were all part of the process.

Right there, I only had a single task at hand: serve those lovely ladies their nice red wine.

Well, I kind of had learned how to operate the bottle opener decently (wines had to be opened at the table, in front of the customers) but I hadn't yet mastered serving it. I was still just serving water. I knew it was a bit risky, but I couldn't let fear stop me from doing what I had to do. I just had to do it.

"Here we go, ladies. Tonight, I'll be the one serving your wine," I said, smiling, trying not to show how terrified I was by such a simple task.

"That's lovely, Carolina."

"So, any special occasion?" I asked them wondering if there was a reason to celebrate.

"Life is always a special occasion, don't you think?" one of them answered in a way just those kinds of ladies can do.

"Absolutely. I love how you enjoy it."

"We came in early to watch the sunset. It's not so busy at this time."

"You're right. In about half an hour, it won't be the same. We're fully booked tonight."

The four glasses were set and I successfully managed to open the bottle. I poured the wine in the first glass for the lady to try.

"How's that?" I asked as we were instructed to do.

"Perfect," she said. "Go ahead and serve us all."

I poured the second glass graciously. Things were going really well until the third. That's when I felt my hand slightly shake. And before I could do anything, I watched the wine bottle fall, in slow motion, perfectly landing on the table, while spilling a significant amount of the red liquid on the floor.

The table cloth instantly turned from white to red, but the ladies quickly reacted and stood up.

My first instinct was panic. I thought I was going to collapse, not to mention, be fired. But I immediately picked up the bottle from the table to avoid further damage. I knew I had to be professional and responsible, so I took the deepest breath I could and managed to get some words out of my mouth.

"I am so sorry," I said slowly, meaning each one of the words. "Is everyone okay?" I looked them up and down trying to identify signs of the spill on their clothes.

"We are," said one of them, laughing. "It was a lucky fall. You did well, darling."

"Right," I said, embarrassed, without losing my sense of humour. "Do you mind sitting on the balcony while I quickly fix this? I'll clean up and also get you a new bottle of wine."

"That's fine. We'll just watch the sunset."

"Perfect, thank you."

I rushed in and cleaned up my mess. I mopped the floor, got a fresh table cloth and in less than five minutes it was all back to normal. I reset the table and asked Juan if I could step outside for a few minutes to get them a new bottle of the exact same wine from the bottle shop across the road. He agreed. I returned and we started again.

"Hi ladies, your table is ready inside. Please come in. Juan will be here shortly to serve your wine."

"That's wonderful. Thank you, darling."

It was intense, but I decided not to let that incident get to me. I was enjoying the job and the last thing I wanted was to spoil everything. I wasn't sure that Juan and I were on the same page, but I kept doing my very best for the rest of the night. We didn't get a chance to talk about it during the shift, but I promised myself that I wouldn't attempt to serve any wine until I felt safe again.

The ladies seemed fine, laughing and chatting as usual. They even sounded happier and louder that night.

About 10pm, they asked for the check. I placed the black leather holder on their table and, minutes later, went back to collect it. When I got to the till, I noticed that there was an extra fifty dollars in there. I went back and told them.

"Here we go ladies. You might have put some extra cash by mistake."

"Oh, no. It wasn't a mistake. It's your tip," said one of them.

"But your check was just under two hundred dollars. You can't leave a fifty-dollar tip for that."

"Well, we can. The way you handled this situation tonight was impeccable. Especially for a young girl like you. We were very impressed. You even got us a bottle of wine. I bet it will come out of your own pocket."

"Well, it was the least I could do," I said with eyes going slightly teary while struggling to hold on to my emotions, but she continued.

"It's not the mistake, it's the way we move past them that matters. Your mistakes can never define you. They can only improve you." A wise piece of advice from one of the other ladies.

"Yes, and the four of us here know that too well. Everyone makes mistakes. Or do you really think we've got this far without them?"

We all laughed together at her little joke, but the real lesson was coming up:

"Here's the thing, darling: when you do something wrong and people still treat you right, you're more likely to treat others the same way when wrong happens in front of you later in life. You'll remember that."

"I sure will. And I don't know what to say. Thank you for your kindness and understanding. Also, thank you for your generosity."

"You deserve it. Just take it," said the other lady.

"Ah, one last piece of advice." It came from the lady who was quiet until then. "Please buy yourself some red wine and have fun, girl! Tonight, you just reminded us of how we used to be at your age. Thank you for that."

"Oh, I hope to be like you when I'm your age too. Thanks for everything. You have inspired me more than you'll ever know."

"Thank you, honey. Just keep smiling."

I'll never forget that night. That story has stayed with me for 20 years. It was one of the best pieces of life advice I ever got.

Kindness, understanding, generosity and owning up to our mistakes. Those four ladies instilled incredible values that gave me a huge head start in life. I hope they're all still alive and having a great time (or still having fun in heaven).

Juan and I also had a little talk after we closed. He saw how everything happened and decided not to get involved.

"Carolina, tonight you showed us that you definitely belong here."

"Really? Only tonight? Why was that?"

"It's easy to be a waitress when things go right. But we recognise the real ones when they don't. Service is an act of humility and responsibility. Your attitude tonight was exactly what we need in this industry. You owned your mistake and you moved past it. Congratulations! You should be proud of yourself."

"Huh, isn't that interesting? For a second, I thought my career in hospitality was over. In the end, you congratulated me and I even got a fifty-dollar tip for that."

"Is that right? Well, those ladies must really like you," he said in a cheeky tone. "They probably knew exactly what was going on. I bet they've been there before."

"Apparently so."

"You see, we're all human. We all make mistakes. And you were lucky, the damage wasn't too bad."

"Agree. It was a very important life lesson, I guess."

"And the ladies had fun. Now, you need some serious training on wine pouring, Brazil. Let's work on that, please."

21. DIGGING DEEPER.

The next morning, on the train, I was back to my book.

> *"I faced a decision. Because of the Manuscript I felt a new direction open in my life, a new point of interest. The question was what to do now?"*

I remembered another writer who talked about similar things: Paulo Coelho. The Brazilian who had become a global phenomenon with "The Alchemist" wrote this:

> *"When you want something, all the universe conspires in helping you to achieve it."*

And he goes further:

> *"Making a decision was only the beginning of things. When someone makes a decision, he/she is really diving into a strong current that will carry him/her to places he/she had never dreamed of when he/she first made the decision."*

Apparently, it was all a mystery. I wasn't even trying to understand anymore. I felt that the wisest option would be to simply trust life. So far, things were going well (even when they went wrong).

I was probably on the right path so I decided not to argue with the Universe. It was apparently on my side. Back to my book, I read this:

> "What's really important is the world view of each historical period, what the people were feeling and thinking."

I had to agree. Humanity evolved with time. In 2005 we were nothing like our fellow humans from the 1900s, for example. Things have changed and so have we. But there's more:

> "History is not just the evolution of technology, it's the evolution of thought. By understanding the reality of the people who came before us, we can see why we look at the world the way we do, and what our contribution is towards further progress. We can pinpoint where we come in, so to speak, in the longer development of Civilization, and that gives us a sense of where we are going."

I wasn't sure I made any sense of where we were going, but those words definitely got me thinking. What could my contribution towards further progress be? Could I even be of any use? Technology was in its early stages. Everyone was still a bit skeptical about future predictions. That's when the next insight came in:

> "The Second Insight puts our current awareness into a longer historical perspective. After all, when the decade of the Nineties is over, we'll be finishing up not only the twentieth century but a thousand-year period of history as well. We'll be completing the entire second millennium. Before we, in the west, can understand where we are, and what is going to occur next, we must understand what has really been happening during this current thousand-year period."

A-ha! I was entering history heaven there. I loved digging into different time periods looking to better understand human behavior and its evolution. Those explanations left me wondering about many things, until a simple truth emerged from the narrative:

> *"After all, you have grown accustomed to having an authority in your life to define your reality, and without that external direction, you feel confused and lost."*

Bingo! That was exactly how I felt: confused and lost. It never occurred to me that I was lacking authority, but they were right. It was the very first time in 22 years of life that I had to make decisions on my own. I was even more curious after that. I kept reading, until I found this:

> *"All the things you took for granted now need new definition, especially the nature of God and your relationship to God. With that awareness, the Modern Age begins."*

Growing up in a Catholic family, I was taught about God and faith very early in life. I prayed every night and always trusted that God was protecting me no matter what. It wasn't hard for me to believe that things had a deeper meaning. I really thought everything was possible if we believed it to be and allowed God to work with us.

I was obviously too young to fully understand all those deeper messages, but certain coincidences and synchronized encounters seemed destined to be. I guess believing that way made things a lot easier for me to process, especially when things didn't turn out exactly as I had anticipated. I still felt protected, even in the redirection stages.

Other times, things simply fell into place like a strike of good fortune. A great example was the job. I wanted it, and I got it. Of course, I still had to work in order to keep it, but everything was perfectly aligned.

I enjoyed working. A lot. I only had one concern: when I had nothing else going on in my life, I'd easily throw myself completely into it. That's why I always tried to live somewhere sunny and near the beach. A little reminder that life shouldn't be all about work. Fun was also a must.

I was really sold on the idea of building my own life, becoming financially independent and all that. That's when a new point of view prompted my attention:

> "Working to establish a more comfortable style of survival has grown to feel complete in and of itself as a reason to live, and we've gradually, methodically, forgotten our original question ... we've forgotten that we still don't know what we're surviving for."

To me, the answer was simple: I was surviving to enjoy life, to have fun, to meet people and have real experiences with them. But I had a feeling that I wasn't even scratching the surface. That's when someone asked the central character an interesting question:

> "How many people do you know who are obsessed with work (...), or who suffer from stress-related illnesses and cannot slow down [their pace]? They fail because they use their routine to distract themselves (...). And they do this to avoid remembering how insecure they feel about why they are alive."

As much as I didn't want to admit it, that really hit home.

> "When you look at the human world now, you should be able to clearly see this obsessiveness, the intense preoccupation with economic progress (...) the preoccupation was a necessary development, a stage in human evolution. Now, however, we've

> *spent enough time settling into the world. It's time now to wake up from preoccupation and reconsider our original question. What's behind life on this planet? Why are we really here?"*

I understood what they were saying but I was literally just trying to survive. I already had too much on my plate to start thinking about an even bigger picture.

I could barely understand why I had moved to Australia, let alone try to figure out why I happened to be on Planet Earth. I instantly switched back to fiction mode and just assumed I wasn't ready to take those profound matters into real life.

Still, I kept reading. Out of curiosity. As you do.

> *"Do you understand that chance encounters often have a deeper meaning? (...) That begins to happen once you become alert and connected with the energy."*

You had to be kidding me! How could I not relate? My life was a series of coincidences. I just didn't know enough to understand what it all meant.

> *"If one can connect and build up enough energy, the coincidental events begin to happen."*

Alright, maybe I was into something — without being aware of it. Could I just get all the insights at once and figure everything out for myself? Apparently not.

We had to discover each one of them in a different way. And I was back in real-life mode. My curiosity wouldn't allow me to ignore the first two insights. I was destined to dig deeper.

Unlike James Redfield and other popular writers of a similar genre, I was a very material girl. My world was very real. I only believed in the things I saw happening in front of my eyes.

That's why I believed in books. To me, they were personal transformation tools. The right words, at the right time, can have a real effect on us.

Fiction or nonfiction, stories help us to amplify thought. It's all about exercising our imagination and our very own interpretation of facts. We choose what we believe in (or not). Often, we see fiction turning into real life. The other way around is also true.

Regardless, words have real power — and not only in the written form.

22. ENERGY MATTERS.

I was still adjusting to the new world around me and absorbing a completely different culture, but I didn't want to fall into a work-study spiral and forget what mattered in life.

If we aren't having fun, what's the point? I didn't leave my old life behind to fall into the same existing traps. My personal goal was to explore and enjoy the new world that had just opened up for me. To do that, I had to deliberately pursue my other interests.

Multicultural by definition, Australia has a bit of everything. It's not hard to understand how diversity has shaped the country's landscape. The "land down under" welcomes humans from every corner of the globe, as long as they understand and respect their values.

A blend between the foundation created by the "world's oldest living culture", the First Nations people, and the British legal and political systems is what makes "Straya" so unique. And I feel that their coexistence over the last two centuries shows a desire to say something about freedom to the rest of the world.

Let people be, whoever they are. Our differences unite us, and make us better.

By the way, have you ever heard "Aussie English"? Well, that's a totally different beast. It can take a while to fully pick up on the accent and all the slang and short-form vocabulary that the laid-back colony down under reinvented. As they say, *"It's gold!"*

Music is probably one of the best Aussie exports, and a huge part of the country's culture. In my opinion, music is not something we simply hear, it's an art form that makes us feel connected.

As one of the capital cities, Perth hosted international tours and festivals. At the time, there was this fairly new multi-genre festival. The first edition was held at the iconic Kings Park, which is one of Perth's most beautiful attractions, and it was called Sunset Live's Botanic Blues, Roots and Soul.

The second, renamed edition, sounded much better: The West Coast Blues 'n' Roots Festival. And it was about to happen at the Esplanade Park in Fremantle.

Paula and I were talking and I asked her:

"Have you heard of the West Coast Blues 'n' Roots Festival?"

"Is that the one in Freo?"

"Yes, what do you think of it?"

"I think it's gonna be fun."

"Do you wanna go?"

"Maybe, who's playing?"

"Wait, let me read it to you: Xavier Rudd, The Waifs, Violent Femmes, The Beautiful Girls," I continued reading the long list of names from the flyer until I became overly excited and almost shouted: "*And* Jack Johnson."

"You love him, don't you?" she said, laughing. She knew I played him, Ben Harper and their crew all day long. They were like friends to me.

"I do. And he's launching a new album. He might even play some new stuff. Please, let's go!"

"You know I love this kind of music too. Is it a day thing?"

"Yes, from 12pm to 10pm. We'll be home early. It's not a crazy party. I promise to behave."

"Alright, let's do it! Get the tickets."

For the next two weeks all I could think about was the festival. I was literally counting down.

My life hadn't changed at all. I was still going to school, working at the restaurant and doing all the same things. But there was a feeling that things were going my way. The entire world seemed prettier, brighter, better.

I also kept reading my book. And I got to the next insight:

> "The Third Insight describes a new understanding of the physical world. It says we humans will learn to perceive what was formerly an invisible type of energy."

It went on:

> "In other words, the basic stuff of the Universe, at its core, is looking like a kind of pure energy that is malleable to human intention and expectation in a way that defies our old mechanistic model of the Universe — as though our expectation itself causes our energy to flow out into the world and affect other energy systems."

I tried to bring that back to my real life.

I was expecting to see Jack Johnson live — right in front of my eyes, not just playing on my CD. That was a pretty big deal to me. And kind of shifted things a little. It made life lighter leading up to it. I had something to look forward to.

"The reality of it is new to everyone. But the interesting thing is that this energy is what science has always been looking for, some common stuff underlying all matter."

One thing I knew: when I really wanted something, I made it happen.

I always just went for things. I could seem quite impulsive, and often, may have sounded arrogant for believing so hard everything was possible. But, more often than not, I got what I wanted.

Could my energy be so powerful like that? Not sure.

All I believed was that everyone deserves to have a good life. Myself included.

23. WELCOME TO THE GOOD LIFE.

The big day had finally arrived.

Paula and I woke up, had breakfast and started to get ready for the festival.

"Let's go, we can catch the 12.30 train," she said, ready to go.

"Coming," I said while checking documents, tickets and cash to take with me.

Freo was only a few stops from Cottesloe. There were extra trains all over town so everyone could safely get to the festival.

From the station to the park, everything was buzzing. I could feel my energy rising.

The park was lightly fenced to justify a ticket payment, but the festival atmosphere was all around. You couldn't escape the great vibes, even if you tried.

I never lacked imagination, but until then I had not yet experienced a day festival on green grass, under a blue sky and with the sun shining. The whole arrangement was a completely new concept to me. I loved it!

I was also trying to understand how to put together so many acts, in a single day, at a reasonable ticket price. It seemed almost too good to be true. Yet, it was a business. Someone must have worked that out. Good on them!

We entered the park and stopped right in front of the first stage.

> *"On a clear day I can see far ahead in front of me,*
>
> *The sky above imagines a God, but on another day I'm...*
>
> *And when I fall the hurt won't show up on me I only hope.*
>
> *And if I follow you along well then I'll rise up.*
>
> *And when the burning sun it falls in my eyes,*
>
> *Is when I come upon another sunrise.*
>
> *Well I will walk alone 'cause I'm not scared to die,*
>
> *On a clearer day in the sunshine."*

"Who is that? I love it!" Paula said while we were mesmerized by their performance.

"The Beautiful Girls," I said, reading from the printed line-up.

Neither of us had heard of The Beautiful Girls until then. They were an Australian roots band from 2001. They already had released a few extended plays and one album. Their music felt so good and those lyrics kept speaking to me as they played their next song:

> *"When I wake into the Morning Sun,*
>
> *Well I feel another day has just begun.*
>
> *I see those clouds up in the sky,*
>
> *And I don't care, everything is going to be alright"*

All those lyrics were about keeping a positive mindset even when things got hard. Is there anything more humanly relatable?

> *"Everybody thinks we'll fall apart*
>
> *Everybody's quick to point their fingers at what*
>
> *They think it is causing the problem*
>
> *And what they don't see is what they won't see, my friend*
>
> *And we've all got to learn ourselves*
>
> *Before we can judge someone else"*

Music engages our heart on matters in which our minds are not open to. Honest, heartfelt songs are meant to stir up our emotions. It's hard to talk about judgement. That's why we let artists do the job for us.

Whoever judges will be judged. But everything has two sides. We really have to learn that for ourselves.

"Wow, they are amazing! I am so glad we came together," Paula said looking at me with that big smile on her face.

"Me too. And it's just starting. Let's grab a drink! The Waifs are next up," I said almost as if I already knew them.

I didn't know their songs, but The Waifs were kind of a big deal. They are an Australian folk rock band from WA who were experiencing great success, especially after playing as the supporting act for no one less than Bob Dylan on his 2003 Australian tour.

On stage, two girls and a guy started making this beautiful mellow sound:

> *"I wonder if you can pick up my accent on the phone*

When I call across the country, when I call across the world

I see you in my kitchen, I picture you now

As you toast to your small town and you drink the happy hour

I'm in London still"

I wasn't in London, but the feelings were so relatable. I was as across the world as one could possibly be from Brazil — and I instantly connected with the band.

"I thought I'd move to Sydney

To get a little piece

Of the city life they talk about

In the nineties

Where everyone I meet

Don't want to know my name

They want to know what I do for a living"

Ironically, their lyrics were on theme. Moving, starting a new life, being unknown. All those feelings were not only relatable, but also translatable.

I would never be able to name or quote every single musician we saw that day. It was overwhelming. In a great way. Fresh, easy-going, real artists. Talented people speaking their truth straight from their hearts.

That festival changed the entire mood of my new life. It gave me hope. I had no doubt I was in the right place. From there, things could only get better. And they sure did.

Around sunset, a young Aussie bloke entered the stage. He sat on a chair, surrounded by more instruments than any human being could manage alone. I wasn't even familiar with half of them. No one else turned up, he was his own band. And I don't say that lightly: he really was.

"Are you feelin'" — His opening words were as beautiful as his presence. An overarching energy was holding the space and keeping all of us under the same spell. I was *over* feeling it, expanded in my own joy.

He started playing the harmonica and an acoustic guitar, simultaneously, while also singing. I know, it's hard to imagine but this is what Xavier Rudd sounds like. He's a real Aussie legend that makes you feel like a friend. He plays like he's chillin' in his own backyard. Music is his nature.

> *"Oh oh, let me be now*
>
> *Hmm hmm, let me because*
>
> *I want to be free now*
>
> *Oh oh, free to see, yeah well*
>
> *Want to walk away, oh oh*
>
> *Let me feel my feet*
>
> *Let me be, free"*

For me, no feeling beats love — but freedom is the closest. The beauty of being free lies in the opportunity to be surprised by the unknown. In freedom, there's always hope.

Art is freedom. Music is freedom. Beautiful melodies, real words, deep reflections.

Nothing is held back when a song comes out. It takes over our emotions and makes us more alive. It touches sensitive spots from a place of love. Art comes from the heart.

"Well, I see, because this is my window

Your questions, with every move I make

So much time, I filled up with answers

To why my feet, will always hold their ground"

A beautiful play of words on authenticity. Xavier Rudd is a free spirit with an unshakeable trust in his own nature.

"When you're pleased

And it's all meant to be

Your heart knows where to go

But your mind can take it slow

It's okay to rest your mind

Let your heart seek and find"

I felt relief and excitement almost in the same way he was able to play all of those instruments: simultaneously and alone.

I heard my own heart telling me: *"Let your relentless search for answers cease for once. Let the answers come to you when you're ready."*

As much as we'd love to be able to tell our own fortune, some questions will always remain unanswered until we get to them — in perfect timing.

Everything I was reading in The Celestine Prophecy was also making sense. It was exhilarating. There was no doubt in my mind that it was all connected.

It suddenly hit me that I only knew Jack Johnson prior to that festival. I had no idea of the entire musical universe that already existed in Australia prior to living there. It was mind-blowing.

Around 8pm, the energy was through the roof. We had great music non-stop for almost seven hours. It was the last act. For me, it was the cherry on top of the most delicious pie I had ever tasted.

It was another dream come true. Jack Johnson live. We found a spot very close to the stage. So close, we could almost touch him.

Jack's new album was titled "In Between Dreams" and it obviously felt very relatable.

Everyone on stage just seemed so cool and unpretentious that day. Jack was no exception. His presence already had an incredible energy on its own. Him and his acoustic guitar alone were creating the first sounds until those amazing drums joined in as his voice came out.

"I know she said, it's alright

You can make it up next time

I know she knows, it's not right

There ain't no use in lying

Maybe she thinks I know something

Maybe, maybe she thinks it's fine

Maybe she knows something I don't

I'm so, I'm so tired, I'm so tired of trying

It seems to me that maybe

It pretty much always means, no

So don't tell me, you might just let it go

And often times we're lazy

It seems to stand in my way

'Cause no one, no not, no one

Likes to be let down"

Flake, from 2001. It's funny how a melody could sound like a memory. I could feel those lyrics circulating my veins. I remembered my university years listening to this on repeat. But, that night, one line got stuck with me: *no one likes to be let down.*

I still had some weird thoughts going on in my mind. I just didn't want to let myself down.

After a few other great songs, he came up with one from the new album:

"I heard this old story before

Where people keep appealing for the metaphors

Don't leave much up to the imagination

So I wanna give this imagery back

When I know it just ain't so easy like that

So, I turn the page and read the story again

And again and again

It sure seems the same with a different name

We're breaking and rebuilding

And we're growing, always guessing

Never knowing

Shocking but we're nothing

We're just moments

We're clever but we're clueless

We're just human

Amusing and confusing

We're trying but where is this all leading

We'll never know"

Suddenly it hit me: I've heard this old story before. I had been through at least four or five heartbreaks in my earlier years. It was nothing new. Yet, it hurt the same.

"Shocking but we're nothing. We're just moments. We're clever but we're clueless. We're just human."

The raw honesty. Jack was an absolute genius in the art of putting words together and translating painful feelings into beautiful songs. Those lyrics just clarified everything for me. Why was I even trying to control anything? I had no power over that.

Songs are like mirrors for our feelings. That's how we connect. I was deeply connected with all the energy around me, just like Redfield had described in the Prophecy.

And there was more. Another classic from 2001:

"She's got it all figured out

She knows what everything's about

And when anybody doubts her

Or sings songs without her

She's just so mmm

She knows the world is just her stage

And so she'll never misbehave

She gives thanks for what they gave her

Man, they practically made her

Into a mmm

She's the one that stumbles when she talks about

The seven foreign films that she's checked out

Such a fortunate fool

She's just too good to be true

She's such a fortunate fool

She's just so mmm"

My overthinking nature was a heavy blessing. All those lyrics seemed somewhat related to what I was feeling — not to mention perfectly aligned to the insights from the book.

I felt like I literally opened this one-thousand piece puzzle and was trying to put it together in five minutes. Ironically, I felt like a Fortunate Fool. Could anyone be so blindly lucky? I kept wondering about life and singing along, as I often did.

If I could describe what a perfect day felt like, it would probably be that. And I knew I wanted more of that in my life. I also wanted everyone to enjoy those kinds of days. It was a highly contagious energy for the good.

Was everything really connected or did I just have too much to drink? I kept wondering, singing and over-feeling it.

"A dream is a dream

And all this living is so much harder than it seems

But girl don't let your dreams be dreams

You know this living is not so hard as it seems

Don't let your dreams be dreams"

A message for the dreamers.

From a very young age, I had this awareness. Dreams are never just dreams. They are divine whispers into our own lives' mysteries. Humans are put on Earth to make dreams come true. We're the vessels through which dreams make their ways into reality. That's why we can't help but follow them — with a human plan.

"This is so much better than I expected, my friend. Thank you for coming," I said to Paula with teary eyes.

"Thank you for making it happen. I loved it!" she said, hugging me, and we both sang the last song together.

As the day was coming to an end, I started to reflect about life and my relationship with music. I seemed to really align when listening to the right songs. Live music was the next level. That one event had just given me a totally new mind frame.

Beach and sunsets always made me feel good. They were my go-to mood lifters.

Right there I knew: music was another reliable source of energy.

I became aware of the simple things I needed to survive.

24. FEELING THE ENERGY.

I was already pretty settled into my routine. There was still a lot of newness, but the novelty had sort of worn off. I started to catch myself thinking of friends and family back in Brazil. I was a very long way from them.

An unexpected wave of deep longing took over me. They even had a name for it: *homesickness*. I wasn't physically sick. I was also not literally missing home. It was simply an instinctive need for love, protection, security and familiarity — things that were usually associated with home.

I was about to turn 23 in a few weeks. My first ever birthday away from home.

I wasn't sure how to celebrate in this new environment and my mind was just trying to adjust to my new reality.

Very few emotions stay with us all the time, they come and go. Still, I thought of ways to alleviate those nostalgic feelings. I needed to find a way to feel "home" again.

I could definitely use some music. More precisely, Brazilian music. Familiar sounds would certainly help to clear my head and restore my sense of familiarity. I knew where to go: The Deen, the place to be on Thursdays.

As soon as I stepped into the Brazilian night, I felt my energy rising. Everyone was singing and dancing without a care in the world. I joined in. I was already having so much fun when I heard this one:

> "Carolina é uma menina bem difícil de esquecer (Carolina is a girl, very hard to forget) Andar bonito e um brilho no olhar (A beautiful way of walking and a sparkle in the eye) Tem um jeito adolescente que me faz enlouquecer (Her teenage way drives me crazy)
>
> E um molejo que eu não vou te enganar (And her sexiness boy, I won't fool you) Maravilha feminina, meu docinho de pavê (Feminine wonder, my sweetie)
>
> Inteligente, ela é muito sensual (Smart, she is very sexy)
>
> Te confesso que estou apaixonado por você (I confess I'm in love with you)
>
> Ô, Carolina, isso é muito natural (Look, Carolina, this is very natural)
>
> Ô, Carolina, preciso te encontrar (Oh, Carolina, I need to meet you)
>
> Ô, Carolina, me sinto muito só (Oh, Carolina, I feel very lonely)
>
> Ô, Carolina, preciso te dizer (Oh, Carolina, I need to tell you)
>
> Ô, Carolina, eu só quero amar você (Oh, Carolina, I just want to love you)
>
> Ô, Carolina, ô, Carolina
>
> Carol, Carol, Carol, Carol, Carol Carol, Carol, Carol

Carol, Carol, Carol, Carol, Carol Carol, Carol, Carol (ô, Carolina)"

Seu Jorge and one of my favorite songs in the world. If your name is Carolina, you instantly feel this song was made for you. You simply can't resist a beautifully crafted repetition of your own name in a love song. You feel the love.

The band called all Carolinas on stage. I felt embarrassed at first, but I knew I had to allow my feelings to come out. Being on stage felt almost cathartic. I danced my shame and sorrows away. I felt free.

That night also brought me closer to some band members. Léo, the Brazilian who went to the same school as me, introduced me to John, an Australian-Brazilian who sang Portuguese better than I did.

We started talking and he mentioned his upcoming birthday party, while also inviting me to that. I couldn't help but think of my own birthday.

"It's in two weeks, on May 8th," he said.

"Are you kidding? Is that your actual birthday?"

"Yes, why?"

"We share birthdays, John!" I said not so surprised about another 'coincidence'.

"Are you doing anything?"

"Not really."

"Let's have a joint party then."

"Are you serious?"

"Why not? It's a party. The more, the merrier."

"You're right. I've only been here for a couple of months so I don't know many people. I'll only invite my closest friends from school."

"You can invite anyone you want, Carol. We can organize everything later. I can only guarantee you one thing: great music and an awesome vibe."

"That's all I need. Thank you, John. You have no idea how much this means to me."

His words were music to my ears. It was amazing how things worked. I left home that night wanting to accept the fact that I was not going to have a birthday party that year. I got home with a real party lined up. How could I not believe in miracles?

I spent the next few weeks studying, working and, obviously, looking forward to the party. Another countdown!

I already had some special friends I wanted to invite. Paula was the first. Along with Rodrigo, her now boyfriend, and a few others from school. Gui was a good friend who was about to go back to Brazil. Plus, my first friends in Perth, the girls I met in the city and went to Margs with. I couldn't wait!

Australians are not like Brazilians when it comes to birthday parties. It's mostly BYO which means "Bring Your Own". In that case, just drinks. They also don't care much about food and formalities like we do. It's actually quite liberating. I basically just had to show up and wait for others to do the same. It was the easiest party ever. I was also allowed to have all the fun.

Still, I wanted to check everything before everybody got there (a bit controlling, I know). So, I went slightly earlier than everyone. Not even sure why, I just felt like doing it.

As I entered the space, alone, I was taken by this incredible atmosphere. It was a shed-like building, perfect for rehearsals and intimate jam sessions. I loved it! There was one single guy doing a sound check. I didn't know him, so I introduced myself.

"Hi, I'm Carolina. Not sure if John mentioned it, but it's also my birthday today. What's your name?"

"I'm Paul, nice to meet you, Carolina. Happy birthday! He did mention. Welcome to your party. I'm just finishing the sound check here."

"Can I help with anything?"

"Nah, I'm all done."

"Perfect, thank you."

"Come, I'll show you the place."

As we wandered around, we continued to talk.

"Do you mind if I call you Carol?"

"Of course not, most people do."

"Carol, do you wanna put anything in the fridge? It's here."

"Oh, not yet. I came by just to check the place first. I'll quickly run to the bottle shop across the road and get something now."

"Are you driving?"

"No, I'll just walk."

"Definitely not. I'll give you a ride. Come on, let's go."

"Are you sure?"

"Positive. It's your birthday! And you shouldn't walk alone anyway."

"Thank you, but I'm used to it. I walk alone all the time."

I liked his attitude. It was natural to him to act that way. Paul directed me to his station wagon parked at the garage. He was a very interesting guy in so many ways. Slightly older, his personality was just the definition of cool. I'd never seen anyone like him. And I must admit: I was curious to know more.

"So, another Brazilian. How long have you been here?" he asked me curiously.

"Not long, only two months."

"Oh, really? Totally fresh. Do you like it?"

"So far I love it."

"You speak very good English, you know. Did you learn that in Brazil?"

"Thank you. Yes, I've been studying English since I was seven. My dad always wanted us to know the language. He said it would help in the future. I have to agree with him. It helps a lot now."

"So, what brought you to Perth?"

"Well, I wanted an international experience after graduation. And last year, I happened to meet someone who said this place was amazing. I guess he was right. What about you? Are you from here?"

"Yes, born and bred. I live in Freo. Do you know where it is?"

"I do. It's a very cool area. So, do you work with music?"

"Yes, all music related. I run a music shop, sell and hire equipment. That's how I know John. I also run a DJ school. Well, I'm a DJ myself too."

"Wow, amazing! And what kind of music are you into?"

"House music, mostly. But I like a bit of everything. Reggae, blues, soul. You?"

"Oh, really? I love house music too. It's mostly what we listen to where I come from in Brazil. I guess I'm not a very typical

Brazilian" I laughed. "But, like you, I like a bit of everything. The other day I went to the West Coast Blues & Roots Festival. I loved it."

"You must have. It's awesome! I was there too. So, where's this place in Brazil? I'm curious."

"South. Santa Catarina. There's a bit of a rave scene there. It's a growing movement. Very organic. We have two big clubs there: Ibiza and Warung. They bring some cool DJs and wild parties. Both right on the beach. But I guess we've just been blessed by nature, really. People make the most of it by promoting independent open-air parties. It could be on the beach or somewhere in the forest. There's a lot of green areas there too. People get creative. Just before I came, there was one at a water park, another at a deactivated airport. Things like that. Wherever they can get away with, to be honest."

"Wow, that sounds unreal. You make me wanna go there."

"You should. I bet you'll love it!"

We instantly clicked. He drove me to the bottle shop, I got a few drinks and we went back. People started to arrive and the party was on.

Perth's music scene seemed all interconnected. People were dancing, laughing, everyone was having a really great time. John played different sets with guest musicians. Even the lead singer from the reggae band was there. That jam session was the highlight of my night! I was stoked. It felt almost like a little private rave, Australian style.

That party meant a lot to me. The vibe was so high, we could almost fly. I couldn't be happier. I kept watching everyone around me, so many new friends and beautiful smiles.

I was finally back in my element. I could be anything in life, but I knew I was born for fun.

And, out of all those people, one got me intrigued: Paul.

He was a chill-out kind of guy. Introverted, but really sexy too. He had an internal confidence, almost mysterious in a way. He was respectful and sophisticated by nature. I was attracted to him, but he didn't feel very familiar.

I must admit: I wasn't used to that kind of man. But he was fun, and I loved that!

He came by in between his sets and we chatted and danced together. There was something about us.

By the end of the night, most people were gone. Only the closest ones stayed around. We wanted to keep going, but we were tired and a bit wasted. Paul wasn't drinking, he was responsibly driving. I thought it was a very grown-up attitude. I liked him even more.

Although we were two strangers who briefly met, the chemistry between us was undeniable.

"I think it's time to go. I'm gonna catch a cab," I told the last ones remaining.

"No way, Carol. I'll drive you home." That was Paul being Paul. I had no way of saying no. The party was less than ten minutes from my apartment.

We got in the car and kept talking. I could've talked to him forever. It was that good.

But my mind started to entertain other thoughts. *Can't he just kiss me now?*

Apparently not.

"Home safe. It was great meeting you, Carol. Can I get your number? I'd love to see you again."

"Sure, I'd love that too. Thank you for the ride, Paul. It was a nice surprise meeting you too."

"I'll call you tomorrow. We should do something together."

"Sounds good."

Paul and I ended up on a slightly longer ride. We spent almost two months dating and he was really special. Hot, clever, fun. Paul was so easy to be with that it made me confused. He had an amazing taste for music, movies, everything. Not to mention he could cook. To be honest, he was probably too good to be true. Just the kind of guy anyone would tell you to invest your time in and marry.

How could he even like me? A young, immature, walking mess. A heartbroken girl still trying to pick up her pieces.

I didn't feel that I deserved him. So, I made sure my actions spoke for me.

Given my family history, I always knew the end: *men left*.

My idea of a relationship was very clear: start, middle and end. Before it was too late.

In my mind, I was protecting my heart.

My beliefs were creating my reality — and I believed that men like that were not real. I preferred to prove myself right than taking the risk of being different.

Paul and I could probably have had a nice, healthy, long-term relationship. We could have dated for years, gotten married and even had kids. We could have been a perfect match, if I believed in that then. But I didn't.

And these are some of the crossways we encounter in life.

I was not ready to face my trauma. So, I just kept repeating my usual pattern.

25. PATTERNS?

Back to my regular routine, another insight emerged from my book:

> *"The Third Insight showed you that the physical world is actually a vast system of energy. And now the Fourth points out that for a long time we humans have been unconsciously competing for the only part of this energy we have been open to: the part that flows between people. This is what human conflict has always been about, at every level: from the petty conflict in families and employment settings to wars between nations. It's the result of feeling insecure and weak and having to steal someone else's energy to feel okay."*

The Fourth Insight felt different to me. I never liked conflict but I had no doubt I caused some. It suddenly exposed what's wrong with us all, but the solution was still unclear.

> *"Understanding the Fourth Insight is a matter of seeing the world as a vast competition for energy and thus for power. The only reason that any conflict can't be immediately settled is that one side is holding on to an irrational position, for energy purposes."*

It made sense that we competed for energy, I just didn't understand what we could possibly do to change that.

> "Once humans understand their struggle, we would immediately begin to transcend this conflict. We would begin to break free from the competition over mere human energy ... because we would finally be able to receive our energy from another source."

That really hit me. I had been caught up in that cycle. At least, I had managed to break free from competing with my own family for energy.

I was curious to learn about new sources. So far, nature and music seemed to do that job. I started thinking about Paul and how love seemed such a foreign concept to me, until I read this:

> "The role of love has been misunderstood for a long time. Love is not something we should do to be good or to make the world a better place out of some abstract moral responsibility, or because we should give up our hedonism. Connecting with energy feels like excitement, then euphoria, and then love. Finding enough energy to maintain that state of love certainly helps the world, but it most directly helps us. It is the most hedonistic thing we can do."

I couldn't help but think about what I truly believed. Not the beliefs inherited from my family. Not even any religious beliefs. Nothing that I had been taught.

For the first time, I began considering my inherent personal beliefs.

I had always been known for my hedonistic lifestyle. In the midst of chaos and confusion, I seemed to somehow find simple pleasures in small things. I had danced my troubles away since I was a child.

Most people judged me for ignoring reality, but maybe I wasn't so wrong. Still, a lot of times I felt guilty about it. How could I dare be happy when everyone I loved seemed to be struggling? It wasn't fair, I had to struggle too.

But I had made some real progress that year. I had been surviving alone for months and I was truly enjoying the little pleasures in my life like sunsets and music.

I also believed in something bigger, an energy guiding our way to what was meant for us. That was the next insight:

> *"The Universe can provide all we need if we can only open up to it. That is the revelation of the Fifth Insight."*

It all seemed perfect until I realised it wasn't so easy:

> *"This state is like leaping ahead of everyone else and glimpsing the future. We can't maintain it for very long. Once we try to talk to someone who is operating in normal consciousness, or try to live in a world where conflict is still happening, we get knocked out of this advanced state and fall back to the level of our old selves."*

That explained why my energy levels oscillated so much. I kept getting knocked out. And the reason why this happened was exactly what the next insight was about to teach me:

> *"We must face up to our particular way of controlling others. Remember, the Fourth Insight reveals that humans have always felt short of energy and have sought to control each other to acquire the energy that flows between people. The Fifth then shows us that an alternative source exists, but we can't really stay connected with this source until we come to grips with the particular method that we, as individuals, use in our controlling, and stop doing it — because whenever we fall back into this habit, we get disconnected from the source.*

> *Getting rid of this habit isn't easy because it's always unconscious at first. The key to letting it go is to bring it fully into consciousness, and we do that by seeing that our particular style of controlling others is one we learned in childhood to get attention, to get the energy moving our way, and we're stuck there. This style is something we repeat over and over again. I call it our unconscious control drama.*
>
> *I call it drama because it is one familiar scene, like a scene in a movie, for which we write the script as youths. Then we repeat this scene over and over in our daily lives without being aware of it. All we know is that the same kind of events happen to us repeatedly. The problem is if we are repeating one particular scene over and over, then the other scenes of our real-life movie, the high adventure marked by coincidences, can't go forward. We stop the movie when we repeat this one drama in order to manipulate for energy."*

The next chapter was called *"clearing the past"*. I noticed it was exactly in the middle of the book.

The main character finds desirable the idea of getting rid of his controlling style in order to accelerate his evolution. I did too. But, just like him, I had no idea how control dramas actually operated. I only knew one thing: I kept repeating a lot of patterns in my life.

I kept reading until I found a real breakthrough:

> *"Each person must reinterpret his or her family experience from an evolutionary point of view, from a spiritual point of view, and discover who he or she really is. Once we do that, our control drama falls away and our real lives take off."*

It appeared so simple. Yet, the hardest thing to do.

To identify our own control dramas, each one of us had to go back in time, to our early family life and observe our relationships with our family members to see how this "habit" was formed.

I instantly found myself as a six-year-old little girl blaming my father for leaving our family.

During my entire childhood, I was the "poor girl". Everyone felt sorry for me. And I couldn't deny: I learned to gain energy that way. Being weak and hopeless.

According to the book, the order of dramas goes like this: intimidator, interrogator, aloof and poor me. I had a strong feeling that "poor me" was my best fit. Often underestimated by my apparent fragility. Ironically, I used to be called a "drama queen". I just never knew those words were actually related to my own drama.

The awareness of my control drama got me thinking, but being aware was not enough to get me out of it.

If I was no longer a victim, who could I be? What could happen next?

The answer came loud and clear:

> "We are truly free to become more than the unconscious act we play. As I said before, we can find a higher meaning for our lives, a spiritual reason we were born to our particular families. We can begin to get clear about who we really are."

I seemed to have unconsciously anticipated my new future when I found the courage to leave my country and family behind. It was my way of slowly breaking free from my old self to follow my dream of becoming who I knew I could be.

The "poor me" was no longer in control. I felt truly capable of surviving and thriving on my own.

I suddenly had no interest in fighting my old ways. All I wanted was to surrender to the new life that was already unfolding right before my eyes.

26. TRUSTING THE UNKNOWN.

I had only been in Australia for three months, but had gone through emotions to last for a lifetime.

My plan was to do a full year away. With only six weeks left on my visa, I was fully focused on making adjustments to ensure I could extend my stay in Perth for at least another six or seven months.

My English course was coming to an end and my goal was to find a Marketing Diploma to extend my visa. I heard about this multicultural agency for international students. They had counselors to assist on school enrolments, visa extensions and work placements. I decided to go there and see if they could help me.

I entered the building through a mall and went up the elevator. The door opened almost directly to a little reception area full of people. I had no idea their services were so popular.

On the wall, I saw the sign: GSH. It stood for Global Services Hub.

I patiently waited in line for my turn to speak to a counselor. Almost an hour later, a fair skinned, blue-eyed, blond man called my name. He sounded European but I couldn't quite pick up on his accent. I followed him inside and he pointed to a chair across his desk.

"Sit down, Carolina. I'm Dominik. Let's see how we can help you."

"Thank you, Dominik. That would be great."

"Tell me your story. How long have you been here and what are you looking for?" He went straight to the point, as he should, with the number of people waiting outside.

"I've only been here for three months, currently finishing an English course. I'm interested in technical schools. I have a degree in Communications, majoring in Advertising. I'm thinking Marketing would be good. Ideally, I am looking to extend my visa for another six months. I also don't want to go to classes every day. I heard some courses are only two to three times a week. I'd like to know my options on those. Ah, reasonable tuition fees, please. I can't afford anything too expensive."

"Impressive. You are very clear about what you want, Carolina. Also, your English is great. Are you Brazilian?"

"Thank you. Yes, I'm Brazilian."

"And you said you have a degree in Communications, right? What's your work experience? Do you have a resume?"

"Well, I'm currently working as a waitress. I don't need work placement right now."

"Sure, I understand. But I'm talking back in Brazil. What did you use to do?"

"Oh, I haven't prepared an English resume for that."

"That's ok, you can do it later. Tell me a little more about you."

"Sure. I have just turned 23. I've worked since I was 17. I've worked as a TV producer, in client services in advertising agencies, marketing, media, events. Different areas, but all within the same industry. In one word, I am resourceful. I like to work and I like people."

"That's brilliant. Would you consider a position here?"

"What do you mean?"

"We've been getting a lot of South Americans through our door lately, but we don't have a South American counselor. We haven't been able to find anyone with the right set of skills."

"What exactly are you looking for?"

"Basically, someone who can speak fluent English and Portuguese or Spanish. But, the most important thing is the ability to handle people. From student enquiries to dealing with schools and universities representatives. We're looking for a negotiator who is also able to handle Marketing efforts in that region. From listening to your story, you seem like a perfect fit."

"Are you offering me a job?"

"Yes, I am. And we have a school that would be perfect for you. Marketing course, two and half days a week. If you are interested, we can make some arrangements to pay for your tuition fees in exchange for your services. That way, you won't need to pay us in advance. You can keep your cash. Would that interest you?"

"Possibly, but I need to know the actual figures before I can make any decision."

"Sure, let's meet again tomorrow to go through everything. You bring your resume and I'll prepare all the information you need: schools, tuition fees and a formal offer to you. This way, you can evaluate the opportunity. How does that sound?"

"Sounds perfect."

"Tomorrow after school? 4pm."

"Done, I'll make that work. Thank you, Dominik. See you tomorrow."

I was still trying to process everything that just happened in that room, especially the potential job offer. Out of all Brazilians in Perth, why me? My mind tried to trick me into believing it was all too good to be true. But I also knew I was fully capable of doing the job.

Even though I was fairly new to the country, my English was decent and I was a good communicator. I just never heard of anyone working in that position before. The job itself was foreign to me.

Whilst my mind was trying to create chaos, my intuition was loud and clear: *Carolina, this is it. You came here to do this. Prepare your resume and come back tomorrow. This is your new job. Trust me.*

It wasn't the first time I heard my intuition, so I went straight into an internet café to translate my resume. I didn't tell anyone. Not even Paula. I wanted to wait until I had the full picture instead of getting ahead of myself. I was learning about patience.

That night, I only remember thinking about Daniel. To me, he was almost like a real angel. Since I'd arrived in Australia, it had been one stroke of good luck after another.

I suspect I would have never gotten here unless we met. Our paths only crossed for those incredible things to happen in my life.

I felt truly grateful. For everything.

I went to school the next day and couldn't stop thinking about that new opportunity. As soon as my class finished at 3pm, I decided to walk to the city to clear my head before the meeting.

I checked my resume about five times to make sure every detail was there with no spelling mistakes. It wouldn't be Dominik's first impression of me. Still, I wanted it to be a good one.

I arrived ten minutes early and spoke to the receptionist. I saw the line and wondered how long it would take for him to see me. In less than five minutes, I saw him coming.

"Hi Carolina, good to see you. Come in, let's talk."

I noticed people looking at me in a very judgmental way, but I just followed him and sat down.

"Did you bring your resume?" he bluntly asked again. His objectivity was natural.

"Yes, here," I said, handing in my papers.

"Great, let me have a look." He took his time reading it while I had a close look around the place. There were a lot of rooms and about six or seven people working.

"You have some pretty solid experience for a young girl." He started talking while I only focused on paying attention. "Here, we get people from all walks of life. Whilst your focus should be on the South American market, you'll also be required to speak to all nationalities. Do you have a problem with that?"

"Not at all. I'll speak to anyone."

"That's what I thought. You'll notice that we may be coming from different parts of the world, but ultimately, we're all looking for the same things."

"You're right. Do you mind if I ask you something?"

"No, go ahead."

"Where are you from?"

"Eastern Europe. Czech Republic. Have you heard of it?"

"Briefly. Not enough to know anything about it."

"A lot of us here are from Eastern Europe. Hanicka, the founder, is Polish. And so are a couple of others who work in admin. But we have a Japanese counsellor and would love to have a Brazilian too. Your community is growing fast here."

"I've noticed. So, what exactly do you expect me to do?"

"Client services. Your clients may require a new school, a job or a visa extension. We can help them with all that. Your role is to speak to them, like I'm speaking to you, identify their needs and pass it on to us."

"And how do we get them what they need?"

"We have agreements with a number of schools and universities for enrollments. Also, employers come to us looking for students and working holiday makers. We place a lot of people here in Perth and around WA, in small country towns. They work in farms, hotels, and pubs. Hospitality industry in general. Our job is to connect students with schools, and candidates with job opportunities. We must find the best solution for both sides. If we can't help, we let them know."

"Sounds very interesting. Sorry, what is a working holiday maker?"

"Have you heard of backpackers?"

"You mean travelers?"

"Yes, young people who come to Australia on Working Holiday visas. They have one year to work and travel, but sometimes they want to stay longer. If they do three months of regional work, they get another year. We help them with that kind of work. That only applies to specific countries though. Eastern Europeans and South Americans are not eligible."

"I understand. So, there's a bit of everything here. English students, University students, backpackers. Do you also offer immigration services?"

"We do, but there's a special department just for that. You don't need to learn about everything. We have immigration lawyers."

"Good. Now, what do you have in mind for me in terms of an offer?"

"Well, you're looking to extend your visa for six months, right?"

"Correct."

"You want a Marketing Course, but only two or three times a week."

"Exactly."

"We have this school here." He showed me a brochure that looked very nice. "Tuition fees aren't the cheapest, but it's the best value for money at the moment. It's actually a good school, you'll like it there."

"It looks great on paper."

"You can go there in person to check it out. It's not far from here."

"I sure will."

"In terms of working hours, we're thinking about having you here three times a week. The same days you come to school. You can come straight here and work from 3 to 5pm. As you probably noticed, it's our peak hour for students. On your half day, you can do 2 to 4pm, mainly with backpackers. It's only six hours a week. You can still work 14 hours as a waitress to make real cash for living expenses."

"And you'll pay for my full semester?"

"That's our offer. You can do your calculations and see if that works for you."

"When would I need to start?"

"We would love to say immediately, but only after you finish your current course. Do you have holidays?"

"Yes, one month. I was thinking of working full-time to make some extra cash."

"Would you work at the restaurant?"

"Maybe. But I heard a few people made really good money planting trees. A friend of mine had gone down south for that. I'm also considering this as an option."

"Would you be interested in that kind of work?," he asked, looking very surprised.

"Definitely. It's only for a month and it would be a great experience. Plus, it's good money. Pretty much double what I can make as a waitress."

"You know it's very hard work though," he said, pondering my willingness to take such a challenging role. "Carolina, are you really up for that?"

"Yes, if she did it, I can do it too."

"Well, in this case, let me call Hanicka. She might be able to help you."

I was a bit confused about what Dominick had just said. He went to the other room and I waited. A few minutes later, he and Hanicka showed up.

"Hi Carolina, I'm Hanicka. Nice to meet you."

"Nice to meet you, Hanicka."

"So, Dominick tells me that you're interested in tree planting. Is that right?"

"Yes, a friend of mine went down south and she said it's a great opportunity to make some extra cash during our holidays."

"It can be, but it's very hard work," she emphasized again, especially the last two words. "I assume she has told you that too."

"She did, but it seems manageable. I'm young and healthy. I'm sure I can handle it."

"Well, we do have a client who needs people in Queensland in two weeks. When does your course finish?"

"Exactly in two weeks."

"It must be your lucky day then. Plus, I just told Dominick that this experience can certainly help you in the job here."

"How so?"

"Imagine when you tell backpackers you have done tree planting yourself. I bet they won't hesitate to go."

"Why is that?"

"Not many girls take up this job. You'll make it sound very easy."

"Hm, I see," I said, laughing, but slightly scared.

"There's another detail: they only take teams. You need four people, including yourself. If you find another three, I'll help you to get it."

"I have a feeling this is my first challenge in this job," I said referring to the opportunity I was being presented by Dominik. "Let's see what I can do. I'll get back to you, okay?"

"Sure, chat soon."

Hanicka left and Dominik continued our conversation.

"So, back to the job here. What are your thoughts?"

"Before I say yes, I'd like to check the school tomorrow, just to make sure I'm comfortable with everything. Is that ok with you?"

"Of course. You're right. Do your due diligence. You can come back here on Monday. You have the weekend to think about everything."

"That sounds perfect. Thank you very much, Dominick."

"Thank you, Carolina. Hope everything works out for all of us."

"Me too."

As I left the office, my mind went wild.

How is this even possible? I went to the agency only to find a course. I ended up with two job opportunities: one that sounded really promising for my future, and another to give me some savings and make sure I wouldn't struggle financially over the next six months.

I had to pinch myself. Was I really that lucky? Apparently, I was.

Before I could say yes to all that, I had another challenge. Hanicka made it very clear: in order to get the tree planting gig, I had to find the right people.

When Paula described her experience, I felt it in my body. But it also had an emotional toll. She specifically mentioned that a strong team was the secret to success.

To me, the whole tree planting experience felt like Big Brother on steroids. Imagine a team working on a tough assignment while spending an entire month living together.

How could I pull that off? I had to put together a tight four-piece team that played just like The Beatles, balancing each other's strengths and weaknesses.

A lot of Brazilians were keen on the opportunity, but not all of them fully understood the extent of the job. They only focused on the money part, which seemed to be the one element most of us were willing to trade our time and energy for.

For me, it was a little beyond that. I knew money was important, but it was not everything. I had found the perfect opportunity to unlock my true personal power and get out of the "poor me" control drama. If I could get through an experience like that, I would be set for life with a new mindset: *anything is possible*.

I was both excited and terrified again. I knew I had to do something to release tension and resistance to allow that new chapter of my life to unfold.

Thankfully it was Thursday afternoon. What better place to forget about everything than the Brazilian night? My regular dose of fun would definitely get my balance back.

I hadn't had time to speak with any of my friends, so I decided to turn up by myself. I learned not to care about being alone. That's how I went to Australia. Somehow, I always seemed to end up with the right people.

As soon as I entered the bar, I saw Mari. She was with a few other girls that I didn't know. Mari introduced me to one of them, Júlia, and we immediately clicked.

Júlia was taller than me, had a perfectly built figure, dark long hair, big brown eyes and a great sense of humour. She seemed determined and strong, with a very confident attitude, but not threatening at all. I felt great around her. We started talking:

"How long have you been here?" I asked her wanting to know if she was fairly new like me or from the 'been here a while' crew.

"Just over three months. My course is about to finish and I need to save money quickly to pay for the next one. It's the only way I can stay. What about you?"

"I'm also finishing my course. I'm pretty much in the same position as you. I wanna stay another six months."

"Are you also gonna work during the holidays?" she asked curiously, since a lot of people had travelling on their agenda.

"That's the plan."

"Have you heard people talking about tree planting? They say it's great money. I'm desperately trying to find where I can get this job."

"Are you serious?" I asked, just wanting a confirmation for another one of those 'coincidences'.

"Of course. If I get that, I'll pay for my full course. Then, I just need to keep working as a cleaner to pay for my expenses. That would be perfect!"

"I don't want to sound 'woohoo' here, but I think you and I were meant to meet tonight, Júlia," I said while trying not to sound overly mystical.

"You mean fate?" she asked, laughing with an almost sarcastic sense of humour.

"Exactly." I looked at her, speaking a little more seriously. "Look, this afternoon I had just been presented with a tree planting opportunity in Queensland. It starts in two weeks. They only take teams of four people. If you wanna come, we'll need to find another two guys so we can balance strengths and weaknesses."

"Are you kidding me?" she asked while I could see her big, expressive eyes sparkling with excitement.

"No, I'm very serious. That's why I said what I said. We're pretty much in the same position. We can make a great team. Do you know anyone else interested?"

"I do. These guys from school. They told me all about it."

"When can we talk to them?"

"They are here tonight. Wait, I'll find them."

As Júlia set off on a mission to find the guys, I took a few minutes to process everything that had just happened. Júlia was a stranger, but I felt great around her. She seemed very down to Earth which was exactly what I needed in a team mate.

"Carol, here are the guys: Hélio and Ivan."

"Nice to meet you," I said while Hélio almost interrupted me and cut to the chase.

"Júlia told us you know something about tree planting jobs."

"That's right. I have just been presented with this opportunity today. They take teams of four. I honestly had no idea that so many people were after this job."

"Everyone needs money, Carol," Ivan quickly joined the conversation.

"True. Why don't we have lunch tomorrow to talk about this? The four of us. I have to check a potential school in the city and I can meet you before that."

"Sounds perfect, Carol. There's a place close to our school. It's nice and cheap." Júlia made sure it was all organised.

"Done. I'll meet you guys there around midday. Just text me the address, Júlia," I confirmed excitedly. "Now, let's enjoy tonight," I said, thinking about the hard work ahead of us. "If we really go, we won't have much time for this in the next month."

"You're right, Carol. Let's have some fun," Hélio said as he left.

Júlia and I kept dancing and chatting about everything but work. She told me about her Aussie crush and her adventures down under. She was the kind of girl I'd definitely be friends with. I was excited with the prospect of having her in my team.

27. WHAT IF IT ALL WORKS OUT?

The next morning, it was school as usual.

As soon as the bell rang, I made my way into the city. It took me 20 minutes to walk to the restaurant Júlia suggested. When I got there, I saw her, Hélio and Ivan sitting at a table, chatting.

I approached them.

"Hey guys, so good to see you all again," I said, meaning every word, without hiding my excitement.

"Good to see you too, Carol," Júlia said with a smile.

"So, can you tell us how this tree planting actually works?" Hélio knew how to get to the point.

"Sure. Here's the deal: they take teams of four people. We'll have a fifth person joining us, probably a backpacker from Europe. We can choose between hourly rate or production rate. If we are really good, production can give us a lot more money. But we can start on an hourly rate until we get up to speed. The average pay is a thousand dollars a week for each one of us."

"What about expenses?" Ivan asked, a little worried.

"They cover our accommodation. We only need to buy food. But we need to make our own way up there. I've already checked the options and it's about 300 dollars for return tickets from Perth to Mackay. There's no direct flight, so we'll fly into Brisbane and change to regional. That must be paid before we go. Can everyone afford it?"

"Well, even if we pay 300 dollars, we still clear 3,700. A little less after food expenses," concluded Hélio. "I can only make around five or six hundred dollars a week here. And I have to pay for accommodation and food. For me, it's a deal."

"I agree," said Júlia. "I can make arrangements so I don't pay any rent while I'm away. It works for me."

"Sorry, guys. I don't have that kind of money upfront." Ivan sounded disappointed.

"You mean 300 dollars for the ticket?" I asked him.

"Yes, I only have 500 dollars left in my bank account. I can't afford to take the risk. What if it doesn't work out?"

We all looked at each other for a minute, in a brief silence.

"But what if it does?" I asked Ivan.

"I'm not a risk taker, Carol. Sorry."

I was confident it would all work out. And I was determined to have this experience with these three people in front of me. I knew we were all strangers, but I felt an unexplainable connection with them.

I knew money was coming in. Plus, I had enough savings in my bank account to pay for my full course and a stable job at the restaurant to cover my living expenses.

On top of that, a potential opportunity to work as a counselor at the agency and not even having to spend on tuition fees. Money was not an issue for me. I could spare 300 dollars to help a teammate. All I would ask in return was his commitment.

"Ivan, what if I lend you this money and you pay me back once you get your first paycheck?" I offered to remove his cash burden.

"Can you afford to do that?" he asked me with a mix of excitement and disbelief.

"I wouldn't offer it if I couldn't. But you must promise me that you'll do your very best to make it work. Remember: this is going to be challenging for all of us. Me included."

"I promise. Thank you, let's do this!" Ivan seemed a lot better after my offer.

"So, are we all in?" I asked everyone as my last confirmation.

"Yes," Júlia answered, excited.

"Yes," Hélio followed her lead.

"Yes," Ivan confirmed once again.

"We're all in then," I said at last. "And we better be ready. It's gonna be a hell of a ride."

The secret to a leap of faith was commitment. None of us had any idea what we were signing up for. We just knew we had to go.

I still had homework to do prior to saying yes to all the opportunities ahead. Choosing the right business college was a fundamental part of it. I left the restaurant and went straight to the one Dominick had recommended.

It was only a couple of blocks away, in a vibrant part of the city. Just walking on those beautiful streets inspired me. Every part of my body came alive.

As I entered the building, I was welcomed by warm energy.

A very friendly receptionist came up to me.

"Hi there, how can I help you?"

"Hi Kate," I said after reading her name tag. "I'm Carolina. I'm here to see Jacklyn."

"Our principal?"

"Yes, Dominick from GSH sent me here."

"Oh, that's right. He called her this morning. She's expecting you, Carolina. I'll let her know that you're here."

"Perfect, thank you."

I looked around and instantly felt the relaxed atmosphere. It seemed like a very easy going, laid back environment. It didn't take long until Kate came back.

"Jacklyn is ready for you, Carolina," she said while escorting me to her office. "I'll let you two talk." Kate politely excused herself and left.

I made my way into the room and sat on one of the nice chairs opposite Jacklyn.

"Hi Carolina, pleasure to meet you. Dominick personally asked me to take very special care of your case."

"Really? Why is that?"

"Well, he thinks you have a bright future here in Australia."

"Is that so?"

"Yes, he wants you to join their team. He's been looking for a South American for a while. According to him, you're the one."

"That's interesting. I was under the impression there were a lot of people just like me here in Perth."

"There are certainly a lot of Brazilians, but everyone is different. You seem to display a very unique set of skills. That's what makes a difference here in Australia. If you can do something none of us can, you become eligible to do a job that otherwise should be taken by an Aussie."

"Hm, I see. So, can you tell me more about your Marketing Diploma?"

"Sure. First, we like to keep things on a smaller scale, with only 150 or so students on campus. Our average class size is around 15 — large enough for the exchange of ideas, but small enough for everyone to be heard."

"Sounds nice. I already like that."

"Our college also has a balance of both international and local students. It's not your regular international school."

"Great, I like the idea of having some Aussie classmates."

"We also prefer relaxed methods of study — it's one of the reasons we are known as the 'friendly college'. Subjects allow sufficient class time not only for training, but for some assessment activities and individual attention as well. Study here is designed to allow time for other important aspects of your life. Classes are held over three days, so you have time for extra study, work experience, or a casual job."

"Yes, Dominick had mentioned that. How is that possible?"

"Subjects are delivered over nine-week periods, with a little break between them for you to recover. Each subject has clear aims and a suitable time frame to encourage lively, structured learning. Your assessment is ongoing and based on a complete learning experience — a lot less worrying than feared final exams."

"It sounds amazing."

"Also, projects are based on real-world situations with trainers providing mentorship and guidance. That's where your experience at GSH comes in. It's pretty much like an internship in your case."

"That's perfect, Jacklyn."

"Let me show you our campus."

As we walked around, a sense of belonging grew within me. I was truly impressed by this college. They seemed to have found balance between study and life. I had to agree with Dominick: it was the perfect college for me.

Jacklyn ended our tour back at reception.

"Do you have any other questions, Carolina?"

"No, I think we covered it all. It's been a pleasure to meet you, Jacklyn. I'll organise everything with Dominick and I shall see you in August."

"We really look forward to it, Carolina. We'll be very happy to have you as one of our students."

"Thank you again for everything. I'll see you soon."

Kate handed me a few brochures, but I handed them back.

"Thank you, Kate. I already have them. You can save these for another student. Have a great day!"

As I left the building, relief took over my body. I remembered the Fifth Insight:

> *"The Universe can provide all we need if we can only open up to it."*

I was open, and I had to remind myself things were not always under my control. There was nothing to be scared of. I only had to accept that things worked out in very mysterious ways, often better than my own plans.

It wasn't the first time I had real proof that a very generous Universe was in charge. Even a stubborn bull like me had no choice but to believe.

I felt very different that weekend. It was like all the weight of the world had been lifted off my shoulders. I only needed to carry my own weight.

I finished my Sunday shift at 2pm and went home.

Only I knew how I would spend my school holidays, but knowing that made me appreciate even more everything I already had. I was gonna miss my life for a little while, but I knew I would be back. Better and stronger.

I realised how lucky I was to be surrounded by so many amazing people.

Our work crew was like my little Aussie family. I loved them. We all became great friends. And one of our traditions was going together to the classic Cottesloe Sunday Sessions. Every Sunday.

Fun is the best way to start any week. At least for me.

28. COUNTING DOWN.

Another Monday morning went by very quickly. With only two weeks left at school, we were getting ready for our final assessments. That was, by far, the least of my concerns. I wanted to make sure I saw every important person before they left.

My friend Gui had just come back from some amazing travels and was ready to leave Australia. Unlike most Brazilians I met, Gui only stayed for six months. We went out for lunch at a nearby all-day pub and I broke the news to him:

"Guess what? I'm going tree planting for my holidays," I said, overly excited.

"No! Are you out of your mind? It's very hard work, girl. I did fruit picking and wouldn't recommend it."

"I know, but it's exactly what I need. You know I'll be fine."

"Can I argue with you?"

"You know the answer. Tell me about your trip."

"Oh Carol, it was unbelievable! Australia is amazing! I know you love to work, but please don't forget to travel. It's beautiful out there."

"Don't worry, Gui. I'll have enough time for that. Why are you going so soon? I already miss you!"

"I'll miss you too, crazy girl. I just have to go. Things didn't turn out great for me here."

"I know. It was not meant to be. You have a great life waiting for you in Brazil."

"Let me know when you are there so we can catch up. And don't get too busy, okay? Keep me posted on how things go."

"Will do. Safe travels, my friend. I hope Brazil treats you well."

"Keep going, Carol. And have fun at the farm."

As we said goodbye, I remembered Paula was also about to leave. She was moving to Sydney for the next six months.

It was the end of an era. My entire group of friends was going through redirection. With the end of our courses, everyone had to make the next move. It was all part of the process. Still, I felt a little emotional.

My life was about to go through some major changes. Again.

That afternoon was going to be my turning point. I decided to say yes to Dominick's offer. I also decided to cherish the tree planting opportunity. I had no clue how I'd come out on the other side of that experience, but my main goal was to prepare myself for the upcoming adventure.

I knew everything was going to be alright. Trust was my superpower.

Back at GSH, Dominik was waiting for me.

"Hi Carolina, good to see you. How was your weekend?"

"It was great! A bit of work, a bit of fun. How was yours?"

"Good. Quiet as usual. So, did you speak to Jacklyn on Friday?"

"Yes, I did."

"And what did you think of the school?"

"I loved it. I definitely wanna study there."

"That's great to hear. How about our offer? Did you have enough time to consider?"

"Yes, I think working here will be a valuable experience for me."

"I have no doubt."

"But, first I wanna take the tree planting opportunity. I found a great team."

"Already? Well done, Carolina. That was quick."

"I know, it's hard to explain but it all just happened. Something tells me this will be a turning point in my life. I don't know why, but I need to go through this."

"I'm excited for you. That will be a life-changing experience for sure. I'll let Hanicka know. You and your team can come here tomorrow to get everything organised with her. Is that okay?"

"Sure, sounds great."

"I'll also prepare your enrolment papers and our agreement. You can sign everything tomorrow when you come in."

"Perfect, thank you."

"Welcome to our team, Carolina. Maybe you can show us how South Americans celebrate."

"Of course, that will be fun!"

On my way home, I kept thinking about how life can surprise us in the most unexpected ways.

I had no real plan when I left Brazil, other than to study and make a living for an entire year on my own. I also wanted to experience love. But as they say: *there's a time for everything under the sun.*

For me, it was time to work.

29. A REAL-LIFE ADVENTURE.

Brisbane Airport. A brief stop to rush into our next tightly scheduled flight. We literally ran to the gate and boarded. Just in time.

An hour and a half later we found ourselves at Mackay Airport, our final destination.

The unusual atmosphere with palm trees all around inspired the feeling of going on a holiday. It helped to ease my mind.

We got our luggage from the carrousel and went straight to Arrivals. Mick was there waiting for us. The sight of him shocked me for a second. He looked exactly like Crocodile Dundee. Dirty clothes, boots, a hat. The whole Australian costume from the movie, but in real life.

All of a sudden, Dundee became a real-life character to me. He was a man of very few words, but they were loud.

"How ya doing?" he asked with an accent none of us had heard before.

"Good, mate," Hélio impersonated the impersonator. A true Aussie bloke.

"Let's go. I'll take you to your accommodation."

Mick directed us to the car park and jumped into a four-wheel drive we could barely recognise. It was fully covered in mud. I took a very deep breath before we all jumped in.

I could have never prepared enough for what was in front of me, but I was fully aware about the nature of the job. Going there was a conscious decision and I wasn't alone.

Still, everything was unknown to us: the people, the place, the job. It was the first time that I literally found myself in the middle of nowhere without a clear picture of what was about to happen.

We had no choice but to trust Dundee. He looked a bit tough, but I knew he would be good to us. He drove for about an hour and then stopped at a caravan park.

Campsites were familiar to me. I grew up camping with my parents. I knew what to expect there. As he showed us our accommodation, a calming feeling finally arised.

"This will be fun!" I said to everyone. "It feels like a holiday!" I hardly missed a joke.

"Except, it's not, Carol," Ivan murmured. He seemed to be having a hard time adjusting to everything. He was not like the others. We had to be patient with him. With time, he would get into the swing of things.

"At least we have our own caravan. I like it here. It reminds me of my childhood."

As I looked around, Júlia and Hélio were already playing in the mud. They seemed to belong there.

Júlia and I started to organise everything, while thinking about what would be required for our new routine. For starters, we didn't have any food. Someone was meant to pick us up later in the day to take us shopping.

After a couple of hours, a new guy arrived. Young, blond, blue eyes. A typical Aussie bloke. He seemed shy and sweet. The complete opposite of Dundee.

"Hey guys, I'm Jack, your manager. I'm in charge of roster and logistics. How are you all settling down here?"

"Getting there," Júlia answered.

"I'm here to take you shopping. You know food is your responsibility, right? Can you guys cook?"

"We're not chefs, but we won't starve, that's for sure," Hélio answered as a twenty-something-year-old student who knew any food goes when you're hungry.

"You'll be working 8 to 12-hour shifts. Most days you'll be too tired to even eat, let alone cook. Make sure you get easy stuff, okay?" he wisely advised us.

"Hey Jack, can you walk us through what's gonna happen here?" I asked him, trying to ease my anxiety.

"Sure, we'll have a debrief session once we get back from the shops. Make sure you get enough supplies for three days. Breakfast, lunch and dinner. Snacks are also nice. The job requires a lot of energy."

"I see. Well, if you don't mind, we just need a few minutes to prepare a list. Is that okay?"

"Sure, take your time."

We got together and wrote a few things down. Breakfast cereal, milk, bread. A lot of bread. Along with every possible filling we can make sandwiches with: ham, cheese, tuna, eggs. Two-minute noodles, muesli bars, chocolate. The list went on. All easy stuff. We were all pretty much eating that kind of crap as students anyway. It was all good.

"Hey Jack, we're ready."

"Cool, let's go."

At the shops, we noticed things were not as cheap as in Perth. We made sure to get all promo packs and stocked up on the things we knew were gonna fly.

Back at camp, Jack gave us the instructions.

"I'll pick you up tomorrow at 6am. Make sure you take lunch and snacks for the day. We'll start with an eight-hour shift for you to get used to the job. You'll be back here by 4pm."

"Sounds good. We'll see you tomorrow, Jack," I said while trying to anticipate what an eight-hour shift at that job would feel like.

We enjoyed a few beers, sandwiches and went to bed early.

A good sleep was the secret to keeping our bodies strong.

30. DAY 1.

I woke up at 4am. I don't like to feel rushed. I prefer to have extra time to do everything I need before a busy day. I had a shower and got ready. I still had plenty of time so I started preparing sandwiches for the day.

When everyone got up, most of our food was ready. We all had breakfast together and said a little prayer. Everyone had their own beliefs, but we were all united by the same faith. Brazilians are faithful people. That seems to help in any situation.

6am sharp, Jack parked a van outside. It was a little chilly so I grabbed a jacket. I only had taken two jackets to Australia: one was white. The other was bright pink. Clearly, neither of them were suitable for the job, but they were all I had. I put my bright pink jacket on and went outside. I was ready to roll.

The four of us jumped in the van with bags of food and really high hopes for a great work day. I noticed Jack checking me out and wondered if there was something wrong. He said nothing so I assumed he was just confused by my dress code.

He stopped the van and we all left the car. The only way I could describe where we were is a million hectares of nothingness.

Completely virgin land ready to be fertilized by the seeds we were about to plant. It was beautiful.

We noticed a couple of kangaroos jumping around in their natural habitat. It felt like the ultimate Australian experience.

We saw Dundee approaching the van with his truck. He jumped off and quietly looked at all of us. He stared at me for a second. I felt terrified. Why was he looking directly at me? It didn't take long until we found out.

"Hey mate," he said looking straight into my eyes. "Are you sure you're fit for this?"

"What do you mean?" I asked, puzzled.

"Look, no offense. But you're the first person who's turned up here wearing a pink jacket. I'm worried you don't understand the nature of this job."

"I totally do. I just have two jackets: white and pink. You'll see me wearing them all the time. You better get used to it."

"Are you prepared to lose them?"

"Absolutely."

"Cool, let's get to work then."

I was fully aware that I didn't look exactly as the usual farm worker. Júlia and I were girly girls. It didn't even cross my mind that wearing pink was gonna make such a statement. Still, we were ready to show them what real girls could do.

They took us through technical training and we learned not only to operate the machinery, but also a sophisticated logistics system behind tree planting. It was mechanical and repetitive, unlike anything I had ever done before. But we understood.

Each one of us took a position in the team and we literally started making holes and moving forward.

We walked for four hours straight. The landscape never changed. No matter how ahead we seemed, it was always the exact same place. An infinite horizon of emptiness. We were in the middle of nowhere going nowhere. But deep inside we knew we were getting somewhere. We just had to trust our hard work would pay off.

A 20-minute break to eat and smoke a cigarette lying on the ground. That's all we had until we started walking for a few more hours. We lost track of time and distance. My personal mantra never made so much sense. "Keep going" was literally all we could do.

We were feeling the hours weighing on our bodies but none of us complained. Suddenly, our truck stopped and the silence felt like a siren. We looked around and saw Jack arriving in a car.

"You're done for the day, guys. Well done."

We had no idea what to do so we all clapped. One day down.

As we jumped in the car, I had a quick look at myself in the rear mirror. My face was fully covered in dust. My arms, and every other exposed part of my body, too. I only had clean hands because I wore gloves.

"I know it was a tough day," Jack started talking in a friendly tone. "But keep doing what you were doing there today and you'll be one of our best teams. The driver said you were amazing for a first day."

"Really?" I asked, excited.

"Really. Girls," he looked specifically at me and Júlia, "everyone was impressed by you two. They didn't believe you could handle it, but you proved them wrong. Well done."

Júlia hugged me and we both smiled in relief. Yes, we could do it!

"Make sure you relax and go to bed early, okay? Tomorrow is another full day. You might wake up sore. After all, it's an 8-hour intense workout. But keep up the pace. Your body gets used to it."

As Jack left, we went straight to the showers. The warm water falling on my head and shoulders made me relax. I felt every single muscle aching. I had never put my body into such intense activity before.

Júlia was showering next to me. We were in those camping showers where you can talk.

"I don't think I've ever been this dirty in my entire life," she said, laughing.

"Maybe when we were kids," I said, trying to keep it light. "But I'm not sure that I will ever feel fully clean again."

"We shouldn't worry about that now. We're gonna do this another 29 times, remember?"

"You're right. Let's worry about that when we get closer to the end. Now, out of curiosity, did you know you had so many muscles in your body? I feel them."

"No. It's like every single one has had a full workout today."

"I think we should call this the ultimate outdoor bootcamp."

"Sounds glamorous."

"I know, very."

"But we wanted this, right?"

"We sure did."

"Just remember what Jack said, Carol."

"I know, he was nice."

"Pink jacket not so bad, hey?" I could hear the irony in her voice.

"Seriously, they must have thought I was a princess."

"And you showed them what princesses can do."

"It's only 29 days. We will survive!"

Between laughter and pain, we kept talking. Any bad feelings just went down the drain. Jack's voice talking about easy meals came straight to my mind. It made perfect sense. We were exhausted and still had to prepare dinner.

Hélio and Ivan were both lying down back at the caravan.

"How are you feeling?" I asked to see if they were any different than us.

"Exhausted," they replied at the same time.

"It was intense, but I feel good," Hélio and his ever-present optimism were contagious.

"Agree, I'm sure we can all make it," I said confident we were fit for the job.

"You're right, pink jacket. We will!" Hélio never missed a joke.

"Tell me about it. I love being underestimated. Who cares about my clothes? Just watch me!"

We all made a choice. Our commitment was to get to the end. There was no turning back. Over the next 29 days, we would experience a different way of existing in the world. I was at peace with that.

Instant noodles for dinner. And a couple of beers. Perfect time management.

They say *"money doesn't grow on trees"*, but if we plant them, money follows.

31. DAY 2.

Same thing, different day.

With expectations out of the way, we got through another eight-hour shift a lot easier than the day before. Our muscles felt stronger. We all knew the rule: *practice makes perfect*.

Our team was hungry. The Brazilian passion was our fuel.

Back at the caravan park, Jack joined us for a beer and made a brief announcement:

"Hey guys, we finished the job here. There is no more land to plant in this region. Tomorrow we move to the next site."

"Where?" I asked curiously.

"To a hostel in the center of Rockhampton. They have a big kitchen and better beds for you to sleep. I think you'll like it."

"It sounds wonderful." Ivan seemed excited.

"Yes, we will have a day off for the transition," Jack added, trying to put us at ease.

"Already? I'm not that tired yet." Júlia was a master at sarcasm.

"It's only one day, Júlia. You'll be back at it in full swing after the move." Jack knew what was about to come. "Let's have a few drinks tonight and enjoy the camp. You guys deserve it."

Jack helped us to light a bonfire as a little farewell to that place. We sat around it sharing stories, beers and a lot of laughter.

"Carol," Jack approached me. "I know we underestimated you yesterday, but I want to say that we are very happy to have you here."

"Thanks, Jack. That's nice of you to say. Look, I'm aware that I'm far from your stereotypical farm worker, but I came to Australia to work. I have done a lot of things I never thought I would. This is just another one of them."

"I bet. Is this your first-time camping?"

"No way. I camped my entire childhood. I love it!"

"And why did you stop?"

"My father left home. He was the one who organized everything."

"Are your parents divorced?"

"Yes, it's been a while. One of the reasons I'm here is to distance myself and hopefully heal."

"How old were you when they separated?"

"Six."

"And now?"

"Twenty-three."

"Do you miss your family?"

"A lot. But since I arrived in Australia, I have never felt so alive."

"Good. Then healing is already happening."

"True. Thank you for your kind words."

Our curfew expired. It was time to move.

32. THE WORLD (REALLY) IS A SMALL TOWN.

The next day we woke up and headed towards Rockhampton.

Bovine statues welcomed us along wide avenues. On the main roundabout stood a statement sign: Australia's Beef Capital.

We stopped at a gas station and while we were talking in Portuguese, a guy approached us.

"Are you Brazilian?"

"Yes, why?"

"Me too. I work for a big meatpacking company here."

"Wow, what a coincidence."

"There's more than 200 of us here."

"All Brazilian?"

"Yes. And you, how did you end up here?"

"We are planting trees."

"For real?"

"Yes. We are actually students, just working for extra cash during the holidays."

"I get it. It's not our case. We are here to stay. We're on work visas. Our lives are here now."

And right there, in the middle of nowhere in Australia, I was surprised by a memory: *some Brazilians move to another country for good.*

It was hard for me to imagine a permanent life on the other side of the world. That idea never crossed my mind.

"Enjoy the city," he said while waving goodbye.

"Thanks, will do."

We headed to the hostel to prepare for our next 28 days of work.

As we checked in, Jack mentioned we should take the rest of the day to get organized.

Food shopping was our priority. We got that out of the way.

Then we had a quick look around the new town. A nice big pub stood out.

"Let's go there one day," Júlia said.

Hope is a beautiful thing. It's always good to have something to look forward to. A pub night in the middle of a work sprint can be life changing.

From there, it was full on work mode. We were all in.

33. WORK HARD, PLAY HARD.

As the days went by, we became familiar with our new routine.

Day in, day out, we kept going.

Our bodies went into what I call "autopilot". The same repetitive moves. Even in our sleep. It was hilarious! I woke up one night to go to the bathroom and literally saw my team "walking in their dreams". They were moving in bed, just like we did during the day. It scared me how humans can become machine-like by repetition. Our bodies are easily trained to do anything.

We lost track of time and space, but things felt a lot easier — and lighter. Every day we simply woke up and walked towards infinity. With an unknown end, what kept us moving was the hope to one day walk into a beautiful forest of trees we planted ourselves.

We accepted that we were living in an alternate reality. It was like a parallel universe. All controlled by Jack. He was always around. His job was to organize shifts and move people from one place to the other. Every day he was there to pick us up and take us back.

I wondered how Jack was able to do that for so many years. He wasn't physically on the ground. Still, it was a tough job. His experience helped us a lot. He was a nice guy. And ironically he was originally from WA.

Sometimes he would stay for a beer and a chat. And he was always happy to share some sound advice. We were getting closer. Somehow, Jack's universe had also become a little bit our own.

To beat the inevitable boredom, we created little collective rituals. Simple things like spending a few hours drinking beer, playing pool or meeting new people for endless chats. They kept our energy high, disguising our exhaustion.

I liked chatting with Jack. On one of those nights, I decided to delve deeper into the work we were doing:

"Hey Jack, what species are we planting here?" I asked, genuinely curious.

"Eucalyptus. They basically dominate the Australian landscape."

"And how long do they take to grow?"

"About 10 years."

"10 years? Are you kidding me?"

"No. That's why we keep planting in different places every year."

"I had no idea they took so long to grow. We'll never get to see our little forest then?"

"We never know. But a lot of people will benefit from what we're doing."

"That's good to know. Our little tree legacy for the next generation. I was just thinking, you know how they say that we all need to plant a tree, have a child and write a book? For now, I'm just mastering the first one," I said, laughing.

"You're funny. I love it."

Jack and I belonged to completely different worlds and led very different lives. But, at that point in time, our paths crossed. He always went above and beyond to help our team in a very practical way. He made our shifts easier by giving us tips to increase our productivity. Somehow, he made life there lighter for all of us. And I noticed that.

After a few beers, I also noticed the way he looked at me. It was subtle, but I could tell he was intrigued. He couldn't hide his attraction. I also couldn't hide that I enjoyed his attention. He often gave me little treats. Always on the way to work. It could be chocolate milk or just chocolate. He learned early on that I loved those. I suspect it was his way to try to sweeten my hard days.

After two whole weeks working non-stop, Jack announced that we would finally have our first day off. We all needed a break. Given the intense pace we were at, a full day to relax and recharge our batteries would do us a lot of good.

We all saw that "night in town" coming. And it finally came. We were ready to hit the local pub.

Júlia and I were excited. As I opened my luggage, I felt an unexplainable joy. I found the only dress I had taken for that adventure (in hopes of finding an opportunity to wear it). I had no doubt: this was the night. Júlia also had a dress. We looked at each other and said: "Let's do it! Time to put our 'girly girls' on."

With a little makeup and a hairdryer that we found at the hostel, we rescued our dusty feminine look that got lost in those two weeks of dirty work. We almost couldn't recognize ourselves in the mirror. We were glowing. And ready for our night out.

I thought to myself: if my pink jacket made such an impression, imagine this little dress. But this is who I am. I just have to own it.

As much as we try to deny this, we have been trained to respond to visuals. Of course, that night everyone saw us differently.

There, we were not the dirty, messy, tree planters. We were two young women ready to have fun. I felt like myself again.

After a few drinks and shots, I noticed that Jack was looking at me. More than usual. He approached us and we got into a deeper conversation. An eye-to-eye kind of interaction. I had no intention of mixing things up, but it was undeniable that we were getting closer that night.

"Can I ask you something, Carol?"

"Sure."

"Is there someone special waiting for you in Perth, or even in Brazil?"

"You mean a boyfriend?"

"Yes."

"The answer is no."

"It's hard to believe."

"Why?"

"Look at you."

"Sometimes what you see is not all that it seems, Jack."

"I'm not just talking about your looks. There's something about the way you are and do things. Everything about you is beautiful, Carol."

"You don't know me, Jack."

"Maybe not. But I like what I do. I don't want you to feel uncomfortable about what I said. I know we work together. Sorry if I crossed a line here, but that's how I feel. I just wanted to let you know."

"I get it. It's just that right now my focus is work."

"I understand, and respect you. Very much. As I said, I just found myself thinking about you more than I should."

"It's not every day that a girl in a pink jacket shows up to plant trees, right?"

"True."

"For me, everything here is very new. It's like a parallel universe, almost like a movie, you know?"

"Is that how you feel?"

"Yes."

"For me, this is normal life."

"I know, Jack. We are very different."

"That doesn't stop me from having feelings for you, Carol."

"I understand, but it's just a story in your mind."

"A story that never happened?"

"Yep. And let me tell you: it hurts a lot less. I speak from experience. I'm still recovering from a story that kind of happened, but didn't end the way I imagined."

"And do you think every story ends the same way?"

"So far that's what happened."

"And what's the idea? Stop living stories?"

"No, living a different one."

"This will only happen if you are open to what's different. I'm different."

How smart was that?! Jack left me speechless. He really got me there. And he was absolutely right. I had so many outdated beliefs about love and life inside of me that I just kept repeating the same patterns.

For some reason, I always went for unavailable men. There was something familiar about them. You guessed it: dad issues. But my strongest belief was rooted in my family history: never get romantically involved with a man you work for or with. Never give up your job for them either. It's a trap.

Why? It will instantly make you dependent on his approval. If his feelings for you change, you have nothing left to hang on to. I've seen too many women go down that path and it didn't end well. Men seem to be better at holding the power when things go sour.

So, the rule was clear: my survival could never be attached to a man's desire. I had to be enough on my own and be able to walk away if my needs were not met in any given relationship.

I was also more comfortable in the familiar. Jack was not only Australian; he was a country guy. A real foreigner to me. But, in that conversation, I discovered that he and I had a lot in common. And this wasn't the job of my life so I could take a little risk.

Next thing I knew was this: Jack found a silver lining in my broken heart. And he got in that way. He was so sure he wanted me that he convinced me of that, just with sensible arguments. Maybe the drinks helped, but his simplicity and honesty brought every single one of my walls down. I surrendered.

For the first time, I didn't make any plans for the future. I was happy to just enjoy what was happening there and then. I remained focused on work, but allowed myself to feel all the emotions. And according to the Prophecy, *"connecting with energy first feels like emotion, then euphoria and then love"*. There was no point skipping the steps.

Over the next two weeks, Jack helped me to see a side of myself that I had previously been unaware of. I could be strong and sweet at the same time. He made a point of giving me a chocolate heart every day. I suspect it was to remind me of that.

Even though love was a distant concept, it was undeniable that I was a hopeless romantic. I was just hurt. Up until that point, love and pain were synonymous to me.

My story with Jack reinforced my somewhat new perspective on the most romanticized feeling in the Universe.

Love can be simple. Not every love needs to be the greatest love of your life. Sometimes love just comes to show us a new place. Physically or emotionally. And through this power, life guides us in some very mysterious ways.

I had experienced it with Daniel. And here I was, connected with my heart's voice again.

When I left Brazil, it never crossed my mind that one day I would plant trees. Let alone fall in love in the process of doing that. And as unlikely as everything was, I felt deeply grateful for that experience — and for the friends I made along the way.

Despite being fiction, The Celestine Prophecy was helping me to understand a lot about life. One of the main learnings was the importance of our connection with nature.

That unusual job made me fully experience that. Every day, on every break, I would lay down on the ground for a rest, and let myself be embraced by Mother Earth. Her warmth and safety kept me grounded the whole time. It was powerful.

The fact that we were far from any city living demands gave me more presence too. I had to be fully there. Nothing else mattered. And for an anxious person like me, it was a brand-new feeling. I could truly breathe. I had endless space to just be me.

One of the main character's teachings in the book, as he became aware of each insight, was that he not only changed himself, he also changed his way of seeing the entire world.

I felt something very deep beginning to change within me. And it extended to all areas of my life, including my relationships. It's easy to romanticize "forever", but life is movement. And it was time for my little adventure to come to an end.

The Brazilian team decided to stay another week, but I needed to go back to Perth. The training for my new job was about to begin and the time off I took from the restaurant was also over. I had a life to go back to.

Jack and I went out for dinner. It was our last goodbye.

"Why don't you stay for another week like the others?"

"I can't. I'm starting at Hanicka's agency next week. And I'm still a waitress. I'm in Australia alone, remember? I need to support myself."

"Are you going to leave one job for another?"

"No. One job for two."

"You shouldn't work so hard."

"I like to. It makes me feel safe."

"Can we meet again when I go back to WA?"

"Maybe, but no plans. I loved it so far, Jack. But life goes on and we need to get on with it. I don't want to get hurt. I prefer to remember us just like this."

It was beautiful. And honest. Just like love should be.

Of course Jack took me to the airport. From there, our lives took off in different directions.

Beginning, middle and end. I never imagined that something so simple and short could inspire me. But it did. I allowed myself to live that story with an open heart and no attachment.

On the plane, I took a deep breath and stopped for a few moments.

Gratitude took over me as this giant, gentle wave. With a lighter heart, I was open to receiving and ready to accept my insignificance in the grand scheme of things.

Since I arrived in Australia, one thing became very clear: *things were rarely under my control.* And I was having the best experience anyone could ask for.

Ironically, I discovered that the most effective way I found to stay at peace was by following some of the teachings of the Prophecy. Seeking to strengthen my own spiritual connection with the energy of the Universe and maintaining a positive attitude towards the facts of life.

Simply put: *just getting out of my own way.* And allowing the great mystery of the Universe to support me in the manifestation of my dreams.

34. A NEW STATE OF MIND.

Back in Perth, I felt a brave new world opening up for me. And while it was fascinating, that didn't mean it was challenge-free.

Before my little adventure, I was already juggling some interesting personalities within myself. The Brazilian, the international student, the waitress, the party girl, the dreamer. As if they were not enough, I also had to find a way to integrate the tree planter. Not to mention, all the questions I had around the spiritual seeker that didn't seem to match the bold, practical, independent woman I was becoming.

At that time, Cosmos or the Universe were not common words in my vocabulary. I believed in the apparent "coincidences" in my life simply because I saw them constantly happening before my eyes. Still, I doubted the idea of hidden messages in the sky, the earth or the wind as Carlos Castaneda or Paulo Coelho dared to describe in their books.

I enjoyed getting lost in their works. I found them fascinating. But it was pure enjoyment. And deep admiration.

As a material girl, I have always done what I could to get what I wanted. I was a doer. Action was the spiritual energy that guided my life. I loved working. My real thrill came from getting things done. Checking the checklist. No matter what anyone needed, I was their girl. Always ready for the task at hand.

A simple attitude that has incredible power and, dare I say, "a little magic".

So, I continued doing what I had to do. At that moment, it was work.

My life was exciting and there was still a lot of new stuff going on, but the novelty of living abroad kind of wore off. I was already well settled into a routine. And for me, that's where danger normally lies.

That unexpected wave of longing hit me again. This time, a little harder.

"Homesickness" was a bitch! For the lack of a better word. I had met her before and I knew we were not meant to be close friends. I just had to find a way to feel love, protection, security and familiarity. I knew I could find all those things within myself, but I was struggling.

Fortunately, these "bad waves" never lasted long. Still, I thought of new ways to ease those nostalgic feelings if they ever returned. Once again, I remembered the Prophecy.

At the age of 23, I may not have understood all the talk about connection and consciousness, but I could easily relate to nature. I already knew that the beach and the sunset were very good for me, along with music and a peaceful state of mind.

Little by little, I learned to face external challenges, using these tools, without losing my internal connection with the higher energy. Quite a step forward for a material girl like me.

My first real challenge was to say goodbye to Paula. I was happy for her move, but sad to see her leaving.

While she wanted to experience big Sydney and travel around Australia before going back to São Paulo's corporate land, I had achieved an unexpected level of stability in Perth. There was no reason for me to go anywhere. I had found work at the agency, started my new Marketing course and still had my great job at the restaurant.

Our lives were very different and we understood that. Even if we were physically going separate ways, our hearts would remain forever connected.

My next challenge? Finding a new place to live. Close to work and to the beach, of course.

As the Universe would have it, Rodrigo, Paula's boyfriend, happened to be moving too. Not to Sydney, but to a house with a few other mates. His apartment became available. I met the real estate agent and managed to sign my first ever rental agreement down under. Next step? Find someone to share the costs with me.

I posted an ad on a website. Pretty simple, right? Well, not really.

Now, let me bring some context into this. 2005 was literally the "dot com" boom. Our social network was Orkut (I can't imagine how many "testimonials" remained unpublished until the invention of "inbox" — yes, we liked privacy). For real-time conversations, MSN. E-mails? Hotmail, Yahoo and the locals (call me vintage, but I still have my Hotmail account to this day).

Facebook was still unknown in Brazil and Whatsapp was just an embryo in the brain of a digital genius. Just like Instagram, Twitter, Pinterest and so many other ideas that rode the wave along with "Mr. Google", who made things searchable at the start of the Digital Era around 1998.

We were thirsty for communication. Instant, immediate, urgent. There was no internet on cell phones and the cost of international calls was through the roof. Believe it or not, we used street pay phones with international cards. Maroon 5 made a song about it. Skype? Still a baby, taking its initial baby steps.

I know it seems like we're talking about ancient history here, but it's only 20 years ago. That's the speed of the world today. Decades are equivalent to eras. And I must confess: a lot of things still seem as new as our digital consciousness (but that's another topic).

Returning to my little ad, it was pretty basic. The website was literally an online community board. There, people who lived in Australia could exchange information and help each other. An incredible concept really.

My post read: "BRAZILIAN IN PERTH". Surprisingly, I got an overload of contacts. I suspected that, for a long time, I may have been the only one who had Perth in their title. That site was mainly used by Brazilians who lived in Sydney, Melbourne, Brisbane and the Gold Coast. So, whoever searched for the West, found me.

That's how I met Carlos. A newly arrived Brazilian, who also chose a homestay to spend his first few weeks. And, just like me, he was ready to move.

We agreed on the cost and I offered to pick him up in person. At that point, I had already managed to buy a car: a White Ford Laser, 1989. Automatic. A real luxury.

Carlos was *"mineiro"* and I instantly loved his positive energy. We connected right away.

With his gear in the trunk (yes, two suitcases, like everyone else) we headed to our new home. On the way, he told me about this great Aussie friend he met in Brazil. A "gringo" who spent six months there. No need to say I was curious to meet him.

In the first week, he came in. Jeff was so much fun. I loved hearing him speak Portuguese with an Australian accent. Always made me think of how foreigners felt about our accent too. Very cute.

We grew closer with time and became great friends. We talked about virtually everything. Including our romantic frustrations. This seemed to ease our pain and spike some good laughs.

He loved joining us at the Brazilian nights. His *"o ariá raio obá obá obá"* singing was priceless!

Jeff only had one little problem: drinking. Not that I didn't have it, but his influence reinforced my negative patterns and that was dangerous.

I was trying to lead an "adult life", juggling between classes and work. I'd go to the agency by day, and to the restaurant by night. My routine was pretty busy, but I still found time for a little party. Sleep? Just enough. This habit used to give me headaches.

I wanted everything at the same time, but it was impossible. With the increased frequency of Jeff's visits, I was no longer able to keep up with their pace.

Almost every night I'd come home to these beautiful castles of beer cans in the middle of our living room. It was funny, but they triggered me.

I had to respect their choice, but it was affecting my life. That was also my home. It was supposed to be my resting place. And it didn't feel like that. At all.

My body went into exhaustion. Even my mood changed. I totally lost my balance. I felt the weight of the world on my shoulders again. It was horrible. I was stressed.

I also missed having girlfriends. I needed comfort and lightness. The high doses of testosterone in the house didn't provide that. It was actually weighing me down.

I missed Paula. And how light it was to share life with her. I missed her help in setting healthy limits for my life. I was going in the opposite direction.

That's when Maria turned up. She was in a moment of transition and "coincidentally" needed a place to live.

There's a saying when we live abroad: there's always room for another one. That's how the two of us shared a double bed for a few months, in a two-bedroom apartment. Me, her and Carlos. Plus, we all saved a few dollars, which always worked well for me.

Of course, sharing a house with three is different, but we found a good balance.

Even with the basic issues, which were absolutely normal, our apartment felt like a good party. I won't deny: all of us still had way too much to drink. But I started to recognize my own limits. I was no longer the last one standing. I knew when it was time for me to leave.

I also kept integrating my multiple personalities. I made peace with all the different Carols that inhabited me. Not to mention, I was learning how to let things go.

I felt like the Universe seemed to really conspire in my favor. Even giving me a break from Jeff. He went on vacation for about ten days.

At that time, I went to a Brazilian night and guess who was there? Yep, Daniel. The original one.

He approached me and said he was very proud of what I had achieved. My work was getting around through word of mouth. He heard I was helping Brazilians to get jobs, courses and essentially better lives. He also asked me about the tree planting experience and acknowledged that it was a massive undertaking for a girl like me.

I looked at him and, for the first time, I saw our encounter for what it really was: a bridge to get me to Australia. And I thanked myself for having the courage to cross it.

We hugged for a little while and I felt comfort. I didn't need him to be anything else. My heart was finally at peace.

But, on the other hand, I started missing someone else: Jeff.

It was a real longing. I thought it was normal since we were good friends and used to spend a lot of time together. I saw him almost every day. It was strange not having him around for that long. I couldn't make up what those feelings truly were, but I decided not to overthink it. A massive challenge for an overthinker like me.

It was Friday night and we (Carlos, Maria and I) went out with some Aussie friends. To my surprise, Jeff showed up just after midnight. I couldn't hide how I felt in his presence. I was higher than ever. There was a spark between us. I felt a very strong pull towards him, but I kept my cool.

He went straight to the bar and ordered a shot. Then he came to hug me. A long warm hug that made me think he had missed me too. We danced a lot and we could have kept going, but Aussie clubs rarely go past 3am. This was no exception.

I was stretching all of my limits that night and I knew why.

Side note: I had to open the restaurant at 5:30am. I know it sounds crazy, but it was the only way to get free nights to have fun. I took the weekend breakfast shifts.

And there was a trick to it. I was allowed to go out, but not to drink. Without a hangover, I could go straight to work and sleep afterwards, still highly functional and with a clear mind. So, I often swapped my hours. Youth is such a blessing if you know how to use it! I also became the beloved designated driver. I loved that role.

I couldn't miss the "after party" though. We all got to a friend's house and they kept going. I was sober, but a little tired. I decided to take a nap and set my alarm for 4:45am.

I woke up to this incredible scene. A bunch of my friends scattered throughout every room, surrounded by empty bottles and cans. Oh, and a classic drunken snores' symphony. I felt very grateful for saving myself that night.

I quickly looked for my bag and headed for the door. On my way out, I glanced at the couch and noticed Jeff was there. He was sitting up straight, like a meerkat, eyes wide open, appearing a lot more sober than usual.

"Cazinha, I need to talk to you," he said.

"Not now, Jeff. I'm already late. You can come to our house later, after I finish work," I replied, saying goodbye and giving him a hug.

And as we hugged, he kissed me. A lip kiss. It left me speechless. And I really had to leave. So, I left.

What was that? Jeff must have had too much to drink!

My thoughts ran wild as I got in the car. But I had no time to entertain them.

I went home, had a shower, put on my uniform and arrived at the restaurant at 5.29am. Phew! A new day was about to start.

My routine was to serve coffee, natural juices and delicious dishes. For eight hours straight. Enough to make me not think about that kiss at all.

Healthy and full of energy, our regular morning customers were living proof that getting older could be wonderful. They were early birds who knew how to make the most of the first hours of the day, enjoying the good things in life, like a sunrise and a swim in the cold ocean. All followed by a hot coffee and a nice warm meal.

Their calm presence gave me this feeling that they had somehow aligned themselves with life's natural rhythm. That day, in particular, I realized that if I wanted to live as long as them, I would also have to learn how to slow down. I acknowledged, there and then, that growing old in Australia seemed to be a great privilege.

After 8am, there was a change in pace. Aussies love their "brekkies". And I love their verbal minimalism. If you can say less, do it.

Breakfast is kind of a ritual. And it can also be a real rush. Everyone tends to go out at the same time and there's just not enough tables and chairs for such demand.

So, for the next few hours, I worked non-stop. There was a certain humility in serving others that I loved. Hospitality made it all very clear. It was crazy busy and very fulfilling.

I looked at the clock. 11am. Time to clean everything up and get ready for lunch.

My shifts were from 5.30am to 2pm. I always had a half hour break at 11.30am. Wait staff were also allowed to eat.

To me, one of the best advantages of being a waitress was the staff discount. As an international student, on a tight budget, having access to amazing restaurant food was a real luxury.

I ordered my favorite dish at the time: Porcinni Mushrooms. Sautéed mushrooms, served on crispy toast with butter. A rich combination that perfectly melted in my mouth. Food heaven!

I sat outside to enjoy my brekkie. As I looked at the OBH (the pub, remember?), I thought I was hallucinating. Jeff was there having a beer, just before noon. Classic. He saw me and waved, smiling. I instantly remembered what happened earlier and totally panicked. *This can't be happening!* — I thought to myself while thinking what to do next.

If there's one area of my life that I'm focused on, it's work. I simply don't like distractions. And this was a massive distraction for me.

So, as soon as I finished my meal, I went up to Juan and asked him a favor to be moved to the balcony from 12 to 2pm. With the ocean view, and open air, I could keep a wider perspective, without overthinking what was happening with Jeff. It worked.

At 2pm sharp, I finished my shift. I went to the locker room, changed my clothes and said goodbye to everyone. I headed towards the car park and, as soon as I walked past the pub, I felt this presence next to me. It was Jeff. He came out of nowhere and started to walk by my side.

"How was work?" he asked.

"Great," I replied, curious to know where this conversation was going.

"I still need to talk to you. Can we do it now?"

"I'm actually just rushing to get home. It's Dani's birthday. You know my friend from school? We're having a party at our place from 4pm. I need to get ready and organize everything. Come and help. We can talk there."

"Sure."

Jeff was one of my best friends. He never missed a party at our house and he knew me well enough to know that any mission given was mission accomplished. That party was my priority. Even if he tried, he wouldn't distract me.

We got home and I went straight to the shower. I loved working at the restaurant, but I hated becoming a total mess by the end of every shift.

I'm a Venus woman. Looks and smells are important to me. Beauty is my thing. I can't help it. Plus, with everything that was happening in the background, I obviously wanted to feel beautiful and confident for the upcoming awkward conversation with Jeff. I had feelings stirring inside of me like a tornado.

After the shower, I took my time until I looked at myself in the mirror and thought: "*I'm ready.*"

Jeff was already on his second beer. I opened myself one and sat next to him on the couch, speaking as we always did: "What did you want to talk about anyway?"

He took a deep breath and began telling me briefly about the fishing trip he had taken with his dad. In fact, it was something he had in common with my dad. Both loved fishing and fisherman stories.

"*Saudade.* I missed you so much, Cazinha." He loved to mix our languages. And I loved that about him. He also liked to use the diminutive, as we Brazilians do, to show special affection.

I thought it was just me, but apparently those ten days we spent apart made our feelings for each other quite evident.

"Me too, Jeff. '*Saudade*' is a beautiful word, isn't it? Why can't it be translatable? 'I miss you' just isn't the same."

"No, it's not. And I'm not done yet. Being away from you made me realize how much I like you. Not just as a friend."

A brief silence. I could not believe what I was hearing. Ironically, I had felt exactly the same way. I just would never have the courage to let him know. I caught my breath and asked:

"What do you mean, Jeff?"

"Do you wanna be my girlfriend?"

And right there he simply popped THAT question. We both knew the answer.

"Yes" is not always a word. It can be a long, passionate, soothing embrace. And a big French kiss.

At that moment, I understood that love can arrive quietly, shapeshifting its way into our hearts. And if we're not paying attention, or have the courage to let it be known, it can end up going to waste.

As I learned from Morcheeba: *"Fear can stop you loving. Love can stop your fear."*

Jeff knew my triggers better than most people. He knew exactly what I was looking for: safety. With him, I felt safe. First of all, Jeff was my friend. A friend usually defends us, especially from the harm caused by our lovers.

He knew my heart was broken. He understood what was good for me. And also, what was bad. And I trusted he would make wise use of his knowledge.

I was finally in a healthy relationship.

Since I was so far removed, I started writing e-mails to break the news to my family and friends. I imagined that each of those electronic reports was an important piece of historical evidence of my existence on the other side of the globe.

I wrote them with the truth and depth of Hemingway's letters, as if my words could also travel through centuries.

Maybe I gave myself too much importance, but that's what we tend to do when we're young. At 23, I truly felt like Carrie Bradshaw in Sex and the City, sharing the joy and pain of my wonderfully crazy Aussie life. For a hand-picked audience.

I was convinced that I would never make a living from a literary career. Still, I loved to play that part, and I was in the perfect setting to do it: a distant country with a fascinating mix of friends, lovers and odd jobs. It was a risk-free way to practice my passion.

I suspect that some things only come to us in writing. Maybe that's why I had so much fun putting my stories on paper (well, computer). I forgot to mention that by then I had managed to buy my own PC (one of those full vintage, beige desktop units).

I'm not even sure if I wrote those stories or if they were written through me. They seemed to have a life of their own. For starters, they hardly followed a classic structure for a successful narrative. At some point, I disappointed my readers. Still, I had a lot of fun living them. And I never gave up on love (even if the world was trying really hard to make me do it).

So, I wondered what was behind those beautiful stories I liked to read, and I decided to dig deeper into the lives of writers I admired. To my surprise, I discovered that many of them were able to write for decades without ever publishing a word. Did you know that?

Apparently, like any craft, writing also requires deliberate practice. Many great storytellers take years to finish their first book. And from there, their careers take off.

You're not born a writer. You become one. By writing. So, *"keep going"* could also apply.

Somehow, it comforted me to know that I wasn't alone in the writing incubation mode. Maybe I would still have a chance in the future. If only I could persist and dedicate time to my craft. Or even if I just had enough courage to withstand all the cruel criticism that would follow if I ever decided to put my work in the world.

Despite being young, I had already learned something important:

> *"We must learn to improve our thinking and not let anyone discourage us from persisting towards the incredible futures that we are all capable of creating. Not even ourselves."*

Deep down, I was aware that, most times, I was my own worst enemy.

Still, I believed in myself. I just needed to live a little longer to find out who I could be.

35. YOU GOT ME IN LOVE AGAIN.

If I could have designed the perfect boyfriend for me at that time, he would have all the characteristics Jeff had. We were surprisingly compatible and that kind of connection didn't happen every day.

I was in the right place, at the right time. And now I had the right person by my side.

Dating Jeff expanded my Australian experience in a very significant way. As his girlfriend, I gained a new identity. I was no longer a foreigner without roots. He helped me to create bonds and restore my sense of familiarity with very simple things: family, his childhood friends and little rituals.

Jeff inserted me into a new world that was very reminiscent of mine. He provided me with unique moments, showing me local traditions and introducing me to new places. He had everything I was looking for: safety, truth and fun.

Our intensity wasn't for everyone, but it was perfect for me. We rarely had any fights, but when we did, it felt like the end of the world. At least for me.

I remember, as if it were today, one particular situation that drove me crazy.

I don't even remember what the trigger was. The memory I have is of performing an unprecedented s#!tshow in front of all our friends. Neither him nor I knew the Carol we saw on our first trip to Rottnest Island.

I suspect it had to do with too much drinking, but all I remember is this: I was in the ferry, just with the clothes I had on, in tears. I literally left everything behind and went home. Alone.

I sobbed like a baby yearning for my mother's lap. I kept looking at the infinite ocean that connected Rottnest and Perth, trying hard not to drown in the waters that flooded my eyes. I was a mess.

Suddenly, someone sat next to me and I felt the warmth and comfort of a hug I knew very well. It was Jeff. Without any words, he managed to calm me down. Just with his presence and the heat of his body. And when the despair ceased, with a soft voice, he gave me reasons to stay.

I will never forget that trip back and forth on the ferry. Another movie-like scene. I'm not sure I would have done the same thing for him, but that was our difference: Jeff was safe in himself. I wasn't.

My emotional challenges were evident and he didn't shy away from them. Quite the opposite. Jeff's attitude in that situation showed me that I could trust my partner to deal with my dramas. Of course, he loved my best. But, right then, I needed someone who could also handle my worst.

After that little episode, we had a wonderful weekend. In fact, Rottnest is one of the most beautiful islands in Australia.

Picture this: sixty-three stunning beaches, bathed by crystal clear turquoise waters, ranging from small bays to great surf waves. There are also some of the best diving spots in the country.

It was so inspirational and amazing, but sport wasn't our thing. Jeff and I liked to party. And Rottnest main pub was our favorite destination.

Still, part of me wanted to feel the other side of that paradise. With the ban on cars, the only means of transport were bicycles or shuttle buses. I had to rent a bike to fully explore the "quokkas" land.

For those who don't know, quokka is a mini-Australian marsupial found only in Western Australia. They are the cutest thing ever. Even the Huffington Post voted them as the happiest animals in the world. I suspect their happiness is directly related to where they chose to live. Rottnest is a paradise. It's hard not to be happy there.

After we returned to Perth, I remained fully immersed in my new routine. School, work, beach, party. And Jeff, of course. There were so many things at once that I barely felt time passing.

It was already September and an opportunity came up for me to make some extra cash at the Perth Royal Show, which is an annual agricultural fair meets carnival festival.

Since I worked at the agency that arranged those jobs, I became the queen of odd jobs. For me, nothing was below my abilities. I had already planted trees, remember? Anything after that was a piece of cake.

So, whenever possible, I increased my income to feel more stable and secure. I like an abundant bank account. Emergency savings are nice to have, even when you're young.

My new odd job was to mind a game stall. It was called "Pluck the Duck". The goal was to catch little ducks that were floating around in an artificial moving lagoon.

I don't even know how many times I repeated the catch phrase *"everyone's a winner"*. Because, in that game, everyone won.

Literally. And somehow, this phrase got stuck in my subconscious: *I am a winner.* That's how I felt.

At that time, I had a revealing insight: I was lucky in all areas of my life. Even in love, which was a rare thing. And Jeff insisted on going there to see me yell at the ducks. He thought it was cute — and funny, of course.

There was a day when I managed to escape for a few hours and we had the best time together. We went on the rides, played at some stalls and laughed. A lot. I loved our unbearably cliché romantic comedy relationship. It was so cheesy!

Then, in November, he took me to the Melbourne Cup (in the Perth Racecourse). It was the first time in my life that I had sparkling wine before lunch. I felt so grown up. Not to mention, I got to dress up.

I had this little pink ruffle dress that I bought because I thought it was so beautiful (and cheap) but I never had an occasion to wear it. Until then. I even put a pink flower on it. I felt amazing.

"You look stunning, Cazinha." Jeff always made sure I knew what he was thinking.

"Thank you, Jeff. You have no idea how happy I am to be wearing this dress."

Jeff and I were a beautiful duo. There was something very special about us. It was so easy to be with him. He made me feel seen, heard, understood, loved. And, even without wanting to create future expectations, I could see us together for the rest of time.

In the second half of 2005, I started to feel almost like an Aussie myself. Truly. I fell absolutely in love with my new country, but I couldn't hide my mixed feelings.

My dream was to live overseas for a year. It never crossed my mind that I'd fall in love with my chosen country (and one of its men) in the process. Let alone wanting to do what I thought to be impossible: stay there for good.

I felt a strong belonging in Australia with a painful longing for Brazil. I was caught in the middle, and my original plan caught up with me. My time was up. It was time to go back to Brazil.

Right there, I fully understood why other people overstayed. One year in Australia was not enough. And I felt in my heart I could live there a lot longer. I just didn't know how.

You know how people say luck is when opportunity meets preparation? I guess they are right.

I was doing well at GSH. I was the right person, in the right job. So a "strike of luck" came out from my efforts. Hanicka offered me this incredible opportunity I could have never anticipated.

"Carolina, do you want to stay here for another year?" she asked.

"I'd love that. I just don't know how."

"Well, we can help you. There's an Internship Visa that allows you to work full-time, without having to go to school. We can apply for that. We'll pay minimum wage, but you can still do some casual hours if you need extra cash."

"Really? That sounds like every international student's dream. What do I need to do?"

"Just say yes and provide all relevant documentation. We'll handle the application for you. But you have to wait for approval overseas."

"That's perfect. I'm going to Brazil anyway. I'll stay there until it's all done."

"Perfect. So, is that a yes?"

"Absolutely. How did I get so lucky?"

"You worked hard for it."

I didn't even need to think twice. All I wanted was another year in Australia.

Hanicka made that very easy for me. Her team was going to take care of my application while I was enjoying my well-deserved holidays in my beautiful country.

I organized all the documents on the list and got ready to take off.

Jeff and I had this beautiful breakfast by the river before he drove me to the airport.

We were both excited about the year ahead. We made a lot of plans.

Life never felt so good. I was in love. And I felt love all around me.

36. A LITTLE CRACK IN TIME.

February 2006. Navegantes Airport, Santa Catarina, Brazil.

It was the first time I felt like I was going back in time. I left Australia on February 11th at 2pm. To my surprise, I arrived in Brazil on February 11th at 3pm.

I never imagined I could live the same day twice. Especially having two completely different stories. But I did. And that was one of the discoveries of living on the other side of the world. Time zones.

So, there I was: in the middle of goodbye and hello. All in a single day.

My mum and two of my best friends, Juliete and Adriana, were waiting for me at the airport. It was an endless symphony of 'saudade', 'saudade', 'saudade' that filled my heart with so much love.

A year is a long time to not see the people we care about.

I was clearly not the same. Even physically.

"You look different," Juliete said straight away.

"I know, I put on weight. It was a crazy year," I said, acknowledging the extra 10kg I was carrying on my body.

Adriana couldn't help herself either. Especially when she saw the length of my hair.

"When was the last time you had a haircut, Carolina Luiza?"

I know they sound mean, but trust me, they meant good.

Over the last few months of my first year in Australia, I was having trouble recognizing myself too. While I was happy in my relationship, my lifestyle became very unhealthy. Too much drinking, smoking and junk food. I wasn't looking after myself at all. I actually let myself go.

That reality check was very important to me. I felt their love.

"You're right. I know I don't look great, but I actually feel happy."

"You can be both happy and beautiful, my friend. That's who you are."

We laughed together. They were right.

I quickly reflected on the whole physical transformation. I could blame anything. My work, the new culture, new food, new habits, new relationships. But I knew they were only excuses. The responsibility for my body was mine.

I just forgot to prioritize myself. And that really triggered me.

I care about the way I look. It's part of my identity. I don't do it for others. I do it for myself. And I seemed to have lost that for a while.

I hugged my mother. She was just watching the conversation. They all helped me with my luggage, not knowing that the heaviest weight I carried was a whole year of emotional baggage.

It's very hard to open up to someone who has never had the same experience as you. I realized that I probably would never be able to explain to anyone what that year in Australia really meant to me. And that's okay. Some things can only be understood through living, and perhaps told in writing.

It was the first time I felt like a stranger in my own home.

For an entire year, I juggled multiple jobs and relationships. I hardly stopped. I was travelling on a highway at a million miles an hour, not only trying to survive, but also getting a head start in life. I went too far the other way.

It was time to turn my survival mode off. At least for a few weeks.

My goal was to relax and let go of control. Not an easy task for someone like me.

I had no idea how long it would take for my visa to go through. All I knew was that I could only buy my ticket after everything was approved.

I had to make peace with uncertainty. And embrace that time as an opportunity to care for myself.

Again, I was in the right place, at the right time.

Between family gatherings and catch ups with friends, I found time and space to focus on a healthier lifestyle. I decided to eat well, exercise and also get all the beauty treatments that Brazil is famous for. I also decided not to drink for a while. It didn't take long until I saw my transformation. I felt a lot better — and lighter.

I still enjoyed going out. As you know now, our little town was a hotspot for e-music. The party scene I described to Paul was on and had such a dynamic growth that even I couldn't believe it.

That year I watched some of the best DJ's of those times play live.

Fatboy Slim was the first. He played at one of the major clubs, Ibiza. I was lucky enough to be lining up, when a gringo was trying to communicate with the bouncers to get in. They didn't speak English. An old friend, who was one of the organizers, saw me and asked: *"Weren't you somewhere that speaks English? Can you help us here?"*

Of course I could. The guy showed me a printed email (I know, those were the times) Norman Cook wrote himself. He was a personal friend to the very headliner. I translated and they let him in. He quickly said: *"She's coming with me"*. Well, there I was. Skipping the line and watching Fatboy Slim backstage with my new friend.

I had to praise myself for that. Having a second language could work wonders even in my home country. And there he was playing me a little reminder: *"We've come a long, long way together, through the hard times and the good"*.

But that was just the beginning. Deep Dish and Sasha took the stage at Warung in the following days. All I remember is that I kept dancing.

It was an endless summer, and I was still "living the dream".

But my heart was far, far away.

I couldn't stop thinking about Jeff. I missed us. We talked on the phone sometimes, and it only made things worse. The longing, now in the opposite direction, was catching up with me.

I had too many uncertainties at the same time. And I was still very insecure. To make things worse, Jeff had his own trauma: his Brazilian ex-girlfriend went on vacation to Brazil and never went back to Australia. It left him heartbroken for years. He couldn't help but think I would do the same. I couldn't blame him.

The stories we unconsciously replay in our minds end up

changing our realities. Not always for the best. It was tough on both of us.

Internal conflicts were stealing my energy and I was back to my old self: the poor me.

I instantly remembered the Prophecy and acknowledged my control drama. I needed to find a way to turn things around, but there was one thing that made this very difficult for me: *my somewhat platonic relationship with my own father.*

In almost two months, we saw each other three times. It didn't matter if I was in Brazil or in Australia, we had a long-distance relationship. And a superficial one too. We shared very few topics of interest and it was very hard to find common ground between us.

I told my father about Jeff and he didn't seem too excited by my description of him. He thought I could "do better". That triggered me and made me question my relationship. In fact, it made me question my choices altogether.

My father wasn't present, but I lived for his approval. I know, silly. But it was hard to fight the program running through my mind ever since I was a six-year old child who didn't feel loved by the man who brought me into this world.

His words were always louder than his actions. And I failed to take notice of that.

Completely dominated by self-sabotage, I questioned whether that visa would actually be approved. I caught myself wondering *"What if this doesn't work out?"* and the tension only increased as the visa process took longer than expected.

I needed a silver lining in case everything went in the wrong direction. That's when my Plan B came to life. I started to prepare myself to stay in Brazil. For good.

I felt hopeless. I knew there and then only divine intervention could solve my case. I kneeled on my bedroom floor and surrendered. In my direct dialogue with God, I asked him for an answer. To be honest, I asked him for a miracle.

It was almost Easter. It felt like divine timing.

On Thursday afternoon, just before Good Friday, I opened my email and there it was: my visa was granted.

How could I not believe in miracles?

I felt truly grateful and ready to pack up and go.

I wanted to call Jeff straight away, but the time zone was cruel. I had to wait until the next day.

I called my travel agent and booked my ticket for the following week.

That night, Jeff made his way into my dreams. He was with another woman. I could almost see her face. Something felt off. I wanted to be wrong, but I was already learning about my intuition.

The next morning, I called him. His mother answered and said he went away with friends for the Easter break. She asked me to call him on the mobile. I hesitated, but called anyway. He answered. A slightly distant tone. I knew what I was in for. To save time and money, I cut to the chase:

"Hey babe, how are you? I called you at home and your mum said you went away."

"Yes, we came to Margs for the long weekend. It was a last-minute thing. That's why I didn't tell you."

"Sure, can I ask you something?"

"Of course."

"Is there anyone there with you? A woman?"

Silence was his initial answer. After the uncomfortable pause, he continued:

"I'm sorry, it's been hard. My mind keeps telling me you're not coming back."

"I knew it. I had a very vivid dream last night. It's okay, I just wanted you to be honest with me. And you were. Thank you."

"I know, sorry, I'm just confused."

"I understand, I'm confused too. I just called to say that my visa was granted."

"Really? Congratulations, Cazinha! I feel like a fool now."

"Don't. We knew there was a risk."

"So, are you coming back anyway? Can we talk about it?"

I couldn't believe his question. *"Anyway"*? What did he mean by that?

For a second, I questioned myself: *was Jeff the only reason for me to return to Australia?* Maybe he thought that. And that really got to me.

I reflected on the entire year I spent there and everything I had accomplished. On my own. By my very own merits. I had to truly believe in myself and be very clear about my decision. And also, about my answer.

I took a very deep breath and replied:

"Sorry, I didn't understand your question. You mean, if we break up?"

"Yeah, we didn't even talk about it properly. I'm still processing."

"Look, Jeff, I'm going to be very honest with you: I have an Internship Visa. I made a commitment with Hanicka to work for GSH for another year. They are waiting for me. I already bought my ticket yesterday. I'll be there next week with or without you. And just so we're clear: I love being with you, but you're not the only reason I'm going back to Australia. You're a huge bonus."

"Let's talk about this in person. I'll pick you up from the airport. When are you arriving?"

"Don't worry, I'll catch a cab."

"No way. I know you're mad at me, but we need to talk."

"I'm not mad, Jeff. I'm disappointed. It's different. It's probably better if we don't see each other. This isn't the first time this has happened to me. Let me manage this, like I always do."

"I'll ask my mum to pick you up then."

"I appreciate your offer but I prefer not to."

I hung up the phone and I broke down. I couldn't believe I was going through all this again. I felt almost as if my father had cursed my relationship. I should have kept quiet.

I also resented my ability to see into the future. I wondered when I would learn to create better outcomes for myself rather than reliving the same old family stories that haunted me. My life was becoming so predictable that it scared me. But I wasn't ready to give up.

I knew the pain was inevitable, but suffering was optional. It was a hard pill to swallow.

Rejection and betrayal were familiar, but not fatal. I'd been there before. All the women in my family had been there too. It was nothing new.

I had more reasons to celebrate than to commiserate. I decided to focus on the good.

I knew, in my heart, everything was going to be okay. I remembered what happened a year earlier with Daniel. That experience changed me. I was able to deal with frustration and come out the other side.

I looked up and spoke to God, again:

> "*What do I still need to learn here? Please help me. I can't do this alone.*"

I took a deep breath and let it all out. A storm took over my eyes. It felt like I was drowning.

After a while, I came back to my senses. I acknowledged that I had no control over anyone's actions, but mine.

While I was trying to write another great love story, I realised that my Australian adventure was all about one single character: *myself*.

I heard this soft but reassuring voice *"every little thing is gonna be alright"*.

And, surprisingly, that was enough.

37. EVERY END IS A NEW BEGINNING.

Internship. A word with multiple meanings. At least in Portuguese. Language is a fascinating thing, don't you think? It can change as it travels.

The first meaning is *"...probationary period, during which a person carries out a temporary activity in a company"*.

It can also be *"phase, each of the stages of a process towards the accomplishment of something"*.

Or even *"the situation between one thing and another, a preparatory moment that precedes something"*

Interestingly, I was experiencing all these meanings at the same time.

That internship was a gift. And some opportunities are too good to pass. Sometimes we need to abandon the path we planned for ourselves and risk taking a new one. Some people will not follow us — and that's okay. We keep walking anyway.

The truth is: everything is always changing. Raul Seixas, a Brazilian singer/songwriter was fully aware of this reality. He wrote *"Metamorfose Ambulante"* (Evermoving Metamorphosis) and no wonder I chose that song to take me to the stage on my graduation day.

I always prefer not to have a fully formed opinion about everything. I'd rather stay open to different points of view and evaluate all possible scenarios as life unfolds. It's what we call critical thinking. Don't believe the hype, you know? Things are not always what they seem. The next big thing can be the next dead thing.

Still, to navigate life we must take our own stands. We can't let indecision take away our power and prevent us from taking action. Unfortunately, we will never have all the information we need to make perfect decisions. We can consider pros and cons (there will always be both in anything) and we must hold space for mistakes and growth.

A little piece of wisdom here: mistakes and growth are surprisingly correlated.

I'll reinforce this: I'm not a *"what if...?"* kind of person. I run towards the fire. One of the most inspirational slogans I've ever seen comes from Nike (the brand named after the Goddess of Victory): *"just do it"*.

Life will never give us absolute certainty. We'd be "waiting in vain", as Bob Marley sang.

I also learned that there is no absolute truth. Everyone has their own. And it's important that we learn to question the truths of the world, because these truths are not always ours.

There are no ready-made formulas for being happy. In fact, some tested formulas can go very wrong and frustrate people. I'm in favor of everyone testing their own formula and dealing with the consequences, especially in adult life. It seems obvious, but we can't act as children once we get here.

So, as Paulo Coelho said, *"once the choice is made, you need to move forward and trust your own heart"*.

And there I was, reading *"The Alchemist"* and starting to open up to mysticism. *Who would have thought?*

My choice was made. I took off to Australia. Alone. Again. At my own risk.

Still on the plane, I met a Brazilian guy. A surfer. Australia seemed like a magnet for those who loved to ride big waves. He was younger than me and couldn't hide his anxiety. I knew that feeling, too well. We had an interesting chat during our endless trip.

It was his first time in Australia and he spoke almost no English. That always worried me, but it was the most common thing ever. We all start as beginners, right?

Since it wasn't my first time, I decided to help him. That was part of my job at GSH. What better opportunity for practice than real life? I did the least that any human being could do: I offered him a ride and a place to shower in Perth. He was heading to Margaret River. No wonder.

After battling my ego, I agreed to have Jeff's mother picking me up at the airport. She called me and I couldn't say no. We were very close and she treated me like a daughter. She was an amazing woman, very kind, and I knew she wouldn't mind helping my new friend.

After almost 30 hours, we landed in Perth and went straight to the baggage claim. Guess who was the first person I saw at Arrivals. Yes, him.

My heart skipped a beat. I was not prepared to see Jeff. But I knew he was there for me. So, I took a deep breath and walked towards him. Slightly embarrassed, I introduced my new friend and felt a huge white elephant standing between us. It was actually really funny.

We all got in the car. An awkward silence mixed with some random conversations. My new friend was a great distraction. We got home, he had a shower and off he went to catch a bus to his final destination.

After he left, I had a shower too. And there was no escape. It was just the two of us. Jeff and I.

He started.

"What happened?"

"Distance? Fear?"

"It wasn't supposed to be like this. I still care for you, but..."

"We are no longer the same people who made those plans."

He looked at me with those bright blue eyes. I was uncomfortably silent.

An entire movie went through my mind. All those times when we were very, very, very happy together. Everything else faded.

Our bodies were pulled into one. A desperate attempt to make up for what we lost. It was good, but it didn't feel the same. Trust had been broken. Our souls had disconnected.

I wanted him so bad, but I simply did not have the emotional capacity to withstand betrayal. I felt like my mother. Stuck in a moment where I no longer felt safe.

Could we ever just go back to being friends? I knew I couldn't. I loved him too much.

"What's left of us?" he asked.

"Memories of a good time."

"Sorry, Cazinha. I wish I had been better."

"I know. Me too."

"Just don't forget all the things we did together."

"There are things we can't forget, Jeff. Even if we try."

"I'll miss you."

"I'll miss you too."

I took Jeff to the door. He knew me like very few people did. He had an innate ability to read my deepest thoughts and knew how much I was suffering from the breakup.

You can't kill love. You have to find a way to reposition it in your heart.

As he headed to the lift, Ben Harper's song started playing in my mind:

"And it's so hard to do

And so easy to say

But sometimes

Sometimes

You just have to walk away

Walk away

And head for the door"

That day, Jeff left my house. And my life. For good.

In the void he left, I found myself in an infinite ocean of unprocessed emotions that were lingering in my soul for far too many years. The betrayal wasn't just his fault, it was the trauma of my life. It wasn't him I needed to forgive; it was myself.

The lesson I was yet to learn was to never let someone take all of my heart ever again.

Digging a little deeper, I also acknowledged something very important: *I needed to forgive my father for betraying my mother (and our family) while also forgiving her, for not having the emotional capacity to overcome what happened.*

Endless layers of forgiveness. And let's just say: *forgiving isn't my strongest suit.*

But, if I had learned anything from the Prophecy, it was this: it is necessary to *"clear the past"* for a new life to unfold. So, from the depths of my heart, I decided to evoke the power of forgiveness. For my own sake.

I let my tears wash over my soul for hours and hours. As delusional as this may sound, I continued to believe in one thing: *true love would eventually find me in the end.*

I knew, in my heart, that there was someone out there who would never betray me, not even in his thoughts. I kept the image of this man in my mind's eye. A man who was willing to love a woman like me until the end of time.

It was probably too early for my happy ending anyway.

After that full round was done, I saw the beginning of a new act. A revolutionary act of liberation from an illusion that anything could have been different. It simply couldn't.

As difficult as that moment was, I had a professional commitment to the people who believed in me. From then on, my priority was to grow and develop myself. I had plenty of room to do just that.

As I slowly processed my disappointment, I also began to learn about something else: *time.*

The teachings of the Prophecy still intrigued me. In Redfield's view, chronological time is not the most important thing, only eternal time is real. According to him, eternal time is always present here and now, everywhere.

Even considering that fascinating concept, my life remained a tangle of past, present and future.

Based on my previous experiences, I was aware that when something didn't work out, better things were coming my way. It was time to leave the past behind and open up to the future. And there is only one place where futures manifest themselves: *in the present.*

I had a simple present mission: *learn how to love myself.*

I believed in what Redfield described as the emergence of a new global culture out of unconditional brotherhood, or simply universal love. But perhaps the idealism of the work was still hardly understood at the time.

The message of the Prophecy sounded familiar, but my little experience did not allow me to truly understand its content.

Maybe that's why we read the same books written by different authors throughout history, over and over again. It must be the way artists cross time to communicate messages essential to our development, in contemporary language.

In Redfield's case, he reminds us that, as children, we are raised in a world of discipline, of obedience, and we are dependent on others. All of this has to be overcome when we reach maturity, so that we can live, not in dependence, but with self-responsible authority. If we are not able to cross this barrier, we could face some serious challenges in adult life.

I still had a long way to go, but I knew I would be okay. I also knew that, if I kept my energy levels high, I could trust the "current" or the Universe to do the rest.

That was as spiritual as I could be at the time, and I swear it was enough.

Maybe that was my true freedom: feeling and acting on what my heart wanted, regardless of others. Living each moment without worrying about anyone else's opinions, but my own.

Somehow, I learned this from Caetano Veloso, a distinguished Brazilian songwriter and musician known for his authenticity and widely acclaimed all over the world. I was still a teenager when I read this in a teen's magazine: *"todo mundo sabe a dor e a delícia de ser o que é"* (*"everyone knows the pain and delight of being who they are"*). I wrote it down in my journal, as a mantra to repeat every day — and as a way of respecting others too.

Every person has a story. One right path does not make the other wrong. Paulo Coelho also knew this when he wrote in The Diary of a Magus:

> *"All paths are magical if they lead us to our dreams."*

My dream was to have an international career. If possible, writing. And that stage in my life was the springboard I needed to be able to achieve it later. A lot later, actually.

Challenges are fundamental for us to develop our best virtues, along with the ability to bounce back when things are not in our favor.

Every hero's journey goes through these stages. Before the reaction and the final triumph, it is necessary to face the defeat and the vulnerability of imminent failure.

I don't know if anyone escapes failure, but I created my own toolbox to deal with these situations. It contains: character, heart, willpower and the winning mentality that I shaped when working with the ducklings at Perth Royal Show.

Also, high doses of patience, resilience and compassion. For others, and for myself.

Even though I was far from becoming a heroine, these were the first chapters of my story as a writer. For a simple reason: faced with all the shame and rejection I felt during that period, my only reaction was to keep living, keep learning, keep writing and keep dreaming.

I was nowhere near the end.

38. GIRLS DON'T JUST WANNA HAVE FUN. THEY WANT (AND DESERVE) RESPECT.

For as long as I can remember, I have loved being a woman. I enjoy everything about the feminine. Dresses, flowers, dancing, long chats, all the usual plays. This doesn't mean that my world is rosy, or that I have anything against men. Quite the opposite: I tend to love men too much. And give them way too much credit.

If you've read this far, you may have noticed that my history of romantic relationships is somewhat frustrating. I take responsibility for my immaturity in the matter. The problem doesn't always lie with them.

What happens is that we, women, have been programmed to feel happy and fulfilled ONLY when we finally have a man by our side. Any interrupted relationship, regardless of the reason, becomes a clue to our inability to hold them in the long term. And, as a result, devalues us from a male point of view. We are automatically labeled as difficult, temperamental, crazy, or simply receive a permanent label that reads: *not marriage material*.

Nobody looks at our emotional history, or the poor behavior of all parties involved. They also don't suspect that we question a lot of things ourselves.

Why does shame and guilt only stay with us? Is it all our fault?

Sorry, I don't have these answers.

The only thing I know is that life goes on. Back then, believe me, without any therapy.

So, unconsciously, I learned to deal with my romantic frustrations in a very productive way: *working my way to healing*.

If there's one thing I love in life, it's feeling useful. And since I was little, I bought into the idea that "work dignifies men" — and also women, if they so desire.

Ironically, I didn't return to Australia for love. At least not for romantic love. I went back because I loved my freedom. And, in the land of opportunities, I saw a possibility for my long-awaited financial independence.

I was about to turn 24 when I learned something very profound: integrity is choosing what is right over what is easy, convenient, or quick. I was never bothered by the long way. I actually quite enjoyed it. Especially if it was seaside.

GSH made an investment in me. They had offered me an opportunity that very few Brazilians had at the time. In addition to my commitment to Hanicka, I really valued our relationship and felt it was another clue on my path.

As soon as I returned to Perth, I threw myself into work. Wholeheartedly. That year, I had one very clear goal: to honor my contract. The rest would follow.

That's when I got a divine confirmation: *trust is a superpower*. If we can only trust ourselves, we can unlock our full trust in something much bigger and way more powerful than us.

Everyone has the right to believe whatever they want, but I tend to question those who don't believe in anything. At the very least, you have to believe in yourself. I know, sometimes it's difficult, but we can't give up on trying.

I also continued reading the Prophecy. In homeopathic doses. I was still trying to understand the dynamics of control dramas. Especially my own.

Initially, I had identified myself with the poor me. But, as life progressed, I started to become "indifferent". In fact, I suspected that most women in my family did exactly the same.

I started to consider a new theory. Perhaps it's common for "intimidators" (the men in my family) to turn into simple "interrogators", while the "poor me's" (the women in my family) numb their feelings into indifference.

I wondered if that could be the root of the overused expression: *I couldn't care less.*

We usually do that after we care too much. You get the idea: we get tired, we let go.

I didn't think it was an upgrade. I also questioned the usefulness of that discovery.

So, I re-read what the priest answered when the main character asked him, *"Once we see our drama, what happens?"* — and, this time, I paid closer attention:

> *"We are truly free to become more than the unconscious act we play. As I said before, we can find a higher meaning for our lives, a spiritual reason we were born to our particular families. We can begin to get clear about who we really are."*

I remember reading that before. And I was not clear about who I was.

Not to mention that every time I faced the *"clearing the past"* chapter, I froze. I was simply not ready to do the clearing. I felt that my past was a big, cluttered, back room that needed an urgent spring-cleaning, but I wasn't up for the challenge.

All I knew was that between knowledge and practice there was a long bridge that inevitably needed to be crossed. That is if we were ever going to effectively change and become who we were meant to be. I had barely taken the first step.

With very limited knowledge about my family history, my goal was to find out where I came from. I only knew some random facts that were thrown here and there, totally out of context.

For starters, my maternal grandmother's dream was to work, but her father wouldn't allow her to do it. She was born in the 1930s. And lost her mother when she was only 15. To escape her controlling father, she got married at the age of 17. Not surprisingly, to another controlling man, my grandfather. They had three children: one boy and two girls.

One of them was my mum. She studied Economics and got a great job at a bank before she was 20. She was flying high on her way to becoming a career woman, until she fell in love. When she was 21, just about to get her Diploma, she fell pregnant. My brother was ready to come into this world. And she never completed her last semester of university. Or considered going back to her career.

Ironically, my mother's dream was to be a mother. All she ever wanted was to have a family. And that's exactly what she did for the next 10 years. That's also when I came into the world, through her.

See? Everyone has different dreams.

My paternal grandmother was another type of woman. She had multiple personalities. A hard-working woman who was capable of juggling two very different professions: cook and dressmaker. All while literally having a ball at her city's theater hall. She was a local legend, highly regarded by the high society.

Right in the theater, she met my grandfather, and just like Elton John wrote, *"married a music man"*. My grandfather was an artist. A saxophonist. But he had a fire in his belly and knew how to make money. He juggled music and business like it was an easy thing to do.

Those two were something. An explosive couple, in every way. I'm not surprised that both of them surrendered to alcoholism. He never accepted her *"genius"*, and she refused to let him control her. Not a great combo.

They had two children. Both men. One of them was my father, who came into this world with the business DNA.

With some clear background, I started putting my own puzzle together.

I shared a lot of my paternal grandmother's traits, including a strong *"genius"*. And I had an *"itch"*, this strange feeling, that I was born into my family to honor the women who paved my way. I had to *"make it"* (whatever that meant). Not just for me, but also for them.

Given the divorce history, I paid extra close attention to those patterns. And possibly gave them a new meaning. I was willing to marry, but only for love. And to a man who could not only love me, but accept me for all that I am.

In the absence of a life partner, I kept sharing homes with people who became family to me. From time to time, my "family" was renewed.

And, in 2006, I had a little all-female family. And a brand-new apartment. Still in the same building though.

Cecília was Brazilian and had that million-dollar self-esteem every woman dreams of having one day. She couldn't care less about others, but she cared a lot about us. On the other hand, Laís enjoyed the simple things in life. She embodied the *"just enjoy the ride"* philosophy in the most inspiring and natural way.

We instantly connected. The three of us made a *"home sweet home"*. A special little welcoming haven. Open, warm and fun. Our home was full of life.

It was around that time that I took notice of something I felt from an early age, but could never name it. It's something that happens when two or more women decide to truly come together to help each other: *sisterhood*.

Sisterhood is a phenomenon that should be included in the list of the greatest universal forces. Nothing and no one can beat women who deliberately choose to be there for each other. It's a simple fact of life. We're just wired to protect the things we love. And when we love our friends, nobody is allowed to mess up with them.

I feel fortunate to be deeply connected to a number of incredible women who have walked by my side throughout this rollercoaster ride that is my life. My real friends sit at my heart's altar where I often go just to rest, recharge and count my blessings.

But over the years, I've also cultivated what I call "transitional sisters". Those random groups that welcome us at specific times, and are the perfect companions when seasons change.

Cecília was from the *"been in Australia for a while"* team. She knew a lot of people and was very much part of the Brazilian community. The Brazilian sisters had this amazing group called "Australian Skirt". In Portuguese, *"Saia Australiana"*. It was the first women's circle that celebrated immigration and the feminine Brazilian-ness. She invited me in.

Right away, I noticed that the members of this group were special and very different from each other. Each one was beautiful in their own way, with their unique personal power. It was a mix of married and single women, a little older than me. They all worked and enjoyed a healthy level of independence while also having a lot of love in their lives.

In that group, there was no competition. It wasn't about belonging either. It was a reciprocal exchange of experiences, a safe place where everyone was willing to learn from each other. Oh, and so much wisdom.

With them, I discovered that a woman's value is not directly related to her ability to keep a man by her side. A true epiphany to the dilemma that threatened my fragile, newfound self-esteem.

They taught me that some relationships are better when they end. Period. And others are proof of everlasting love. There isn't just one single happy end that fits everyone. We should all learn that. Sooner rather than later.

I will never be able to thank them enough for what that sisterhood represented at that stage of my life. And, regardless of my lack of clarity about life and the future, I began to feel the kind of love that Redfield talked so much about in the Prophecy.

I noticed that the more I trusted people, the more they trusted me. We helped each other for no apparent reason. Just in the belief that this is what humans do. We really are all in this together. Whether we want it or not, we're all connected.

In my 2006 retrospective, I travel in little fragments of distant times. Looking at my photos (in an old hard disk), I remember the Canon Powershot 6.0 megapixels I used to carry everywhere. Nightclubs, weddings, parks, beaches. And, a lot of "home shots" (pun intended). Yes, the drinking happened there too!

I delved into the dreams and frustrations of a group of people who shared a good part of my unconventionally wild life, before digital was even a thing. I get lost in the time-space of an ultra-real era that I find hard to believe was just two decades ago.

In each "power shot", a laugh or a cry. I can't help it; nostalgia always gets the best of me. Even though my mantra is "keep going", there are times when we need to look back and remember just how far we've come.

I tend to agree with Steve Jobs when he wisely said:

> "You can't connect the dots looking forward; you can only connect them looking backwards. So you have to trust that the dots will somehow connect in your future. You have to trust in something — your gut, destiny, life, karma, whatever. This approach has never let me down, and it has made all the difference in my life."

Thank you, Steve. Wherever you are, I second that.

We can't explain the nature of this crazy ride we're all in. Life is a box full of surprises, and we must be open to receive the goods. Whatever they are, and exactly as they come.

Little by little, I learned to live one day at a time. Comfortable with my own freedom, I decided to *"enjoy the ride"* and welcome everything Perth had to offer.

And, right there, when everything was *"just fine"*, another man made his way into my life. As they often did in those times when I finally made peace with it all.

Luca, an Australian-Italian, five years younger than me, literally swept me away and changed a lot of my misconceptions about love in very subtle ways. I was impressed by his certainty and presence at such a young age. He was not only hot, he was smart, hard working and caring. Our chemistry was almost impossible to put in words. Let's just leave it there. You get it.

But, by then, I had already learned that love doesn't always last forever. It can have a beginning, middle and end. And be wonderful anyway.

Was he "the one"? Nope. But that brief romance sparked a fire within me that I almost forgot I had. It reminded me of a Rumi's saying (Rumi was a 13th century mystical poet, who no one really knew but a lot of us quote):

> *"You have to keep breaking your heart until it opens."*

Not sure if my heart understood what "open" really meant, but it had the most wonderful collection of cracks I had ever seen. And it was still beating. Hard and fast.

To me, there's no better medicine for heartbreak than music. I sync my heart to the beats. I'm a pro at dancing my sorrows away. Judge me if you like. And my Brazilian soul discovered that, even far away, she could feel "at home" anywhere.

Patife landed in Perth that year. It was magical. He had no idea how much love I had for his work that blended electronic beats with Tom Jobim's poetry in an unlikely "Tupiniquim" remix.

Our Brazilian DJ was the man of the hour in the drum'n'bass world scene. And Perth was huge on that. He won the whole crowd over by sampling *"reco-reco"* and *"agogô"*. And we were all loving *"sambassim"*, without *"pandeiro"* or tambourine.

Patife and Marky showed the world new beats that simply accelerated our hearts.

> *"It's the way that we play this sound. It's the way that we bring this sound to you."*

But not everything was about Brazil.

"If you're fond of sand dunes and salty air, quaint little villages here and there" like me, you can imagine that watching Groove Armada play in a Fremantle garden was 'another dream I didn't know I had' come true. The English know their tunes.

"Whenever I'm down, I call on you my friend."

Closing my eyes, the *"life is made of moments"* cliché became a true feeling. Even now, as I type these words.

What remains in our memories are those magical moments. Don't ever say they don't matter. They do. Wait until you get older.

Cecília and I melted in the middle of this wide ocean of people in full motion. All dancing as one. Yeah, we were Superstylin' — and fully living. Just like twenty-somethings should do.

2006 ended on a very high note. In that annual review, everything seemed possible. Even living in Australia for another year.

Inspired by the Red Bull Air Race and the many planes flying across the Swan River, I felt a new wind blowing.

"I see you baby, shakin' that ass" — and working your ass off. All at once.

Carol, Carolina, Bela: you've already learned how to walk your talk.

Hold tight, baby. We're gonna teach you how to fly.

39. THE (IM)PERMANENCE OF THINGS (AND PEOPLE).

In 2007 came my biggest surprise.

According to Hanicka, I was doing very well at work and I had all the requirements to qualify for permanent residency in Australia. With so many people aspiring for a permanent visa, I knew the opportunity was too good not to try.

Was there a risk? Of course. Rejection. But, by then, my rejection threshold was higher. Much higher. I could take another punch. And I still had my *"if you never try, you'll never know"* mentality. Here's what I said: *"Screw it, let's do it."*

So, we applied. And guess what? It all worked out.

I was officially a Permanent Resident of Australia. I didn't just have another full year ahead of me down under. I had achieved the freedom to stay there as long as I wanted.

But with freedom comes responsibility. I was also committed to working with Hanicka for at least another two years. Enough time to learn how to live with a split heart.

As I entered the third year of my Australian adventure, I started to question the exact same things I used to question everyone else before living here.

> *How do you manage to be away from your family?*
>
> *Don't you wanna go home?*
>
> *How long can you continue living like this?*

Like this could mean "one day at a time" or simply "away from home".

Yet, there I was. Living in a way I once considered "impossible". And with life coming at me at 25, the pressure was on. I had so many unanswered questions.

> *Do you want to live in Australia forever?*
>
> *What are you gonna do?*
>
> *Do you want to get married?*
>
> *How about children?*

Those questions. And I simply didn't know what I wanted to do with the rest of my life at 25. Honestly, I believe hardly anyone does. If you do, good on ya. Go be it.

In my case, I also suspected that I didn't have as much control as I thought I did. If it was that simple, everyone would get it right, right? Wrong.

You can't just script life and go into production. Life isn't this straight line some people like to make it. If we're honest with ourselves, it's humanly impossible to go through this journey without some kind of contradiction. Let's face that for once and have some mercy for each other, please.

A "one size fits all" formula simply doesn't cut it for everyone. Even if it fits a lot of people just fine. Some folks still need different sizes and custom-made lives.

So, what to do when the idea you had of life just doesn't fit in yours?

We keep trying. We look at what is available and experiment. We go in and out, just like kids. We fall, we fail, and we learn.

Of course, it's not that simple. The trials start weighing on us. We try things we really shouldn't. They don't fit us, but we wear them anyway. Or we simply go naked. Have you ever seen those kids walking around? I find them adorable. The little rebels of life.

Or, we just suck it up. More than we should. And then we break. We have our little tantrums. I know, shame on us. Shouldn't we just grow the hell up? Yes, we're trying here. It's a process, for anyone who doesn't know it yet.

So, instead of resenting my growing pains and unwanted feelings, especially the anger of it all, I decided to go on a personal quest to reframe those questions.

> *What kind of life am I trying to create here?*
>
> *Can I do this from anywhere or do I have to choose one place?*
>
> *If I stay here, who could I be?*
>
> *And if I go home, what happens to this life?*
>
> *Do I just leave it all behind?*

I decided to search for some facts about life. That's when I developed an interest in biographies. I started to study other people's lives to see if I could get any insight into mine. I was looking for references to recreate my own life. And nothing spoke louder than experience.

What I discovered was really eye opening: between success and failure, there is always a new world in creation. A million untapped opportunities to become oneself. So many different paths. No better or worse. Simply different.

I noticed that the ones I liked the most all shared a common trait: *they learned from their mistakes.* And never gave up on creating the life they wanted, even if it literally took them a lifetime. I kept cheering hard for them!

And I began to admire the way they were capable of overcoming seemingly impossible obstacles, while also integrating positive and negative aspects of themselves for the entire world to watch. They were whole — and immensely powerful. And I wanted to be just that.

So, I began to see beauty in my very own contradictions. For the very first time in my life, I was comfortable in my own skin. I accepted my imperfections. I was quite happy just experimenting. Two years wasn't even that long. If I managed the first two, how could I not double that? I gave myself some credit. *Come on, girl! You've got this!*

And, despite my external instability, that year, I learned to value all the good I had in my life. The places I'd been, the people I'd met and all the things I'd achieved on my own. I remained focused on extracting the best from all of my experiences, including the negative ones.

That was a big turning point.

People would still question my behavior and way of living. But, even without a clear path forward, I knew I was on track.

I also noticed I had two internal voices who would often talk over each other: one who was my cheerleader and another who was my worst enemy. I made a deal with myself. *Let them be. You can't please both.*

We would learn to be friends along the way. Just give it some time.

Confusion may cloud our hearts, but it also points our way. When we learn to quiet down our minds, we open the space for our own song to play.

My song was playing out and loud. But, as they say, you can't have it all.

At home, some things were changing. Laís decided to move in with her boyfriend. We were happy for her, of course. But that meant Cecília and I had to find a new flatmate to make our budget. Life as usual.

Within my limited experience, I had learned that worrying alone does not solve problems. All of our power lies in aligning ourselves with the solutions. And that's exactly what I did. I trusted that the right person would show up, and I kept an open eye.

Work was busy. A different day, every day. I was taking on a lot more responsibility and truly enjoying it. We were helping a lot of Brazilians to settle into new courses and jobs. It felt so good to see them thrive. And our little community kept growing.

I'll never forget the day this Brazilian guy came to GSH. Vinícius. He was in his thirties, which wasn't very common for a fresh arrival. I was amused by his very calm and centered nature. He had left a stable accounting job in São Paulo to seek a new lifestyle in Australia. He seemed very comfortable with his decision and confident it would all work out. I was amazed by his courage and determination. The least I could do was help him.

His English was basic, but he had a fire in his belly that I knew I could trust. We had a job opening at a restaurant and I offered him the position. Kitchenhand. He humbly accepted. It was hard work, but he was smart enough to know it was only a means to an end. A first of many steps. That's how we all start. Doing what we have to do. Until we can do what we really want.

I felt connected to him. And as we kept talking, he said *"I'm also looking for a place to live if you know anything"*. Right there I knew. It wasn't a coincidence.

"How much can you afford a week? We have a spare room. If you want, I can show you the apartment."

"For real? Where?"

"Mosman Park."

"Perfect. When can I see it?"

"Tomorrow?"

"Done. Just give me the address. I'll be there."

And just like that we had our new flatmate.

Sharing part of my journey with Vinícius was one of the best things that could have happened to me. I guess to all of us. He is one of the very best human beings I was fortunate to know. An honest, generous and very committed man. He had no vices. No drinking, no smoking, and enjoyed just the right amount of partying.

He was a great influence on me. Hanging out with him helped me to see a different side of life. I felt safe with him. I found another big brother.

The three of us got along very well. He was clean, organized and extremely sensible. Side note: he was a Taurus. For anyone interested. Cecília was too. We were all "down to Earth" buddies. And we loved a beautiful home.

With one less thing on my plate, I started planning my year. I had two clear priorities for 2007:

1. Professional growth

2. Traveling (as Gui had wisely advised me in 2005 and I nearly forgot)

At that time, it wasn't so common for women to travel alone. But, given I had gone all the way to Australia, it wouldn't hurt to go a little further.

My plan was to go somewhere in Asia first. I pictured 10 days of pure beach-side bliss, doing absolutely nothing. From there, I'd choose two or three countries in Europe.

Spain was a must. One of my best friends was living there. And then, Brazil. It was time to see my family again. And I wanted it to be a surprise, just after Christmas.

I had a few good months to get everything sorted and I went straight into action mode.

First things first: budget. Yes, I was as practical as delusional. Real world thinking, you know. They may say I'm a dreamer, but I like to get my dreams checked "done".

To be able to afford my dream trip, and enjoy my well-deserved vacation, I needed to have a very clear financial goal. I would need to do something that although seemed quite simple, it wasn't: save money.

Since I was already living on a tight budget, and was not willing to compromise on the little comfort I had created for myself, I made a short-term plan: for six months, I was willing to work even harder than I already was. I had a pot of pure gold on the other side. And I knew my way through the tunnel.

So, let's get into the specifics. I was already a full-time office girl. How could I squeeze more hours in? With a little lifestyle adjustment, I opened my schedule to a number of other jobs. Instead of partying, I worked.

A few nights a week you'd find me still working in the same restaurant as a waitress. On Saturdays, from 9am to 4pm, I was all over this home cleaning gig. A giant four-bedroom home with loads of washing to get through. Pure joy!

And, to top it all up, on Fridays and Saturdays, from 8pm until the early hours of the morning, people knew where to find me: doing whatever was needed at a kebab shop in Northbridge. Yes, I managed to stay around the party scene, but I was on the other side for a change, serving others. My duties included, but were not limited to: handling the till, frying chips, cleaning up tables and even trying not to be too rude with the drunk guys who often went there to chat me up.

You read that right: I literally went straight from the kebab to the cleaning gig. And then back to the kebab. I had showers in between, of course. Sundays? Rest and reset.

I remember it was just about the time when Ben Cousins, a famous Aussie footballer who won the Brownlow medal in 2005, got that iconic tattoo: *"such is life"*. Very wise. And so real.

But, when things got really heavy, I made sure to have a day off (something I learned during tree planting). It was important to remind myself that life was not all about work. I was allowed to have my share of fun.

I even managed to go on dates. I know, quite an achievement! And since I was juggling a number of jobs, I also kept two guys on a casual basis. It was easier than going out and trying to find someone new every time. Sometimes, you have to make the Paradox of Choice work in your favor. Less is more.

Some people would question the fact that I lived in a somewhat fancy neighborhood. I did. But I liked it. And I wanted to stay there. Living in a nice area was always a big part of the experience for me. I wasn't ready to trade that. And moving it wouldn't necessarily mean cheaper. I shared the luxury, remember? There was always a way to make things work. It's knowing what you can and can't compromise.

And with the ever changing life, Cecília decided to move on. I already knew the next step: we needed a third person to make our budget, again. I also knew that the right person would come along. The perks of *"being there, done that"*. You know the way out. No need to panic.

And, no surprise, there she was: our new flatmate. Martina, another Brazilian girl who had become a great friend over the years, had just ended a long-term relationship and was looking for a place to live. Well, she found it. The two of us shared a room. In fact, I always did that from the beginning. The trick for keeping rent and bills low.

It didn't take long for a friend who worked with me at the restaurant to introduce us to a recently arrived Brazilian, Thainá. She also needed a cheap place to live. *Didn't we all?*

As I was about to travel for seven full weeks, we made a deal: Thainá would take my place for that time. And we would squeeze her in for a few months prior to that.

It's amazing what we can do when everyone comes together towards a common goal. The four of us wanted the same things: to live well, to save money and to have a little fun. If three is too much, imagine four. It was a party!

But, can four people really get away with sharing a two-bedroom apartment? Absolutely. It was the most common thing for young adults like us. And for that brief period of time, our very organized mess worked wonders.

Just like brothers and sisters, we shared rooms. Martina and I, Vinícius and Thainá. We truly cared about each other. It felt like a real family. A home away from home.

So much so that we gave our little quartet a nickname: *"familião"* as in "big family". And instead of last names, we would all call each other with the Portuguese augmentative suffix *"ão"*. Carolão I was. And it didn't stop there. Our family kept growing. You know how they say *"the more, the merrier"*. We were into that.

The memories of those times evoke a "feel good" nostalgia that is hard to describe.

Shared love is a timeless thing. What survives of us is love. Nothing else. And, sometimes, even love is not a big enough word to express our feelings.

Our lives have completely changed since then. But, even apart, we still care and cheer for each other from a distance. Always will. All of us.

You guys are reading this. You know how much you mean to me.

Thank you for being part of my life.

40. WORK HARD(ER), PLAY HARD(ER).

Hard work really does pay off. After spending so much time working non-stop, I was ready to press "pause". Or, at least, enjoy life in slow motion.

November came quicker than I expected, and it was time to take off.

With butterflies in my stomach and a comforting warmth in my heart, I reflected on the last few months: *I made it. Job done. A big tick on my to-do list.*

I heard my cheerleader voice whispering in pure joy: "*Good girl! You're a star!*"

And, once again, I entered one of our incredible, modern, shared flying machines towards a new destination: Thailand.

It was my first-ever time in Asia. Arriving at the newly opened Bangkok airport was an experience in itself. (Note: it opened in 2006.) I had never seen an airport like that. Imagine a series of angular, wave-like forms as a building. It was quite sculptural. I was in awe.

I decided to catch a taxi to the hostel. It felt like the safest option. The taxi driver was nice, but we just had trouble communicating.

He barely spoke any English and that surprised me. Not to mention his adventurous driving. Very Bangkok style. But, in the absence of a better option, I had to trust him. He was my first Asian guide.

He drove towards Khao San Road and stopped in a very odd spot. He just pointed to this historic-looking building and said: "Here, ma'am". He helped me to get my luggage out of the boot, said *"bye"* and left.

I crossed this huge door that looked like a portal or something and started laughing. It wasn't a hostel; it was a pub. I turned around and the driver was gone. It suddenly hit me: *I'm alone here, and lost.*

I won't lie: I wanted to cry. I panicked. For five minutes. I even tortured myself with the least helpful question: *"Did you really think you could do this? Alone?"*

But I knew I had to turn my solution mode on. So, I left the pub and went outside to get some fresh air. The street looked nice. I sat down and started to think. *"He wouldn't leave me in the middle of nowhere. I must be close."*

I noticed this guy on the street, with a huge backpack, looking a little displaced too. He was right in front of me so I went up to him.

"Hi, I'm a little lost here. Do you know this address by any chance?" I asked as I handed him a little piece of paper with the address on it.

"Not really, but I can help you find it if you want. I'm Klaus. I just got here too. I'm from Germany. You?"

"Carolina. Nice to meet you. I'm from Brazil, but I live in Australia."

"Wow, two of the best countries in the world."

"If you say so. I tend to agree, but I'm biased. By the way, I'll take your offer. Let's find this place."

We checked our surroundings and asked one of the Asian looking guys who was walking past us. He was Thai and spoke great English. Thank God! He said it was right there, just a little further down. It was along a "no through road". Cars were not allowed past that point.

Mystery solved. I knew I could trust the taxi driver. He just needed some English classes to be able to provide better customer service and full directions.

We walked about 100 meters and found my hostel. I checked in, not knowing I was in for another interesting surprise. I had booked a single room and paid a relatively high amount for it — but it wasn't quite like that. They literally left me alone in a room with six beds. I started laughing at myself, but I accepted it. *"I must learn something from this."*

I left my belongings in the room and went back to the reception. Klaus was still there. He needed a bed too, but the hostel was full and he had no booking. I looked at the receptionist and asked her:

"Can he stay in one of the other five beds in my room?"

She answered, "It's your room, up to you."

"Okay," I said. "He can stay."

Sharing accommodation was never a problem for me. And I wouldn't let this guy who just helped me wander around the streets at that time of the night trying to find a place to rest. I offered him a bed and he accepted, of course. But he insisted on going halves with me on the full cost. It was a win-win, just the way I liked it. The Universe is fair.

I was only there for two days. It was nice to have a new friend to share part of the journey with.

Klaus and I walked the streets of Bangkok together, trying local delicacies and avoiding the pushy street vendors. We also had a great night out at the corner pub. It felt so good (and different) to go in, empty handed, for all the right reasons. We had a ball!

It didn't take long for me to notice the synchronicities in that trip. I was living my own Prophecy, with every detail perfectly orchestrated.

Life is like a test with consultation. You'll face challenges, but the answers are always there if you're willing to wait and look for them.

After the madness of the capital, my next stop was Koh Samui. I safely placed my Europe-Brazil suitcase in one of the lockers at Bangkok Airport and went to check in just with my summer backpack. The unbearable lightness of simply being.

I had a week there. This time, I checked into this beautiful resort by the beach. I had a rather luxurious bungalow, with a king size bed, an extra single bed and a wonderful bathtub. I felt like a princess receiving the rewards of my own hard-earned labor.

I put my bikini on and went straight to the beach. For hours. On my way back, I sat by the pool and started talking to this nice Swedish couple. Astrid, the girl, soon introduced me to her brother and we all decided to have dinner together that night.

Thai food is an attraction in itself. And they have options for all tastes: from a milder pad thai or egg rice to many variations of curry, with very spicy flavors. To end our night, we went to Chaweng Road, one of the main streets on the island, where most of the action happened.

The best part of traveling alone is being open to meeting people from all over the world and having truly unique experiences with each one of them. That same night, we met Jessica. A Canadian backpacker who became my travel buddy on some of the craziest nights of my life.

I noticed there was a guy looking at me. He was wearing jeans, a white t-shirt and our world-famous Havaianas. He was my type of guy. And despite having brown hair and tanned skin, he had an Australian vibe. Very laid-back.

I shyly reciprocated his look. He came straight towards me. In his first sentence I could tell I was wrong. He was French. I had barely landed in Asia and the Universe was already preparing me for my next destination. We French kissed all night and he gave me a list of things to do in Paris. It was perfect!

This is one of the pros about being single. You can enjoy spontaneous *"love affairs"* wherever you go. A guilt-free pleasure!

On the second day, I decided to rent a scooter and went out exploring. It was all very different from anything I had ever seen. This part of the world gave me a sense of calm and confidence. I felt safe there.

I arranged to have dinner with Jessica that night. That's when she told me about her accommodation arrangement. She was sharing a hostel room with 11 people. I remembered I had an extra bed in my bungalow. I didn't even think twice:

"Jessica, you can have that extra bed in my room for the whole time that I'm here."

"Are you serious?"

"Yep, on me. You still have a lot of travelling to do. It will save you money and you'll sleep much better. I really don't mind."

She took it and we spent the rest of our trip somehow connected. We had our own individual quests, but we shared some pretty amazing adventures too.

One of the reasons I chose Thailand was for its spiritual side. It was all new to me, but I wanted to learn more. So, I took a whole day just to visit the "wats", the famous temples. I hired a local guide to tell me their stories and advise me on the best times to visit.

As the name suggests, a temple is a sacred building. The general rule was simple: be sensible, don't do anything you wouldn't do in a church. This included how you dressed and behaved. You needed to cover your shoulders and knees. And keep quiet.

Oh, one other detail: shoes had to be left outside. Another important thing was not to point your feet at sacred images.

With all of that in mind, we started with one of the most famous temples, Wat Phra Yai, better known as "Big Buddha". Built in 1972, the imposing 12-meter-high golden statue can be seen from various points on the island and has been a frequent destination for lovers of culture, religion and history.

We arrived just before the sunrise to join the Buddhist monks for a spiritual experience.

It all started with a climb of about one-hundred steps. The staircase had a serpent as a handrail on each side. It led to a small islet from where the Big Buddha watches over Koh Samui island.

It was also one of the highest points in the city. The view reminded us that every experience was a matter of perspective.

In a sacred place, everything is symbolic. And despite being very touristy, the experience in places like this remains individual. You make it your own.

Every morning, devotees light incense, say prayers, sing songs and bring offerings of fruits and flowers to the Buddha statue. It's impossible to be immune to the presence of this giant in a meditative pose, with a calm and serene face, receiving so much grace.

Inhaling the sweet aroma of incense, I fell silent and surrendered to the local ritual. I took the opportunity to contemplate that moment of reverence in a complete state of gratitude, which led me to a profound experience.

Closing my eyes, I can feel myself there.

I could spend hours and hours just observing the details, the colors, the textures, the shapes carved into the adornments of each symbolic element, purposefully inserted into that great Buddhist atmosphere that represented the culture of those people, but there was still a lot for me to see.

Although it is a religious site, tourists were always welcome. After the morning ritual, the atmosphere changed when visitors of all nationalities mixed with local traders who set up their stalls to earn their living. That in itself was a beautiful thing to admire.

Next, we went to Wat Plai Laem, a temple complex next to the Big Buddha. Completed in 2004, the relatively recent project at the time sought to recreate some traditions through the creativity of distinguished Thai artist Jarit Phumdonming.

In addition to the vibrant architecture, with buildings that merged Thai tradition and Thai-Chinese style, the complex had several images that represented Buddhist deities, all very colorful and imposing.

It is impossible to talk about every detail of the place, but I will highlight three points that caught my attention and what they mean in their culture.

Hotei, better known as "Fat Buddha", is the representation of a Chinese monk — one of the seven gods of luck in Asian mythology. Chubby and smiling, he is believed to attract health and happiness. His popularity is unquestionable. After all, who doesn't want both?

Another highlight was the Wat Laem Suwannaram Temple, a sacred site with pink lotus borders, over a fish pond, which blended into the blue sky in a surprising landscape. Its facade was so detailed that it would be impossible to describe all the guardians that protected its entrance.

Let's just say that, in this place, we have an example of the manifestation of faith and symbolism of a culture that worships and respects a diversity of gods, including elephants and snakes. I would say it is a celebration of respect for all beings and their infinite beliefs and specificities.

Images and gods can also contain different representations in different cultures, as is the case with Kuan Yin (or Guanyin) herself, which made me stop to reflect during my visit to the complex.

When I came across that image of a woman, with eighteen arms, which represented her ability to provide assistance to all beings in need, anywhere in the world, I asked myself: *How does she do it?*

I had a brief epiphany about the very essence of the feminine, evidenced in that work, which was not the only way in which the Goddess of Compassion and Forgiveness was represented.

Kuan Yin can also appear sitting on a lotus flower, or floating on several of them, highlighting her spirituality and spreading Buddha's love and compassion symbolized by the flower.

The most important thing is to respect the moral and human values that tend to lead us to compassionate and loving behavior towards any and all forms of life.

In addition to these, some smaller images of Ganesha, Vishnu and Shiva were also spread throughout the complex, which generally takes us to a state of peace and tranquility, characteristic of sacred places.

I continued my journey in Thai, experiencing the sacred vs. profane paradox, just like any human being walking on Earth right now.

I had nowhere to go. I was already at my destination. So, I allowed myself to spend the rest of my days doing absolutely nothing. I suspect I got one of the best tans of my life during that little trip. Every day was a beach day. Blissful living is what they call it.

There was just one thing I wanted to check off my Thai "to do list": The Full Moon Party.

Created in the 1980s by a group of travelers, the Full Moon Party takes place on Koh Phangan Island on every full moon of the year, with extra editions at Christmas and New Year. It attracts thousands of people to Haad Rin Nok beach, also known as Sunrise Beach.

As we were between full moons, I found out they had a Half Moon Party. A slightly smaller version. I got all the information about times and the boat trip from Koh Samui to the party island. It felt in alignment.

I invited Jessica to go with me. She said yes, of course. The next day, we literally jumped on the boat, carrying nothing but ourselves, with no idea of what to expect. It was thrilling!

Big electronic dance parties were nothing new to me, but that island had something magnetic and slightly surreal. I didn't know if it was the neon paints, the famous "buckets", the diversity of people, or just the fact that I was nobody in that place.

All I know is that I fully surrendered to the experience. Of the memories I have, dancing for hours by the beach is the most vivid of them. I also remember playing with fire, even knowing the risk of getting burned. That night, even though I met some interesting guys, I just truly enjoyed myself until the sun came up.

That Half Moon Party made me rethink what I thought I knew about partying in a very profound way.

Jessica and I made it to the pier just in time to not miss the return boat. Sure, I was a bit crazy, but I was also ultra-responsible. I always kept myself out of trouble everywhere I went.

That trip to Thailand showed me facets of my personality that even I didn't know existed. It was magical and eye-opening. Just like any travel should be. Inspired by a new place, I found myself deep diving into my own internal world. It was wild.

And after the easy island life, it was time to explore another part of the world.

Next stop: the "City of Lights".

41. WHEN IN PARIS.

Being a traveler is amazing, but having a local to help you out always comes in handy. Especially when you have one of those late-night arrivals at Charles de Gaulle.

Pierre, my French friend who worked with me at GSH, was the kind soul who welcomed me to his hometown. He conveniently lived very close to the airport and offered to pick me up at those odd hours. He also offered me a mattress in his living room for the night. It was just perfect.

We woke up the next morning, had a nice breakfast catch up and he took me to the train station on his way to work. Nice, easy and joyful.

Thank you, Pierre! That little gesture meant the world to me.

When travelling on budget, you must be aware of everything — and I was.

For starters, I knew Europe was a lot more expensive than Asia. There was no way I'd have any luxury in this part of the world. So, I booked a nice hostel, good location, in a shared quadruple room. All female, just in case.

The "coincidences" started right at the check-in. My roommates were a little Aussie trio who were traveling together. *Seriously? I'm in Paris. What are the chances?* But that's what happens sometimes. We got lucky! My room was a little Aussie land that made me feel home.

On the first night, I went down to the common area and joined a multicultural group who was brainstorming ideas to get to know Paris on a budget. It suited me perfectly.

We started with a night walk, perfectly safe in a group. Zero dollars for a priceless experience.

Our investment would go towards something important: dinner. So, we stopped at a very "chic" restaurant (at least by our standards) and everyone agreed to share a little French feast. We started with escargot. Most of us had to learn the trick to eat it. It was hilarious! For main? Duck with orange. Yes, we went for the classics. To end on a high note, an authentic crème brûlée. Dessert heaven!

I often say "don't believe the hype", but this place honored French fame. Their food was incredible, and not at all over budget. We hit the sweet spot there!

Now, let's make something clear: Paris isn't just about food. Or fashion. Or art. Although these are some of the things that put the city in the spotlight. But it's not all you get.

French people, like Aussies and Brazilians, love a good party. And I would never miss an opportunity to party French-style.

I had a friend who was living in London at the time and was into clubbing like me. I asked if he knew any hidden secrets. Of course, he did. I can't remember the name, but he told me about a famous little club where you had to be "in the know" to access it. I invited my new friends to join me. Two of the girls came along.

There was a huge line, as expected. But lines never bothered me. I learned to wisely use the waiting time to make friends. I started talking with three young French guys, who were right in front of us. They gave us all the insider information about the club. In no time, we were in.

My mantra for that trip was *"dance like there is no tomorrow"*. I was young, wild and free. The girls left after a couple of hours and I stayed with my new "French buddies".

When the club closed, I was ready to catch a cab. One of the "buddies" came up to me and said: *"I'll drive you"*. It felt like a genuine offer and I accepted. I had no idea that a ride home would be an experience in itself.

We walked to his car and I almost couldn't believe it. He had a Smart (you know the tiny little car?). I had such curiosity about those little beauties. I was finally getting into one, and it was surprisingly comfortable. No wonder they were included in the permanent collection of the Museum of Modern Art in New York as a "contemporary design classic from the last decade of the last century". Small is beautiful too.

Late at night, Paris streets are like Aussie deserts. An empty wilderness. He drove around and showed me his city in a totally new light. Only as locals can do. There I was, living another real-life movie. My very own Paris private tour, way before Woody Allen brought Midnight in Paris to life.

We visited some of the iconic tourist spots, without the crowds. I couldn't stop thinking *"how lucky am I?"*.

Did we French kiss? No, not this time. This was a pure, uninterested gesture of human generosity. How could I not believe in the best in people? They usually showed me pretty good sides.

On the next day, I went to the Palace of Versailles to recreate the memories I had of Marie Antoinette, the film directed by Sofia Coppola, which was largely shot in that palace, under special authorization from the French government.

I would like to take this opportunity to express how much Sofia Coppola inspired and continues to inspire my life. The Italian-American filmmaker, screenwriter, producer and actress was one of the first prominent directors of my generation, gaining notoriety for her films composed, in the majority, of female protagonists in moments of fragility and change (and even both together). Any similarity to my real life is not coincidental.

One of my favorites was "Lost in translation" from 2003, with Scarlett Johansson and Bill Murray. A film that earned her an Oscar for Best Original Screenplay, in addition to being nominated for an Oscar for Best Director, making her the third woman to be nominated in the category.

The mastery with which Sofia portrays cultural aspects that are not so easily translated between people, even with the correct use of the language, is fascinating. What enchants me about her is her ability to demonstrate delicacy and sensitivity when reporting stories of privileged people who get lost in their ideal world and end up disconnecting from reality.

In the case of Marie Antoinette, the film tells the story of the young queen of 18th century France. However, in Coppola's version, the plot does not exactly follow the traditional historical panorama.

Anchored in the stunning performance of actress Kirsten Dunst, a new look at the personality of the dauphin emerges, who, despite all her privileges, was treated with disdain because of her Austrian nationality.

What touched me most about the work was the humanization of the 14-year-old teenager who cannot escape displacement and the inability to meet the expectations placed on her. While oscillating between material excesses and emotional emptiness, Marie Antoinette was forced to adapt to a new environment, pre-revolutionary France.

Without any idea of the great abyss of social inequality and suffering that surrounded her, the rich young queen used all available devices to survive the intrigues and fantasies that took place inside the palace. A bittersweet journey that doesn't escape a tragic ending.

The film received mixed reactions at the Cannes Festival after its world premiere, causing discomfort among the most conservative. Some critics disagreed with Coppola's decision to insert contemporary elements into the classical context, and summarized the work as something "cute, but empty".

In my view, that is precisely where her genius lies. When Sofia bets on challenging some traditions to connect with new generations, she seeks to show that Versailles can happen anywhere in the world and at any time. Even now.

The combination of the real period with touches of boldness and modernity creates a more familiar atmosphere and contributes to the audience's identification with the narrative.

In addition to the impeccable photography and costumes, she bet on a soundtrack based on the 1980s, which includes The Cure and The Strokes.

An example of this creative boldness is the iconic scene in which Marie Antoinette and her friends enjoy a shopping spree and feast on luxurious sweets, champagne, clothes, shoes and jewelry, to the sound of "I Want Candy" by the Bow Wow Wow band.

Although they are disturbing elements to the status quo, and clichés in other contemporary works, such devices convey the rebelliousness of a young woman, frustrated, bored, isolated and, yet, always on display.

I would dare to say that Sofia simply anticipated, through art, a reality that is somewhat familiar today. And that's why there are poetic licenses. For questioning unquestionable questions.

Despite the controversy caused among the public and critics in 2006, the legacy left by this work is undeniable, which, despite not being a commercial success, became a cult classic and one of the most beloved films in Coppola's filmography.

Between applause and boos, I believe that the historical-biographical drama is an example of how contemporary art has the power to engage new audiences in conversations necessary for the evolution of thought, even if it takes some time for the artistic vision to be understood.

In 2023, where I write from, the excesses of luxury and ostentation, portrayed on social media, by thousands of people completely oblivious to the pains of the real world, represent not only the youth and alienation of Marie Antoinette, but of the majority of young people who go through times until they become aware of the world they inhabit.

Life and art are intrinsically interwoven. Art inspires life. And life will never cease to inspire art.

Now, returning to the Palace itself, I lack words to describe such opulence of the extravagant monument-museum dedicated to "all the glories of France".

Since 1979, the Palace of Versailles has been listed as a World Heritage and is one of the greatest achievements in French 17th century art. Louis XIII's old hunting pavilion was transformed and extended by his son, Louis XIV, when he installed the Court and government there in 1682.

For over a century, Versailles was a model of royal residence in Europe until the French Monarchy was shaken up by the French Revolution.

Curator Pierre de Nohlac began conserving the palace in the 1880s, but it did not receive the necessary funding until the donation of 60 million francs by John D. Rockefeller, between 1924 and 1936.

Its promotion as a tourist site began in the 1930s and accelerated in the 1950s and 1960s. Considered one of the largest in the world, the Palace-Park is one of the most visited tourist attractions in France and has an absurd number of rooms.

We spent the entire day immersed in gardens, museums and small palaces spread across the entire length of the complex which, over so many years, had undergone successive expansions and transformations.

One of the highlights was the Hall of Mirrors, which, in 1919, was the stage for the signing of the controversial Treaty of Versailles. The room, 73 meters long and 12.30 meters high, was lit by seventeen windows that have mirrors in front of them that reflect the privileged views of the gardens.

The other highlight was the Petit Trianon, Marie Antoinette's refuge from the excesses of Versailles. It was there where she reconnected with nature and with the people she truly loved, including her daughter. It was probably my favorite place there too.

To fully process all the visual and historical information I was being presented, I spent the next day walking. All by myself. But, when in Paris, your daily walk can be on Champs-Élysées which is an attraction on its own.

Even without a budget for extravagance, I was allowed some

simple pleasures. I could delight my senses in the beauty of the city and experience a "princess day" on my own terms.

I started with a croissant. Sitting there, having the Eiffel Tower as my view, was already an immense privilege. I took it all in.

I couldn't deny: I had a passion for fashion. And a fascination for brand creation. But I was 25 and my life was just getting started. I was nowhere near the ideal customer for any luxury brand.

But I took the opportunity to do some research. I was allowed to enter and feel the private universe created by all those iconic luxury brands, without purchasing any item.

An imposing building caught my attention. I was at one of the most famous corners in Paris, standing by one of Louis Vuitton's most successful stores. It was impossible to ignore the presence of the brand. I went in.

And while the LV monogram stamped bags were not really my thing, I truly admired the brand and its long-standing value. The store was impeccable.

What I didn't expect was to bump into a childhood friend there. Yes, another one of those "coincidences". Fernanda was with her husband. It was their honeymoon. *"What a small world!"* None of us could believe it, but it happened. And I loved the feeling of familiarity that little moment brought to my solo trip. I also reflected on the totally opposite directions our lives were going. I felt happy for her.

To make the most of our chance encounter, we decided to catch up properly the next day. Both of us were planning a visit to the Louvre and we could do it together.

After my pseudo retail therapy, I got overwhelmed by the whole idea of desiring things I knew I didn't need. I felt like taking a break from city living. I kept walking until I found this interesting garden with statues spread all over it: The Carrousel Garden. It instantly took me to another state of mind. It grounded me. It made me feel fully alive.

I knew it was time to go back to nature for a while so I asked if there were any other gardens around. One of the locals told me that, not far from there, I could find one of the most beautiful gardens in Paris, The Tuileries Garden.

I followed her instructions and in less than 10 minutes found myself in this incredible green oasis right in the middle of the concrete jungle. Every big city needs a big garden. That's how they breathe life into it. Otherwise, humans can't survive the pressure.

I spent a few hours there, just relaxing. People watching. Life wandering. Daydreaming. For a few moments, I felt like a Parisian. A true sense of belonging. I could simply enjoy that space without spending a cent. To me, that's a real privilege.

One of the most extraordinary discoveries about travelling was this idea of being just another ordinary tourist making myself comfortable in the priceless attractions of someone else's home. Think about it. Some people marvel at the place you live. And sometimes, you don't even notice. Or simply rush through, literally taking it for granted.

After a while, I was ready to continue my city adventure. And since I haven't spent any money on extravagant purchases, I still had my allowance for simple pleasures.

I decided to try Ladurée's famous macarons. Back then, those sweet little treats were not available everywhere in the world like they are now. So, I bought some as gifts. For my mother and a few other people. I know, food always gets me.

As the night fell, I saw an opportunity to create an eternal romantic memory for myself. I spun on the extinct *"grand roue"* (great wheel), which was located on the Place de la Concorde. I don't think I could have been any more cliché than that. Spinning the love wheel all by myself. It was fun!

I lost track of time and got carried away by the beauty of the lights that made Paris so famous. My heart lit up too.

The next morning, I had breakfast and went straight to the Louvre to meet Fernanda and her husband. The most important museum in France, and also the most visited in the world, needs no introduction. It is, in itself, already a beautiful work of art.

We are talking about 400 rooms, 35 thousand pieces on display and a number of tourists beyond average. It's humanly impossible to see the endless galleries of the former royal palace in just one day. That's why we didn't even try.

Like most tourists with limited cultural artistic repertoire, we made a selection of historical pieces we simply couldn't miss. In about four hours of immersion, we managed to see some of the rooms and were quite inspired by all the artists that worked themselves up to that level of recognition.

Among so many works of beauty and value, my favorite was Venus de Milo, or Aphrodite, who in Greek mythology is the goddess of love and beauty. Two of my favorite things in the world.

Carved in white marble, the statue, without the arms, leads us to deep reflections on the simple fact that they were broken somewhere in the past and instigate the imagination of many about what those arms could have been doing before they had been lost. *Who knows?*

And how could I forget the enigmatic Mona Lisa, by Leonardo da Vinci. Often referred to as *"the most famous woman in the world"*, the painting measuring just 77 x 53 cm is one of the most valuable works of art in existence. Valued at more than a billion dollars, it is a small concrete proof of the intangible value of art.

While art nourished our souls, we also needed food to nourish our bodies. By now, you know the value I place on my meals. I literally can't live without them.

We left the museum to go after a nice place to eat. On our way out, we noticed some tables on the covered terrace overlooking the Pyramid and the entire Cour Napoléon, the museum's courtyard. Fernanda's husband said, "How about here?" and we instantly agreed that it was the perfect place to relax and enjoy the heart of Paris.

Le Café Marly is a restaurant strategically located under the arcades of the north wing of the Louvre. It occupies the dining rooms of Napoleon III and was the perfect setting to immortalize that brief crack in time with contemporary nostalgia, honoring the luxury of other times.

Fernanda and I toasted to life and our happy encounter around the world. We said goodbye, without a date to meet again. As you do when you don't live in the same city. Or country.

The next day I went to Montmartre, the neighborhood where people like Salvador Dali, Van Gogh, Monet, Picasso and all sorts of musicians, painters, writers and the like led free lives and were considered somewhat hedonistic.

I also wanted to get a taste of Parisian bohemia, at least for a day.

Leaving Abbesses station, I came across the Wall of Love. As I read "I love you" in more than 300 languages, the phrase echoed within me, like I had never felt before. Maybe because I never stopped believing in it. Or, perhaps, because, for the first time, I repeated it just to myself.

And even if you want to avoid clichés, it's impossible to ignore the classics.

Montmartre's best-known attraction is the Sacre Coeur, the Basilica of the Sacred Heart. Impressive, both outside and inside, this historical icon, which combines religious, cultural and political elements, demands a long pause to admire each of its details. And it doesn't end there.

Located at the highest point of the French capital, the infinite view of Paris meeting the sky can be considered another one of its sacred elements.

The neighborhood also has an unusual tourist spot: Café des deux Moulins, which I discovered through the film "The Fabulous Destiny of Amélie Poulain". I, who already had an identification with the dreamy waitress, for a few moments, imagined myself in that story.

Like her, I also had my complexity. And a tendency to navigate the intersection between the real and the imaginary in search for the meaning of life — in addition to being an incurable romantic who, despite all the romantic setbacks, had an unshakable faith in my own Prophecy.

Inspired by Amelie, I felt an immense desire to change destinies, starting with my own. And while my destiny was still being designed, I enjoyed every single moment I walked through every corner of that neighborhood that embraced the most diverse forms of art.

Montmartre has a Musée and a Galerie. I went to both, in addition to admiring the street art at Place des Tertres, where pulsating artistic souls expressed their freedom. No pretension. Just creativity, lightness and intention.

As another night fell, another classic waited for me: Moulin Rouge. At the height of my 25 years, and somewhat influenced by pop culture, I was humming Christina Aguilera's "Lady Marmalade" along the streets. And funny enough, it was the eccentric Australian director Baz Luhrmann, and Aussie actress Nicole Kidman, who made the Parisian cabaret even more famous in the 2001 film.

My budget didn't allow me to enter the show, but I took a photo with the beautiful background. As you do to remember "I was here". We had no need to share anything on social media. It was just a collection of moments we were lucky to live.

As a good Latina, I chose the Latin Quarter, known for being a bohemian region and a famous intellectual hub, to complete my brief tour of Paris.

The Mighty Saint Michael was quite a host for those who arrived on Boulevard Saint-Michel and came across that fountain. In fact, right behind it, was where an illustrious Brazilian, described as *"the most significant creative figure of the 20th century in Brazilian classical music"* once lived.

The plaque on the building's door confirmed: the composer Heitor Villa-Lobos lived in this house from 1923 to 1930. The apartment, on the third floor, was lent by a Rio tycoon who, in some way, made his contribution to Villa-Lobos's success, supporting him on his way to becoming the best-known South American composer of all time.

As I walked through the small streets, deeply inhaling an air composed of creativity and nostalgia, I could feel the soul that still inhabited that region that attracted tourists, students, philosophers and artists.

The Latin neighborhood had a peculiar atmosphere and invited us to a new way of thinking.

Great thinkers and revolutionaries in their fields have passed through the iconic Sorbonne, which coexists between bars, bookstores, theaters and museums. Created with the aim of teaching theology to the most in need, the institution became France's first faculty of letters and human sciences. A name so strong that, even without having actually existed for almost 50 years, it continued to exert its influence as the most famous French university.

Among the extensive list of illustrious alumni are the scientist couple Marie and Pierre Curie and the libertarian intellectuals Simone de Beauvoir and Jean-Paul Sartre. A very special and well-deserved highlight goes to the Brazilian artist Lygia Clark and the former president of Brazil, Fernando Henrique Cardoso, who also studied there.

It is understandable that some defend the theory that Paris is called the City of Light, not because it is very illuminated (which is also true), but because, for centuries, it has attracted the most brilliant minds in the different aspects of arts and sciences, and in the most diverse expressions.

It's also impossible not to imagine Simone de Beauvoir walking through those streets, while immortalizing some feelings in words.

> *"Let nothing define us, let nothing subject us. Let freedom be our very substance, since to live is to be free."*

And this freedom, which I was so desperately after, came precisely from the mix of ideas and exchanges that livened up cafes and sidewalks. Whether wonderstruck tourists or hurried Parisians, everyone wanted to find their own play while life happened in all its subjectivity.

Welcoming intellectuals, romantics and the distracted, the Latin Quarter also housed Shakespeare and Company, the English bookstore that has served as the setting not only for several films, but also books. For those who appreciate literature, like me, it is a true "trip down memory lane" that goes back to a time of literary and cultural effervescence in Paris.

I entered that small, chaotic and brilliantly organized space, and I felt the souls of Ernest Hemingway, F. Scott Fitzgerald, James Joyce, Gertrude Stein, among many others, still hovering in the air. Shakespeare and Company is a true living novel, which stands the test of time, and reminds us why Paris is a party and continues to inspire artists and writers to this day.

I enjoyed every single minute the French capital had to offer, but I had to keep moving.

I was about to get a taste of what life would have been like if I had chosen England over Australia.

42. LONDON CALLING.

The most incredible thing about being in Europe was the ability to get from one country to another at high speed.

In just over two hours, I crossed from Paris to London, thanks to Eurostar. And from St Pancras International Station I went to Kings Cross to take a tube to London Bridge. I had to change lines to get to Canary Wharf, London's so-called "Wall Street". I bet the English despise the comparison. They have my respect.

I had dived into a whole new world. The contrast between Parisian nostalgia and the modernity of London's financial center did not go unnoticed. Luckily, I had an angel waiting for me there.

Ash, a good friend of a friend from Perth, offered to be my host on this part of my trip. He was not only kind enough to offer me a room at his place, but also made sure he'd pick me up at the subway station. Side note: he drove a Porsche, which we both quickly discovered was not the best vehicle for transporting the 32 kg suitcase I had been carrying around across the world.

I sat in the passenger seat, hugging my backpack, a little embarrassed, and we both cracked it. The laughter instantly brought us together. What better way to break the ice than making a fool of yourself? It was hilarious!

On the way to his home, Ash told me a little about his life. At 40, my host had built a solid career as an international model and seemed to have achieved the financial stability he had dreamed of. Tall, elegant and polite, Ash was a lovely Englishman. Proudly black. He had an amazing life story that inspired me in a very profound way from his very first words. Strange things that strangers can do.

Let me make a point here: I'm fascinated by stories that rip off any kind of pre-established labels made by who knows who. I'm one of those people who quickly connects with strangers for a very simple reason: I like people.

It may seem a bit crazy or even scary to some, but I believe life talks to us through these synchronized encounters. Trusting the unknown is a powerful way to strengthen our connection to Source and accept that life is working out its best for all of us.

That wasn't just in the Prophecy, it was also my way of life.

As soon as we got to his apartment, I thought to myself: *"I must have done something right to deserve this"*.

Ash lived in a beautiful triplex, with a contemporary interior that looked like it came straight out of a magazine. His kind and respectful nature made me feel not only welcomed, but especially safe.

He took me to one of the ensuites, accommodated my suitcase and left me alone.

I felt very humbled and grateful by his generosity.

After a shower, we chatted a little and went out for dinner. The advantage of having a local host was having access to experiences that you would probably never have as a tourist.

The restaurant he took me to that night was one of them. I don't remember the name, but it was West Indian. At first, I felt a bit confused, until Ash explained to me that it was not the Indian as I knew, from India. It was from the West Indies, the Caribbean. That was his heritage.

It stayed with me the fact that some European explorers believed they reached Asia by sailing west, and named a lot of places as India, until they finally realized it was a "new world". Isn't it ironic how even history is not 100% accurate?

Back to the food, I lack the words to describe the flavors. The waitress kept bringing all the right dishes, without any need for Ash to order. He was a regular. I fully understood the depth of that relationship. I had similar bonds with our regular clients.

Our West Indian feast was divine. And after introducing me to this peculiar cuisine, Ash also offered me valuable tips to make the best of London. I had a full schedule for the coming days.

Again, I didn't escape the classics that most tourists experienced in the English capital. I loved watching the changing of guard at Buckingham Palace and took a nice shot in front of the Parliament. I know, so cliché! But I resisted the London Eye. I just observed from a distance and it was enough.

My focus was to enjoy the cultural part of the city. I started at the National Gallery, one of the most famous art museums in the world, which was located in Trafalgar Square. As it was a very busy area, I took advantage of the fact that it was a weekday and went very early to avoid the crowds.

At 25, I was no art expert. I'm still not. But I have this long-standing relationship of love and admiration with any artistic expression. On a soul level. To me, it's inspiring to see those artists who are capable of overcoming their fears and insecurities to bravely express how they feel, while also giving up control over the reactions that their works may cause in others. Even if that was discomfort or rejection.

Art is courage at its highest form. I suspect that most artists don't even realize how brave they are, or how much influence they have on humanity.

Museums and galleries are responsible for conserving the countless works produced over eras of creativity. It is quite a feat to organize them so that people like us can get to know and admire historical pieces of art in modern times. It remains a resistance to the spirit of each time and proof of the constant changes in the way of thinking.

Many consider the National Gallery to be the grandmother of galleries. It is impossible to disagree with the artistic ancestry that the institution carries with more than 2,300 paintings that span seven centuries of Western art, carefully organized by periods.

Among the immense collection, some classics are widely known and celebrated.

"La venus del Espejo", "Vênus ao Mirror" or "The Toilet of Venus" stands out not only for what it represents, but for highlighting the complexity that exists in the translations.

Completed between 1647 and 1651 (four years of work) by the main artist of the Spanish Golden Age, the painting presents the goddess Venus in a sensual position, lying on a bed and looking into a mirror held by her son Cupid, the Roman god of physical love. The one who introduced me to Daniel, remember?

Diego Velázquez did not hide his sources of inspiration, the Venuses of Italian painters, whom he met during his stay in Italy. It was the only female nude work made by Velázquez that had survived to this day, having lived in some Spanish courtiers' homes before being publicly exhibited. It remained preserved in the Buenavista Palace in Madrid, until it was taken to England. It was hung in Rokeby Park, Yorkshire, where it was nicknamed "The Rokeby Venus".

In 1906, the painting was purchased by the National Art Collections Trust for the National Gallery. Despite being attacked and seriously damaged in 1914 by suffragette Mary Richardson, the work was fully restored and remains on display today.

Another classic was one of Van Gogh's "Sunflowers", spread across the world's main museums. For him, the flower had several meanings. The blossoming bud, the fullness, the maturity and even the eventual decay.

"The sunflower is mine," once declared the Dutchman, who made the yellow flowers, considered coarse and unrefined at that time, synonymous with Vincent, exactly as he prophesied.

No other artist has been as closely associated with a flower as he has been. For Van Gogh, sunflowers represent the celebration of the beauty and vitality of nature. Furthermore, they have become a symbol of friendship around the world.

It's hard to believe, but his painting only gained value after his death. Van Gogh did not have commercial success with these works during his lifetime, even though he was responsible for the flower's worldwide fame. Still, he was honored with countless of them at his funeral. A classic case of posthumous recognition.

Perhaps art is a great enigma on its own. Or just too simple for our human understanding.

I could write a lot more about the subject, or about the gallery itself, but London goes beyond art. And I only had four days.

One of the most iconic places in the city, for example, had the Eros fountain surrounded by huge luminous panels, proving that history and modernity could inhabit the same space. And that advertising made its way into virtually anything — for good or bad.

It was impossible not to recognize Piccadilly Circus, an invitation to immerse ourselves in the busy streets of Soho. I couldn't escape Oxford Street, one of the busiest and most popular shopping streets in the world. I repeated what I had learned in Paris: I went into some of the boutiques, updated myself on the main fashion trends, and purchased absolutely nothing.

The temptation became greater in department stores, where things started to fit in my budget, but not in my suitcase. This was definitely not a shopping trip and I was at peace with that.

Cultural diversity and freedom of expression caught my attention in this area of London, especially when I walked through the Carnaby Street portal.

The unusual mix of fashion brands and independent stores left no doubt as to how this London street became an avant-garde symbol in the 1960s. Known for its modernity, creative freedom and good taste, Carnaby became extremely popular at the time London exported culture all over the world.

I passed Berwick Street Market and continued walking until I was seduced by one of the many cafes that brought together all kinds of people on the sidewalk. Only those who love to have breakfast at any time of the day can understand and appreciate the joy of being able to order eggs benedict in the middle of the afternoon. I particularly love an "all-day breakfast". In London, I found many. That meal made my day.

I walked a little further and took the subway to Ash's house. After a well-deserved shower, we went to dinner at another restaurant, also in Soho. This time, one that served dumplings, gyoza, among other oriental delicacies.

Ash also took me to one of those incredible jazz clubs for a complete experience. This connection with my host made me perfectly understand the insight from which Airbnb was born. At that time, the world was open and blossoming. Experiences were meant to be shared. That was the spirit of 2007.

Even though I prioritized living in English, I loved meeting my fellow countrymen who lived in other parts of the world. Orkut was the social network of the time for Brazilians. But, on that trip, I decided to join Facebook to connect with the foreigners I met along the way.

Some Brazilians were also there (mainly the ones who lived abroad). Marcos was one of them. He knew I loved electronic music (he gave me the Paris tip, remember?) and asked me to keep a free night to join him in London. I simply obeyed.

The next morning, while Ash and I were having breakfast, I told him about my Brazilian friend and our planned night out.

"We're going to Fabric tonight."

"Oh, that's a big one!"

"I think so. I'm more likely to be back tomorrow morning," I said, laughing.

"You sure will. But you're never going to be 25 again. This is it. Enjoy yourself, girl! You deserve it!"

Anyone who's in the scene knows what Fabric means. For the ones who don't, it's a famous London club known for being an incubator for DJs and a platform for artists. That year, it had been voted the number one club in the world in DJ Magazine's "Top 100 Clubs" survey.

What a night! That's all I can say. With the finest line-up, I danced like there was no tomorrow. But there was. And I woke up at Marcos' house with one of the biggest hangovers of my entire trip.

Of course, we ended up having "a thing" and decided to spend the next day together. I remembered what Ash said before I left:

"You're never going to be 25 again. This is it." So, once in London... make the most of it!

I just had to call Ash to let him know I'd only be back for dinner. He got it.

Apart from the hangover, our day turned out to be amazing. Marcos knew me, and took me to a place I simply couldn't miss: Camden Town.

Colorful and lively, Camden is a mix of old buildings, courtyards and open-air markets. You could feel creativity buzzing on the streets. For a creative person like me, that was Disneyland. I mean, *"where dreams come true"*.

In the 1970s, Camden was huge on alternative culture, always challenging the status quo. Pink Floyd and Ramones used to play there. Driven by the music scene and youth culture, the neighborhood had established itself as a stronghold for punks, bohemians and alternatives, the place where all tribes met.

No wonder it gained fame as one of the most modern places in town. Amy Winehouse, who we forever miss, was a distinguished resident of Camden. Attracting interesting and original people, it was also the birthplace of emerging fashion. Where real style was born.

We briefly passed by the canal, which was behind the Camden Town gallery. According to Marcos, it was one of the coolest places to meet friends on a sunny day. I imagined that happening, but that day was grey and freezing. So, we kept walking while he shared insider tips only people who live there got to know.

I was ready for some food when we got to Camden Market. Divine timing! I ordered an easy warm noodle soup (a little too spicy), in an attempt to cure my hangover once and for all. It worked. I was all spiced up!

And I still wanted to see Hyde Park before leaving London Town. Marcos was all in for that. As soon as we got to the city's heart, I knew, there and then: if I had chosen London, I would have spent a lot of time in those green gardens.

Marcos and I didn't have a future together. But real connections were not always about forever. I already knew that too well.

We sat on the grass, feeling nature's energy surrounding us. It was beautiful. Another reminder that there's nothing more powerful than truly living in the present and enjoying things for what they are.

Back at Canary Wharf, I also had my last dinner with Ash. I couldn't have had a better host for my time in London. I realized some encounters were just impossible to predict. They were true blessings to remind us we have so much to be grateful for — if we can only open ourselves to experience the unknown.

Next stop? Spain.

43. HOLA, BARCELONA!

As soon as I left the plane at BCN, my heart warmed up. I had no idea I'd be so taken by the Catalan capital, but something there really connected with me.

It may sound like an overstatement, but I believe that everyone should visit Barcelona at least once. Really, everyone. And I know there are so many beautiful places to see in the world, but Barcelona gives you all these different feelings.

I remember saying: "*I could totally live here*". And I could. I'd just need to sharpen up the language to do so. I like to communicate well.

Just for the record: Portuguese and Spanish are very distinct languages, although they can have some similarities and a lot of gringos get them mixed up. Now, Catalan was a totally different thing. Even compared to Aussie English.

Still, I often practiced my not-so-great *"Portunish"* (Portunhol, as we know it in Brazil). It was basically a self-made language that we, Brazilians, tended to speak very poorly, while showing our willingness to meet other *latinos* halfway in their culture. That's how we bond with *los hermanos*. And we get along just fine.

I only had four days to explore the Catalan-speaking city. Elisa, my Brazilian (almost Spanish) friend, had given me some amazing insider tips to make the most of them.

Here's a great tip for travelers: *find your locals. Wherever you go.*

Elisa knew I was a bit of everything. I'd want to see architecture and art just as much as I'd need to eat, drink and dance all night.

To make things easier, I booked a hostel just off La Rambla. I know, quite touristy. But it was the best way to truly experience all the layers of this bustling city that lived up to its reputation.

So, my Barcelona's to-do list was just like me: *simply complex*.

I often started with the simple things. An unpretentious long walk on La Rambla was all I needed to get a feel for the new surroundings. And that was truly a one-of-a-kind boulevard. It was hard not to get a little overwhelmed by the amount of action a single strip could hold. No wonder it's a landmark.

But, as most of you have probably already heard, you have to watch yourself not to be fooled by the not-so-well intended people of the world when in Barna. Every great place has its downfalls. Do your research, be street smart and stay safe. You'll be fine.

I must say that my Latina look had probably steered away a lot of these people. So, whilst I didn't walk alone at night (as everyone advised me), during the day, I did Barcelona my way.

And for a foodie like me, La Boqueria was non-negotiable. Just around the corner from my hostel, one of the most-visited attractions in Spain was once the Convent de Sant Josep monastery, which was destroyed by a fire.

The history-rich site was then converted into Barcelona's oldest market and had become a fundamental part of La Rambla's fabric for centuries.

While this picturesque market had a distinctive stained-glass Modernista gate and metal roof to engage all visitors at first sight, it was its interior that brought every single one of our senses to life.

Sure, La Boqueria is a feast to the eyes. But it also challenged us with loud noises and mixed smells. It could feel overwhelming and uncomfortable for some, especially while each one of us is trying to find personal space within a crowd.

My suggestion: *just surrender*. You'll be rewarded with the most exquisite mouth-watering tasting experience ever. I'd say give it a go and let La Boqueria swallow you into its own magic. I found it worth it.

And since I was starting to truly enjoy magic, I was instantly taken by this fantasy café hidden away in a small alley just off La Rambla. The Bosc de les Fades was really an alternate world waiting to be discovered. I went in, unpretentiously, and had what I recall to be my first real immersive experience. There were lights, sounds and a magical atmosphere that kept me there until later that night. I had found my new enchanted forest in the middle of a city. It was surreal.

On the second day, I went straight into Gaudí's world. His art meets nature architecture was just one of those things that got you thinking. The more you looked at it, the more you wondered what kind of mind could possibly imagine those buildings.

If you go deep into his story, Antoni Gaudí had a very contemplative childhood. His delicate health made him observe the very patterns of nature from an early age and he obviously connected with and followed them later in life as the very basis of his work.

Gaudí himself once said:

> "*Originality consists of going back to the origins.*"

That meant you had to strip back everything that the world threw at you if you ever decided to be original. Quite literally, go with your gut and do what's right for you. The risk of being disliked would always be there, even if you produced incredible work.

We all agree that opinions are often divided. Everyone is entitled to their own. But, whether or not one enjoys his aesthetic is subjective. Few are the creators, architects, artists, designers, and such, that have managed to transcend generations and are said to have built a piece of history.

Gaudí was an inconsistent student, but he showed some evidence of brilliance that opened doors for him. When he completed his studies at the School of Architecture in 1878, the Director, Elies Rogent, declared:

> "I do not know if we have awarded this degree to a madman or to a genius; only time will tell."

And time always tells. Gaudí was an undeniable genius ahead of his time. An absolute legend who had not only achieved the great feat of becoming a big part of a town's identity, but also the most universal architect that Barcelona had ever known.

Always respecting its laws, Gaudí did not copy anything from nature, but rather traced its course through a process of cooperation, and in that context, he created the most beautiful, sustainable and effective work possible through his architecture.

Given my time and budget restrictions, I chose four of his sites to visit: Basílica de la Sagrada Família (the most controversial one), Casa Milá (La Pedrera), Casa Batlló and Parc Güell.

I could write an essay on each one of them, but I'll keep my opinion to myself. I will only say this: very few places can make you feel something so profoundly meaningful like those four do. If I were you, I'd definitely experience them for myself.

After my deep dive into the art-chitecture of Gaudí, it was time for a sea change.

La Barceloneta was one of those places that integrated modern-city living with a unique historical feel. The narrow alleyways held old buildings, churches, stores and restaurants that looked just as they did 200 years ago. The contemporary beachfront was a breath of fresh air. A peaceful atmosphere that smelled of the Mediterranean Sea and welcomed locals and visitors with an uplifting energy.

And while it was a very touristy area, citizens maintained their old traditions. At sunset, you could still observe how the fishing boats unloaded their catches and then auctioned the fish. A perfect example of how old and new could still co-exist.

Of course, I couldn't leave Barcelona without paying a visit to the Parc de la Ciutadella.

The lush greenery breathed life into several species of birds, ducks, geese and other living creatures, including us humans. This is where you'd go to relax, have a picnic, play sports, take a walk or simply be with your very own nature.

Home to several notable buildings and spaces, one of the park's most emblematic attractions was the Monumental Waterfall. A collaboration between the architect Josep Fontsére and the young Antoni Gaudí. It was one of those beautiful man-made things that enhanced Mother Nature in a very gentle way.

After my cultural bucket list was done, I was almost feeling like a local. Cruising every night, enjoying tapas and sangrias. Not a care in the world. So, I decided to turn my party mode on and spent my last night in Barcelona at a beachfront club I can't remember the name of. All by myself. Honoring my mantra: *"dance like there is no tomorrow"*.

I must admit, I have a lifelong affair with dance floors. There's a magnetic force that brings us together into this otherworldly experience. It awakens my internal senses. It's liberating. And while I was there, contemplating the idea that a DJ actually saved my life so many times, I felt a strong pull towards this guy next to me. All by himself too.

Our eyes met and we started to create our own synchronized rhythm. We naturally started a conversation and it didn't take long until I tasted some very fine Spanish kisses. Dancing alone is amazing. But, sometimes, we've gotta dance with somebody.

Being young, wild, free — and single, gave me so much space to experiment in that area of my life. My heart was wide open. Love is an overflowing force. The more we give, the more we get. I always had this strong belief: *we should never hold love — even if it only lasts one night.*

We danced and kissed until the early hours of the morning. It was nearly 6am when I realized I had a 9:30am flight to Seville.

I kissed my "dance floor love" goodbye and caught a cab straight to the hostel. I had the quickest shower of my trip. Another cab driver was already waiting for me. I asked him to go as fast as possible to the airport and he took my request to heart. It was probably too fast for our own safety, but we do what we need to do. And we made it — just in time.

On the plane, my mind wandered in another one of my many deep reflections.

> *How amazing is this idea that we can have crazy wild nights with strangers that will stay in our memories forever and, at the same time, be a person who values long-term relationships for life.*

Nothing compares to spending time with our people. The ones who truly feel like home, no matter where we are in the world or in our lives. And I wouldn't miss the opportunity to see one of my people. Ever. I always made an effort. I'm an effortful person. I care.

Elisa and I were lifelong friends. We went to school, and to University, together. Our friendship spanned almost the entire two decades we were both alive at the time (and still does after another two decades too, just for the record).

She was one of the smartest women I'd ever met. No wonder she was doing a master's degree in Seville back in 2007 when she was just 25 and we said *"let's catch up in Europe"*.

I had no other reason to go to the capital of Andalusia, apart from her. And I'm forever grateful for one of the best surprises of my trip.

I can't find a better word to describe Seville than vibrant — as in having a real good vibe. You could feel the youthful spirit on the streets and the overall excitement literally took you in.

I tended to blend into new cultures quite easily, especially when I had local guides. So, between tapas and flamenco dancing, Elisa and I enjoyed our days together as real Sevillanas. It was an overdose of love and laughter. Pure bliss!

Our last night was December 24th. Yes, Christmas Eve. And, by then, both of us had come to terms with the fact that this sacred date could be celebrated in many different ways, anywhere in the world. We toasted to our freedom and the courage we had to pursue the lives we truly wanted for ourselves.

As I look back on those experiences, I realize that they really shaped who I am today.

From a young age, I unconsciously lived moment by moment. I had no idea of "the power of now" or any concept about "being present". I simply walked that talk.

And, as frivolous as my life may sound to some, I keep all those memories in my heart.

All the people I met, even for a brief moment, had an impact on me. I may not have evidence of it, but my soul does. And it keeps guiding me from its depth and experience, always forward and overflowing with love.

My European chapter was coming to an end. I had saved the best for last.

44. A LITTLE BRAZILIAN SURPRISE.

All my people in Brazil knew I was traveling that year. What they didn't know was that I had decided to kick off 2008 in Brazil. I only told one friend: Adriana. I trusted her to keep it a secret and asked if she could pick me up from the airport. We were both excited!

To this day, I still can't believe how I managed to keep that secret for so long. I guess it was the price I had to pay to see my mother's face when she saw me standing by her door. Love is what they call it. The things we do to turn words into actions.

Adriana did the same. She prepared this unpretentious get-together at my mum's house. It wasn't a stand-alone thing. They did visit my mum from time to time, but it was the 25th of December. The excuse my smart friend used was that my mum was probably missing me and it would be nice for my friends to pay her a visit and cheer her up on that date.

It was the best present I could have never asked for. Love is a gift that keeps on giving.

My Brazilian itinerary was back-to-back booked. I wanted to revisit a lot of the places that made me, including Garopaba, where all my madness began.

Gui, the friend I met in Australia (the one who told me to travel, remember?) agreed to go on this four-day road trip along Santa Catarina's coast with me. He was from São Paulo and we made a deal to literally stop at as many beaches as possible up until Santa Marta's Lighthouse in Laguna.

I hear a lot of people saying that men and women can't be friends, without benefits. I totally disagree. I have some amazing male friends who make my world so much better and often enlighten me with the best insights into our differences. Gui is one of them.

We hired a car and left on the 26th of December. Without a single booking. And everything worked out just fine. Maybe we were lucky. Or maybe there's still room for a little spontaneity after all.

In our endless chats between places, Gui often mentioned my personal mantra *"keep going"*. It stayed with him.

So, when we were at Ferrugem beach (yes, where I met Daniel), after one too many *"caipirinhas"* (a very strong traditional Brazilian drink), I made a decision: I'd get that little phrase tattooed somewhere. And guess what? Right next to the bar there was a tattoo parlour. How's that for a sign?

I went in, got a little piece of paper and a pencil, wrote it down with a tiny star on each side and said to the guy: "Can you do this?"

"Sure," he said. "Where?"

And just like that I got my mantra stamped on the back of my neck as a constant reminder to keep me going. People don't see it. It's not for them, it's for me. Mind you: I never got any other tattoo in my life. That was enough.

The next day we got to our final destination: Santa Marta's Lighthouse in Laguna.

It's definitely one of those special places on Earth. Maybe because it's still very raw and real, but also because you can watch one of the most breathtaking sunsets from a little mountain top — for free.

So, on the 31st we made it back to Itajaí to join a few of Gui's friends on a Brazilian style big white New Year's Eve. Never too many dance floors for a girl like me.

Between his friends and my friends, we had a massive party crew that stayed together until sunrise in this beautiful beachfront club. It was one of those moments you wanted to freeze in time. And it obviously messed up with a lot of my feelings.

I couldn't deny: I missed that part of my life. I missed that part of the world. The energy, the language, the culture. Everything. And I had to face it: I couldn't have it all.

To live in Australia any longer, I'd need to make peace with the fact that those things were never going to be part of my everyday life, if I chose to stay down under. And that was easier said than done.

I was also enjoying the comfort of my family home. It would have been so easy to stay within the boundaries of the familiar back then. But, once you see something, you can't unsee it. And I knew that the opportunity I had in front of me was too good to be wasted.

I couldn't stop The Clash from replaying in my mind: *"Should I stay or should I go?"*

The Paradox of Choice. Multiple options don't make it easier. It actually requires more effort to make a decision. The endless possibilities waiting to be revealed in front of someone could have a paralyzing effect. Isn't that ironic?

We all know decisions have power. But how do we know we're making the right ones for ourselves?

I had been given this incredible opportunity to spend another year (or many) in a country that I learned to love. I still wasn't finished with Australia.

Why settle when my heart wasn't settled yet?

If all that remains of us are our stories, I was in a good place.

I had an open road both ways. There was really no right or wrong answer. Both were good. Time was still on my side. I had a job, money, and freedom. It was nowhere near as risky as 2005.

Once again, Jack Johnson turned my feelings into a beautiful song:

> *"And all of these moments*
>
> *Just might find their way into my dreams tonight*
>
> *But I know that they'll be gone*
>
> *When the morning light sings*
>
> *And brings new things*
>
> *For tomorrow night you see*
>
> *That they'll be gone too*
>
> *Too many things I have to do"*

There was no combination of words I could put on the back of a postcard to say how much I loved and missed my family and friends. That's why I had to go there. In person.

> *"Love is the answer, at least for most of the questions in my heart*
>
> *Like why are we here? And where do we go?*
>
> *And how come it's so hard?*
>
> *It's not always easy and*

Sometimes life can be deceiving

I'll tell you one thing, it's always better when we're together"

But, our dreams are made out of real things. And I had real things waiting for me on the other side too. So, I took my shoebox of photographs with sepia-toned love and I boarded that plane. One. More. Time.

You can't be sitting, waiting, wishing your entire life. Sometimes, you just have to pack up and go to see what happens next.

45. THE NATURE OF THE UNEXPLAINABLE.

We, humans, often fear change. We also fear the idea of breaking the rules or deviating from the norm. Yet, we are all constantly changing, along with the world around us. And guess what? Breaking a number of rules for evolution's sake.

It's hard to explain something we can only experience. But I'll make an attempt to unpack some of my personal feelings about what it means to have a life of your own.

Each human being is unique and unrepeatable, right? We're one in however many billions scattered around this massive blue dot. Can we all agree on that? Good.

Now, some of us seek adventure, while others seek security. There are those who dream and those who can only believe when it happens. Those who like to start and those who can't wait to finish. We have givers and takers. We also have the ones who want to be, and a whole bunch who simply are.

With so many nuances, it's astonishing to me that we could all believe there's a norm or a standard for living. If we are all different, isn't it easier to just accept that no one fully fits into any made-up labels? Wouldn't it be better to just drop the script and all unrealistic expectations and let people be whoever they are?

I get it. We, humans, seek a sense of belonging. As Brené Brown has clearly articulated:

> "Belonging is being part of something bigger than yourself. But it's also the courage to stand alone, and to belong to yourself above all else."

To me, it's owning your uniqueness and taking it with you everywhere you go.

But, whenever asked about *"why live abroad?"*, I found myself unable to describe my real feelings. Words do not solve all the demands of language or communication. Some human issues do not fit into a simple argument, they go through the most human condition of all: *emotion*.

And perhaps it is precisely our current lifestyle that has suppressed our very human nature that is *"to feel"*. With increasingly repetitive routines and new technologies at our fingertips, we are all becoming a little machine-like without even taking notice. We have this false feeling that it is possible to control everything, but we have no control over the mysteries of our own creation.

Even though it's hard to admit, my biggest war remains between my mind and my heart. They often feel disconnected. I can be too smart for my own good. I also find myself believing things that don't make sense to my heart, just to feel accepted in a world that values facts more than feelings.

So, I created my own way of proving myself right (or wrong). I like to face the wilderness, to go out there, on the edge of my own fear, and let it swallow me. By doing this, I can register a new fact in my brain that I can actually do it. I can act, despite my fear.

It's just that to survive the unknown, we undress ourselves, layer by layer, until there's nothing left. Without protection, at first, the experience tends to cause fear, insecurity, and strangeness. It's terrifying, as close to death as you can get in life.

But, when we finally see our vulnerable and helpless essence, in the midst of so many strange and mixed people and feelings, we feel part of everything. And at the same time, part of nothing. And that is as confusing as it is empowering.

Maya Angelou put some magical words to this feeling:

> *"You are only free when you realize you belong no place - you belong every place - no place at all. The price is high. The reward is great."*

The price is high because you have to let go of your ego. You discover that you are much less important than you thought, because life goes on without you. It's not what we leave behind that scares us, it's what stays with us wherever we go.

In my case, I look at my life, and the two countries that support it, and realize that I am now two separate people. No matter how much my countries represent and fulfill different parts of who I am and what I like, no matter how much I have formed bonds with people I love in both places, no matter how much I feel truly at home in either place, I'll still be divided into two parts. Two identities. For the rest of my life.

What I discovered was that it was impossible to be in two places at once, and based on the choice I made, I found myself thinking about all the things I was missing in at least one of my homes.

For anyone who also experiences this, I'll expand a little.

Think about holidays, birthdays, weddings — every event you miss in either of your homes. They become a footprint of your unlived experiences. Until one day, you simply look back and realize that you were a part of almost nothing. In your absence, you yourself become a turned page in a place where you once belonged.

And the longer you stay in your new home, the deeper the changes will be, and they become more and more ingrained. "Home" stops being a specific place and becomes the search for a deeper meaning in your journey.

Your soul unconsciously begins to alternate desires to be here and there, to dive back into the person you were before you moved. There are those who stay so long that they can never return. It's a risk some people are willing to take. And there is nothing one can do to avoid it.

If there's one thing I can share about my personal experience, it's a very humbling conclusion: *there is simply no tested formula for this.*

I understand it may not sound very helpful at all, but it's a reality that will catch up with you at some point if you choose to go down this path yourself.

Living abroad (or even in a different city) is not for everyone. And it's better this way. We need people to stay, exactly where they were born. We need people to light fires and bloom flowers in their homelands. For the greater good of all.

Living in a new place can be beautiful and transformative, but it can also be frustrating and make people feel very unsettled. Getting on that plane (or even in a car or a bus) comes with a cost that a lot of people aren't willing to pay. It's not even a financial matter here. It's an emotional toll.

It takes courage to inhabit your skin and actively engage in a new world. But those who manage to transcend fear and judgment are blessed with a little secret for life: *you are your own home.*

And, if you feel the internal impulse and desire to take the risk of trying a new life for yourself, I must leave you with a tiny piece of wisdom to carry in your pocket:

No one can offer you a guarantee of anything. Only yourself.

Still, I'll say this:

Allow yourself to experiment. Go out there. Feel the fresh air of a simple walk along a new road. Learn other ways of being. Explore, within yourself, a new place — and the person you become in it. And don't beat yourself up if you don't like it. Go back and say: I tried. I no longer need to wonder. I found my place.

In my case, I like the idea of new and unknown places. I love the version of me that emerges when I am out in the wild. The openness, the kindness, the expansion of my soul beyond the streets I grew up in. I am at my most comfortable when I'm out in the world.

And the idea of relying only on myself to trust my feelings and surrender to every moment always appealed to me.

The beauty of being self-aware of your best qualities and your own limitations is that you can work with yourself to heal in your own way.

I am my biggest challenge — and I know it. But I have always been at peace with the crazy part of me. And as long as I could support myself, I could keep going.

Yep, the tattoo says it all.

46. BACK ON THE AUSSIE SIDE.

Living as a foreigner in a new country can be financially burdensome and limit our basic survival. Naturally, the dream of everyone who arrives fresh and intends to stay is to achieve a fundamental right: *the ability to live there legally, to work and pay the bills.*

On a practical level, this is something I always tell people: *make sure you can survive before risking everything.* It doesn't matter where you go, or what you do, you must have a roof over your head, food on your plate and optimal health. With those things checked, you can only grow.

Now, let's fully acknowledge that a large part of the world's population has not yet achieved these fundamental rights until this day. But we all should. And if we can help each other get there, we would witness a massive jump on our overall wellbeing as a collective.

Love one another enough to extend a hand when times get tough. We can all do it with a little help from a friend. Or a stranger.

I did experience a fair bit of struggle in my first years in Australia, but it was all manageable. All I needed to do was work. Hard. Sometimes, too hard. But doable.

In 2008, things started to change. I was probably in the most comfortable position I'd ever been in Aussie land. I had achieved PR (Permanent Residency) and had a full-time job. I pinched myself and thought: *"Am I all grown up now? What next?"*

There is great security in having Permanent Residence in your chosen country. It basically means having almost the same rights of a citizen, except the right to vote and obtain a passport. Other than that, most countries provide access to public health, education and even the possibility of taking some family members to live with you. Not to mention the endless new job opportunities that open up with the new status.

It gives you freedom to truly come and go and explore a much broader life out there. But it's not an easy thing to get. It takes years (literally) — and commitment.

In my case, I had to live in Australia for at least 12 months within a five-year period to not lose my Permanent Residency. So, to be truly free, one must acquire Citizenship.

In Australia, if you choose to go down this path, you'll undergo a general knowledge test about the country, which includes history, geography and cultural aspects. To call yourself Australian, you must embody the Aussie spirit and represent the nation in the best possible way.

If you pass the test, you'll be part of a Citizenship Ceremony where you sing the national anthem, swear loyalty to the Australian flag and receive the right to own your Australian Passport.

Then you can come and go as you please. You can even take a gap year to live elsewhere (which is a very Aussie thing to do).

I was entering my fourth year in Australia and becoming one of those *"I have been here for a while"* kind of people. Isn't it funny how we become the very things we never thought we would be? And there I was, even considering a citizenship path for myself.

And while my career was going in a great direction, the missing feeling was still there. I had no idea what I was missing, to be honest. I just felt "not enough".

It didn't take long for me to notice that the emptiness was coming from my relationships. Or the lack of them.

I was away from my family and close friends. Nothing (and nobody) in my life was permanent or lasting. I became quite used to being alone.

For over a year, I had nothing but superficial flings with a few guys. I accepted that casual sex and zero commitment was all I could get. I found it very hard to trust anyone, but me. I had become so unattached that it scared me. It was almost as if my heart had gone numb. I completely forgot what my feelings were for.

I couldn't understand why, but I was curious to find out.

And when we ask, we receive — whatever we need.

47. REDEFINING LOVE.

In my search for what love was, I received a timely email with a chronicle by Martha Medeiros, a wonderful Brazilian writer, that made me think about what I actually believed love should be and why it was such a messed-up concept for me.

Here's the translation:

> *"They made us believe that love, real love, only happens once, usually before the age of 30. They didn't tell us that love is not rationed nor arrives by appointment.*
>
> *They made us believe that each of us is half of an orange, and that life only makes sense when we find the other half. They didn't tell us that we were born whole, that no one in our lives deserves to carry the responsibility of completing what we lack: we grow through ourselves. If we're in good company, it's just faster.*
>
> *They made us believe in a formula called "two in one", two people thinking alike, acting alike, that this was what worked. They didn't tell us that this has a name: annulment. That only as individuals with their own personalities can we have a healthy relationship.*

> *They made us believe that marriage is mandatory and that untimely desires must be repressed. They made us believe that the beautiful and thin are more loved, that those who have little sex are old-fashioned, that those who have a lot of sex are unreliable, and that there will always be an old slipper for a crooked foot. Nobody told us that old slippers also have their value, since they don't hurt us, and that there are more crooked heads than feet.*
>
> *They made us believe that there is only one formula for being happy, the same for everyone, and those who escape it are condemned to marginality. They didn't tell us that these formulas go wrong, frustrate people, are alienating, and that we could try other, less conventional alternatives.*
>
> *Oh, they also didn't tell us that no one is going to tell us all this. Each one of us will have to find out for ourselves. And then, when you are very much in love with yourself, you will become very happy and fall in love with someone else."*

Wow, that was so refreshing! It was almost like a new insight from the Prophecy.

Someone had found the perfect words to my unspoken feelings of disconnection from love. Thank you, Martha, for making it so clear. Your words, at that time, somehow saved my life.

I suddenly realized that they (whoever they were) made us believe so many unreasonable things that it became very hard to question the truths of the world.

The only way to undo the damage of my limiting beliefs was to find a truth of my own.

Deep inside, I knew I could never fully drop my heart into someone else's hands. I had done that too many times and it never worked. I was always the one left with the broken pieces of my own heart to mend.

And with my *"keep going"* attitude, I just kept moving on. I always seemed to find the right people for every stage of my life. Just like in the Prophecy.

Maybe I was starting to grasp what people now call *"flow"*. *Be like water, my friend.* You know, those things. I was too good at letting things go. What I never knew was how to keep them. Should I drop the "going" if I wanted something to "keep"? Maybe.

But, first, I wanted to figure out love for all that it was worth. Such a loaded word. Probably the one that carries the heaviest weight in any language. A big feeling word.

Love is not just a feeling though. It's kind of an art. And, like any art, inspiration is not enough, it also takes a lot of work and consistency to master it.

The best place to find love is wherever you are. Often, the way is not out — it's in. It's just hard to really believe in that. Or feel real love for ourselves. Especially when we're young.

But, when love is not served to us, we are allowed to let it go. Close some doors. Not because of pride or arrogance, but because they no longer lead anywhere. We haven't found love there.

What we can't stop doing is opening new doors, even if we're terrified of what we may find on the other side. We can't let our previous experiences run the new show. It's a mind game that keeps playing on and on. And it often sabotages our evolution.

> *What good is it for me to fear what has already happened?*
>
> *And how many things do we lose for the mere fear of losing?*

Morcheeba has a beautiful song about that. I quoted it earlier in the book, and I will quote it again because it's always on replay:

"Fear can stop you loving. Love can stop your fear."

Yes, falling in and out of love can make us quite cynical. With all the disappointment and sadness we face running towards it, it's hard to believe that love can do us any good. But the problem isn't love in itself. It's how much responsibility we place onto other people when it's something we simply are.

"You're frozen when your heart's not open."

Madonna knew this and wrote one of the most beautiful definitions of love for us to sing out loud.

"Love is a bird, she needs to fly. Let all the hurt inside of you die."

We must wisely accept the fact that the path is full of contradictions. There are moments of joy and despair, confidence and lack of faith, but it's worth moving forward.

Love is a real thing — and it lives in all of us. Love is also a shapeshifter. It has infinite forms.

Giving too much love is never a sign of weakness. It's a sign of abundance.

You only regret the things you didn't do.

You'll only ever regret the love you didn't give.

It took me years to learn this. I am still learning.

So, forget about what they told you. Be the love you search for.

Be love, wherever you are.

Live now what others will only have the courage to live in the future.

You'll thank yourself for it.

Too many things end up dying inside of us.

Love should not be one of them.

And just like that, I decided I was ready to give love another chance — if it ever came my way.

48. WHAT ARE WE LIVING FOR?

As soon as I got back to Perth, in January 2008, I heard some heartbreaking news.

Heath Ledger, a Perth born, Australian actor, who was only three years older than me, had his life cut short. He was 28 years old. Too young, too talented and with way too much love for life to leave our world. Especially having a two-year-old daughter.

Grief took over the entire nation. It just seemed unfair. He was one of the most brilliant actors of our generation. And a genuine good-hearted human being. Why check out so early?

I had only watched two of his movies: "10 things I hate about you" and "Brokeback Mountain", and I became a fan.

In "10 things" he made me fall in love with him, just like Kat (the main character in the movie) did. Her strong, challenging personality resembled my own. She normally would come across as a know-it-all and a snob, but she had a kinder, more vulnerable side that people didn't often see, unless they took time to explore. She wore an armor of protection to hide just how frightened she was of falling in love and being seen. *Aren't we all?*

I had repeated her classic speech in my mind so many times (and even created my own inner dialogue lines for specific guys along my life):

> *"I hate the way you talk to me, and the way you cut your hair. I hate the way you drive my car, I hate it when you stare. I hate your big, dumb combat boots and the way you read my mind. I hate you so much it makes me sick — it even makes me rhyme. I hate the way you're always right. I hate it when you lie. I hate it when you make me laugh — even worse, when you make me cry. I hate it when you're not around. And the fact that you didn't call. But mostly I hate the way I don't hate you — not even close, not even a little bit, not even at all."*

It made me think of all the times I tried to hate the guys who hurt me, but I couldn't. Not even close, not even a little bit, not even at all.

"I wish I knew how to quit you" is one of those lines that I wish I had written. It's the most famous line from Brokeback Mountain. It makes us feel the entangled love and pain that Jack holds in his heart for "wrongly" wanting Ennis. And, regardless of your sexual orientation, we all know it's humanly impossible to fight our feelings. Even when we try so hard to do it.

Sometimes we get "stuck in a moment" and need to find our way out of it. Or, perhaps, simply surrender our way in.

Brokeback Mountain has to be one of the most influential films of our times. It was 2005 and they turned Annie Proulx's book into a masterpiece. You don't have to be LGBTQIA+ to support it. Like you don't have to be a woman to acknowledge we deserve equal value. These are just human rights.

Art can give so much more meaning to these equations than any discussion could. Imagine if we all learned to read between all these very blurred lines? Think about it. We surely would have space for a lot more colors than just black and white.

Heath received an Oscar nomination for playing Ennis in Brokeback Mountain, but he didn't win. Ironically, his award recognition only came from his iconic role as The Joker in Christopher Nolan's *Dark Knight*, released in July that year. He was posthumously awarded the Best Supporting Actor Oscar for a memorable performance that transcended his untimely death and achieved legendary status.

Almost 20 years after his passing, Ledger's performance as The Joker has proven to be groundbreaking in terms of redefining and unlocking the dramatic possibilities that could be explored within the superhero film genre. Many films have tried and failed to match the gritty realism of The Dark Knight and Ledger's unforgettable gift.

Portraying a variety of roles, from romantic heroes to tragic characters, Heath had an internal wisdom about his role as an actor in society: *"I feel like I am wasting my time if I repeat myself"*.

He described in a very articulate way this tendency people have to label you for something:

> *"People always feel compelled to sum you up, to presume that they have you and can describe you. That's fine. But there are so many stories inside of me and a lot I want to achieve outside of one flat note."*

What a wise soul! Yet, he struggled with his inability to be happy with his work. *Does anyone relate?* He once said:

> *"I feel the same thing about everything I do. The day I say, 'It's good' is the day I should start doing something else."*

I might have to challenge you on that, Mr. Ledger. It's so important for us, human beings, to learn how to celebrate ourselves for our own achievements. We fight too hard for the things we believe in to simply discredit them. We're changing that as I write this.

Creatives are on an evolutionary roll. We're healthier now. You'd be very proud of us.

The other thing I admired about Heath Ledger was his ability to draw from multiple sources of inspiration to create something truly unique. For instance, he based his Joker performance on various punk influences, most notably Malcolm McDowell's sociopathic character Alex from Stanley Kubrick's 1971 dystopian crime film "A Clockwork Orange" and the 1962 Anthony Burgess novel of the same name.

Like Alex, Ledger's Joker is a mass-murdering psychopath who is devoid of empathy and seemingly aspires only to, in the words of Alfred in "The Dark Knight", watch the world burn.

One of the most frightening aspects of his portrayal of The Joker is the character's seemingly complete lack of a typical criminal motivation. In the words of Ledger's Joker, his reign of terror isn't about money but rather making a statement.

Great performances like that should only stay on screen. Please do not copy that in the real world. We certainly don't need any Jokers around.

And, as sad as that was, I find it fascinating how death evokes an urgency for living.

None of us are born with the awareness of our expiry date. Still, everyone goes through life at a different pace. *Have you noticed?*

It surely isn't the norm for someone to die at 28, having achieved so much in life. Heath Ledger was one of those people who had a rare maturity beyond his years.

I suspect our souls know something we don't. And they keep pushing us on our individual paths, asking that we trust their guidance as much as the timing of our lives.

It's this underlying soul intelligence that guides us to do the things we're meant to do in order to avoid wasting an entire lifetime. Heath's soul knew this. And it masterfully guided him to be this bright, fast comet running back to the sun.

He was often praised for his creativity, seriousness, and intuition. In his own words, acting was about harnessing "the infinite power of belief", thus using belief as a tool for creating. I'm with you on that, Mr. L.

He also liked to wait between jobs so that he would start creatively hungry on new projects and always follow his intuition. Side note: he was not all "woo-hoo" about it.

Marc Forster, who directed Ledger in *Monster's Ball*, complimented him as taking the job "very seriously", being disciplined, observant, understanding, AND intuitive.

There you go: Intuition is a superpower. Especially when combined with a realistic view of the world and focused action. To the very skeptical people out there, please do not underestimate or discredit intuition. Even if you don't agree with us.

Christopher Nolan has also expressed his amazement over the actor's working process, genuine curiosity and charisma:

> "I've never felt as old as I did watching Heath explore his talents."

It's a shame that Heath wasn't able to acknowledge how great he was and how much he inspired us. Still, we all know the role he played best: *himself*.

With an eye-opening start to the year, I felt 2008 was already smelling a lot like change. At least for me.

I was starting to feel unsettled. Again. That "itch" to do something different. *Why can't she stand still?* I could almost hear external voices questioning my inner knowing.

I couldn't answer. Maybe because my soul was born to move. I was born for the dance of change. If change was precisely what moved me, then when I didn't change, I was dying. And guess what? I wanted to live. As many lives as I possibly could.

Just like Heath Ledger, *"I feel like I am wasting my time if I repeat myself"*. You don't need to be an actor to play different roles. Life is an open stage. Go pick your favorite ones and put on your best show.

I guess there was a prophetic hidden truth behind my graduation song's choice: I definitely preferred to be an *"evermoving metamorphosis"* than having an old-fashioned opinion about everything. But let me tell you, it's not always easy to stay true to that.

The longer we live, the harder it becomes to recreate all the characters we have been. It's also hard to keep up with everyone who played such fundamental roles along with our many different versions.

For some strange reason, stability never appealed to me as much as the thrill of challenging myself over and over again. I admire stable people though. Often, I almost envy them. I wish I could be as happy as they are with routine, but I'm not.

As in every long story, it is necessary to identify the theme that moves it along. The single drive that remains within us, in every situation. The very concept of our lives. The thing we always go back to when we feel lost. To me, that's love.

You're either walking into love or towards fear. You must make a choice about the feeling that leads your life. My choice was very clear.

And since the Universe is aligned with my deepest desires, I soon saw "The Sign". And I started an internal review of myself.

49. REALITY CHECK.

With a full awareness that *"I still hadn't found what I was looking for"*, I decided to make an inventory of my own negative tendencies to see how I could help myself. I know, a terrible idea. But here it goes:

#1 Co-dependency

My default mode was to play with fire to (try to) avoid abandonment. I relied on external approval to validate myself. That could be from anybody, really. Family, friends, lovers, co-workers. My receiving love language was *"words of affirmation"*. Not surprisingly.

But, at least, I knew. And that led me to too many meaningless interactions with guys who always used the right words but never followed with aligned action.

Britney Spears was right on the money when she wrote:

> *"With a taste of your lips, I'm on a ride*
>
> *You're toxic, I'm slippin' under*

With a taste of a poison paradise

I'm addicted to you

Don't you know that you're toxic?"

No, they didn't. And neither did I. So, we kept going, being toxic to each other. Until we couldn't go any more.

#2 Binge eating

I could blame the stars (after all, I'm a Taurus), but the truth is: number one and two are correlated. I relied on food to fill this giant void that existed in me. I often ate a lot more than I needed, especially after a party (where my void usually grew into a big black hole). As a result, I set off on this on-and-off battle with my weight throughout my entire life. With low self-esteem as a side effect. Yep, we're getting real here. It was devastating.

#3 Anxiety

I wasn't even aware of this word back then. I just had zero patience to wait for anything to happen. All I wanted was to get over and done with things ASAP. Almost as if I had to rush through life before it all ended.

Maybe the whole Millennium Bug had bugged me. And since I survived after 2000, when we all should have ended, my new mode of action was to hurry through life like a maniac, too scared *"to miss a thing"*, with the Aerosmith song from the 1998 Armageddon movie stuck in my head.

Therapy would have done wonders here, I believe. But we were not into that.

#4 Insecurity

A constant feeling of inadequacy and uncertainty. The belief of not being good enough.

Again, it's linked to number three and can make us anxious about our goals, relationships, and our ability to handle certain situations. No safety net for my feelings either.

Let's face it: it wasn't a pretty picture. And I fully understood that it would take all of me to cross that huge deep valley of hopelessness if I truly wanted to grow up. And, in all fairness, it was all I ever wanted. To grow up.

Surprisingly, insecurity is the only path to growth. Facing danger is the only way to grow. Accepting the challenge of the unknown is the only way to grow.

You read it right. That's why they call it *"growing pains"*. We underestimate how much it actually hurts to reach higher levels in our existence. Life is phased for a good reason. You can't throw a kid out in the world without any training. It's fatal. We all know it.

So, becoming aware of our limitations is just another one of those boundaries we must cross on our way to "owning our own greatness". *The brighter the light, the darker the shadow.* Read that as many times as you need.

Right about that time when I was starting to get real with myself, I learned a super effective "life hack" (that wasn't even a thing back in the day, but I'll use contemporary language to help you here). I started using my own negativity as ammunition for growth. I channeled anger for the greater good of me. *How badass was that?!*

Without our belief in them, destructive thoughts self-destruct. They too are co-dependent. They need our validation. So, teaching them to stay put becomes another superpower. "You're welcome." we tell them politely. "We're not your biggest fan, but we respect your opinion. The final word is ours though. Is that okay?"

And the more we're exposed to something, the better we become at it. So, it doesn't matter how many times we get attacked by destructive thoughts; we keep improving our reaction to them. We become gentler every time.

It's a beautiful thing to watch someone battling their own demons with grace. Pay attention when you find them. So heavenly human.

I know this may not sound that beautiful, but I promise it wasn't all doom and gloom. Like any other human being, I had my fair share of positive tendencies too. Balance as we call it.

Often people described me as the most hopeful optimist they ever met. And I was.

Maybe it was part of my coping mechanism. If things weren't great, they could only get better, right? And they normally did. I always found a way to turn horrible things around almost like magic.

"It's not how many times you fall, it's how well you learn to get back up."

With enough analysis of my past, I was ready for the future.

"Hey girl, hey boy, Superstar DJs, here we go".

You got it! The Chemical Brothers were in town for the Future Music Festival, a huge event that toured every major Australian capital. And they were in great company: John Digweed, Sven Vath, Roger Sanchez, Eddie Halliwell, Shapeshifters, Markus Schulz and Laidback Luke.

A stellar line-up. All in one day. Sunshine and good music were my safe remedies, remember? Nothing beat a summer music festival to bring all my senses back to life.

I was about to dance my way "out of a funk" by the Swan River and let myself get hit with a high dose of those "happiness hormones". It was as if another dream I didn't even know I had just came true.

And with it, an urge for expansion.

I was back on the fully hopeful bandwagon. And I knew something had to change.

Perth was a great place to be, but I didn't see enough room for growth. Let's just say that I was settling for what came my way rather than chasing my real dream.

I still wanted a career in advertising and the most isolated Australian capital just wasn't the ideal place for that to happen. The agencies were not there.

That "itch" started to poke me again. *Where can we go? Sydney?*

It was always an option, but for some reason my heart never responded.

I started to research other cities. Things were also changing in the world, and that included the way we connected with people.

I still had my Facebook account for foreign affairs. A lot of people were joining that. I guess it was the start of the social revolution. You could make friends with people you never met in real life. It sounded bizarre, but also amazing. It opened up infinite possibilities.

And I knew that's where it could get dangerous for me. The Paradox of Choice, remember? I must avoid too many. Less is more.

But life has a funny way of helping us out. If you are old enough, you may also remember this feature called *"poke"* on the earlier version of Facebook. It was kind of a first move, something like: "Hey, I thought you were interesting. Wanna talk?"

I didn't have many connections, but I got quite a few random pokes. I ignored most of them. They were a bit creepy. But a particular one caught my attention. *"Love your smile"*. It was cute. It felt like a match. Maybe that's where they got the whole dating app idea from. *Who knows?*

Anyway, I responded, and we started talking.

Justin was an English-Australian who lived in Melbourne. We went from Facebook friends to speaking on the phone — daily. It was getting serious. It felt odd, but also heartwarming.

I really loved talking to him. He seemed to get me on a much deeper level than most people. Perhaps because we didn't engage physically. We were taking our time to learn about each other and the things that made us tick, rather than letting our animal hormones run the show. We got closer and closer, until he came to Perth and we met in real life.

I wrote a little story about it to all my friends (the famous e-mails). It went something like this.

50. FINDING MR. RIGHT.

I know, what a cheesy title. But that was me, at 26, with my very soft spot for rom-coms. Please forgive me. I still love rom-coms though. I'm a hopeless romantic. I can't help myself. Yep, it's cliché for a reason. People relate — and we're people.

Once upon a time there was a girl who lived between dreams and realities. To be fair, more dreams than realities. But she always believed that each dream was a future reality waiting its turn to breathe life. And if we believe in our hearts, any dream can come true.

One of her many dreams was to find love. But not any kind of love. Real, everlasting love. She wanted a man to sweep her off her feet and show her that, despite any heartbreak, love always wins.

That's when a Melbourne guy showed up. Justin. He was traveling to Indonesia for work and made a stopover in Perth on his way back home. After the longest two weeks ever, she was finally going to meet him. In the flesh.

At 6am she went to the airport to pick him up. As it happens, the flight was delayed, but she had a book: "The Celestine Prophecy". Yep, she was still trying to make sense of all the insights and kept on re-reading it until it was all clear. A bit nerdy, but that's her. Read it until you get it.

So, she sat down and waited. Impatiently. One eye on the book, the other on Arrivals. When she finally let go, and focused on reading, there he was: Mr. Just(in) Right.

They had never seen each other before. He simply dropped everything he had on the floor and picked her up, spun her around and gave her the biggest kiss ever. Yep, the cheesiest romcom moment you could script. Right there, in real life. As if it wasn't enough, he starts singing their chosen "theme song":

"You are just too good to be true

Can't take my eyes off you

You will be like heaven to touch

I wanna hold you so much"

It was one of her favorite songs. The Lauryn Hill version.

She drove him home and they started exploring each other little by little. Mr. Right felt very right. They had so much fun together. She showed him why she loved Perth and he understood completely. It was beautiful, warm and fun. Plus, she had a lot of friends and an expansive life.

After a dream weekend came true, he left. And planted a little seed in her mind: she should give Melbourne a chance.

In her heart it was yes, but her mind literally froze. She didn't like the cold. At all. But she liked him. A lot. So, she decided to pack up and check it out, right in the middle of winter. It would be a love or hate situation, but, you know, *"screw it, let's do it"*.

On arrival, at 6am, it wasn't cold, it was freezing. But that was just the beginning. Between them, things were only heating up.

He prepared a full-on tour to show her why he loved Melbourne. And he was determined to convince her that she could be happy there too.

Victoria's capital was aesthetically pleasing to most people's eyes. The European feel and the winter clothes were totally different from Perth. But Melbourne had multiple personalities. It brought art, fashion, food, coffee, design, shopping, and everything in between, together, in a culture of its own that was both vibrant and easy-going. It's very hard to explain. One must experience it to understand.

Quality was another thing that stood out there. Everyone in Melbourne gave their all to deliver unprecedented experiences. It was impressive. They built their culture around that, since the weather was never gonna draw people in. You could feel the effort to make things great.

So, there's this special flair for all things fine. And more than enough contrast to make it overly interesting. Ironically, she really warmed up to a city that had never even crossed her mind before.

She thought to herself:

> *I could totally live here.* And that's exactly what Justin wanted her to do. Her artistic soul whispered: *Thanks for showing me a little more of this beautiful world. It's inspiring. I feel alive.*

It was probably too big of a city for a small-town girl though. A little overwhelming too. But what could be better for growth than a bigger place? Still, it felt like a big move.

Justin knew she needed to feel safe to take a risk like that. And that's all he tried to do: to make her feel safe. The whole time.

As part of his actions, he introduced her to his entire family which was another very big move. Their general comment was:

"She must love you to be introduced to everyone just like that".

They were right. She really did. It was better to do it that way than to find out later that she didn't belong there. In the early days, one can always run away. *Runaway Bride anyone?*

But he had a really nice family. They were all lovely and made her feel very comfortable and welcomed.

After a whole week of getting to know Melbourne, she went back to Perth. The sunshine tested her will. *Can we really have it all?* She kept asking herself.

She knew the answer. *We can. But, sometimes, only one thing at a time.*

51. BIG DREAMS, BIG MOVES.

In life, you'll never have a one-hundred percent guarantee of anything. Full control is an illusion.

But, if that's the case, how can big life decisions be made?

Well, there are no rules. You can follow manuals or other people's stories and opinions.

I always preferred to use my personal experience, practical research and intuition to evaluate risk. More often than not, I simply faced the imminent dangers of the great unknown. A lot of people avoid this, but they also miss out on a lot of the fun.

Love takes courage. Brené Brown has this amazing question that helps people to understand that vulnerability is courage. It goes like this:

> *"Can you name one act of courage that you've ever been involved in or witnessed that did not involve uncertainty, risk and emotional exposure?"*

We all know the answer.

I am comfortable with my vulnerability. I have a very brave heart. Tapping into my previous experience, I found that everything I ever did up to this point was worth the risk.

You may disagree with my view of life. I don't need you to change.

But, when my heart says *"go"*, I follow. Even if my results turn out to be completely different than I imagined. It's the only way I can stay true to myself — and evolve.

I believe our stories are the very thing that make our lives interesting. And, unless you have such a perfect storyline that you can stay there from beginning to end, without any real change, you must be prepared to live more than one story in a lifetime.

Or maybe I'm just one of those impractical people with an unshakeable faith. *Who knows?*

But Brené also says that:

"If you know how it's going to turn out, it's not courage."

She's right. Here is where I can safely state that my courage was always greater than my fear. In retrospect, all I ever did in life was to show up and let things unfold.

So, I packed 130 kilograms worth of "stuff" I probably didn't even need and sent it to Melbourne. I literally doubled my belongings in Australia. But those were the things I was holding on to, to make me feel safe.

For someone who moved to the other side of the world, moving to the other side of the country felt slightly easier. I was also no longer alone. Justin was waiting for me.

Did I have everything figured out? Of course not. But I knew I could trust one person: myself. If things didn't go as planned, I would surely find my way out.

So, I wrote that beautiful story to all of my people to let them know I was still me.

Their response? Nothing short of love and support.

Here are some of their replies:

> *"Oh, that's so beautiful! I got emotional. Missing you, crazy girl who moved to Australia! You're right: you can never make a mistake when you follow your heart! And even if you make a mistake, it's always worth it! And if it wasn't worth it, you can tell it later and laugh once it's over."*

> *"My dreamy sister-in-law, this was a home run! I loved, loved, loved your crazy story! Just keep loving! Everything will be alright."*

> *"I'm in the office reading your email with an unexplainable happy smile on my face. It's so good to know that a friend so far away is happy. Keep smiling!"*

> *"Carol, you are already 'love' by nature. You just found someone to share it with because otherwise you would die of love, right?"*

> *"Carol, I showed your email to my mother. She said that, regardless of whether love lasts or not, for you to publish the story. She said that you should become a writer. Her bet is that it will be a bestseller."*

I knew, there and then, that what made me so strong and determined wasn't my ability to fly. It was the size and strength of my roots. I was grounded in love. Pure unconditional love.

You're only free when you know you have somewhere to go back to. It doesn't have to be a physical place. Sometimes all you need is your people. The ones who will be there for you, no matter where you are.

In the current world, we hear people saying that everyone is bad and they just envy you. This way of thinking makes me squirm a little. I disagree. Every time I made a real big move towards one of my dreams, I felt the love. The real ones were always there cheering for me. Some of them worried, of course. But my clarity made them believe I could do it.

We didn't have social media back then, but I always found a way to keep in touch, to be present and to stay close to the ones I love — no matter the distance.

How can I not believe in the good in people?

They are all still in my life. And most importantly: they're still helping me to stay alive.

They may pray, cross their fingers, kick my ass, listen to my BS. Whatever is needed.

They know I'm real. And they are real too.

This book is dedicated to everyone who stayed with me in the ups and downs of my life.

You know who you are. You are my world. And you give me an unshakeable faith in humanity.

Thank you for loving me just the way I am.

Yes, I may be crazy, but we all know this: *love always wins.*

52. YOU MAY SAY I'M A DREAMER, BUT I'M NOT THE ONLY ONE.

When Martin Luther King said *"I have a dream"*, he was inviting others to dream it with him, inviting them to step into his story.

A new story, shared in a vulnerable and open way, can give us a sense of possibility. It's an invisible force which pulls us forward. We imagine other ways of thinking about our world and our futures.

Imagining new futures makes it more possible. When we see the world differently, we begin behaving differently, we step into new stories. That's how change effectively happens. The stories keep changing.

> *"The most unrealistic person in the world is the cynic, not the dreamer. Hope only makes sense when it doesn't make sense to be hopeful."*

That's Paul Hawken. *How profoundly clever is that?* It's also a nice reminder for current times.

> *"You know what the issue is with this world? Everyone wants a magical solution to their problem, and everyone refuses to believe in magic."*

Again, that's not me. It's Alice in Wonderland. But in a world where magic formulas are being sold off the shelf, it rings true, doesn't it?

And there is more. From Walt Disney. The man who made a dream world come true had a very realistic take on what "being a dreamer" really means:

> "I dream, I test my dreams against my beliefs, I dare to take risks, and I execute my vision to make those dreams come true."

Spot on. I've been to his world. It's very real — and fun.

Liza Minelli, the legendary actress, has a more rebellious view (as we, women, tend to have):

> "Dream on it. Let your mind take you to places you would like to go, and then think about it and plan it and celebrate the possibilities. And don't listen to anyone who doesn't know how to dream."

Sometimes we have to mute the naysayers for our own good. Let their beliefs limit only themselves.

There's also Oscar De la Renta, the Dominican fashion designer, who perfectly articulates the correlation between a vision and a dream:

> "Things never happen by accident. They happen because you have a vision, you have a commitment, you have a dream."

You can read that backwards: you have a dream, you have a commitment, you make your vision happen. On purpose. Get it?

And last, but not least, I'll stand by the Aerosmith song that inspired the title of this book:

> *"Dream on, dream on, dream on. Dream until your dream comes true."*

Repetition plays a trick too.

"Fake it until you make it" really means *"practice until you learn"*.

Don't let your dreams be just dreams. Take action. Now.

> *Keep living, keep loving, keep writing, keep dancing, keep changing, keep working on the things that matter to you. Keep surprising yourself and shocking the world with what can come to life through you. We need babies too. Mothers and fathers are real artists in life-making. Never underestimate them. Life needs life. We see you. We celebrate you. Your work matters.*

Your real duty is to save your own dream. Whatever that is.

Your soul will thank you for that.

Consistency is key. Do your own keeping. Just keep going.

You know that change you want to see in the world?

It's up to you to make it happen.

And don't worry, life will tell you when you hit *"the end"*.

Until then, just remember: *nobody can play your role.* There's only one you.

To all the self-published writers out there, good on you! It's a hell of a ride!

But we can't stop. And we won't stop.

We were born at this time for a reason.

We can be whatever we give ourselves the power to be. And, right now, we need life-lovers, peace-makers, wound-healers, trail-blazers, bridge-builders and truth-sayers.

We need dreamers who believe this isn't the end: *it's just another new beginning.*

Let's rewrite humanity's story. And, this time, let's make it beautiful.

I'll leave you with a remix from Nelson Mandela's legendary quote:

> *EVERYBODY WILL TELL YOU IT'S IMPOSSIBLE.*
>
> *UNTIL **YOU SHOW THEM HOW** IT'S DONE.*

Here you go: I'm a writer, after all.

Thank you for reading until the end.

The dream goes on.

BIBLIOGRAPHY

Real life interviews, quotes and chronicles:

Extract from Dave Grohl's interview

Extracts from Troy Brooks, Roy Powers and Neco Padaratz's interviews at the 2005 Salomon Masters.

Extract from a Steve Jobs speech

Rumi quote

They made us believe, a chronicle by Martha Medeiros published at Brazilian Zero Hora newspaper

Extracts from Heath Ledger's interviews

Extract from Marc Forster's interviews

Extract from Christopher Nolan's interviews

Extracts from Brené Brown's interviews

Books:

'wild spirit, soft heart', butterflies rising

Daring Greatly, Brené Brown

The Celestine Prophecy, James Redfield

The Alchemist, Paulo Coelho

Diary of a Magus, Paulo Coelho

Featured Song Lyrics:

Down Under, Men At Work

Don't stop believin', Journey

Times like this, Jack Johnson

Mas, que nada!, Jorge Ben

Mr. Jones, Counting Crows

Falling in love again, Eagle-Eye Cherry
Save tonight, Eagle-Eye Cherry
Rock and roll all night, Kiss
It's a long way to the top (if you wanna rock 'n' roll), AC/DC
Champagne Supernova, Oasis
Master Blaster, Stevie Wonder
Free, Donavon Frankenreiter
Ironic, Alanis Morrissette
Wild World, Cat Stevens (Yusuf Islam)
Diamonds on the inside, Ben Harper
On a clear day, The Beautiful Girls
Morning Sun, The Beautiful Girls
Learn Yourself, The Beautiful Girls
London Still, The Waifs
The Waitress, The Waifs
Let me be, Xavier Rudd
Fortune Teller, Xavier Rudd
Things meant to be, Xavier Rudd
Flake, Jack Johnson
Never Know, Jack Johnson
Fortunate Fool, Jack Johnson
Dreams be dreams, Jack Johnson
Carolina, Seu Jorge
Fear and Love, Morcheeba
Praise You, Fat Boy Slim
Metamorfose Ambulante (Evermoving Metamorphosis), Raul Seixas
Walk Away, Ben Harper
LK (Carol Carolina Bela), DJ Marky, XRS, Stamina MC

Sambassim, DJ Patife

At the river, Groove Armada

My friend, Groove Armada

I see you babe, Groove Armada

Better together, Jack Johnson

Frozen, Madonna

Toxic, Britney Spears

Can't take my eyes off you, originally written in 1967 by Bob Crewe and Bob Gaudio and recorded by Frankie Valli and many artists

Featured Movies:

Dundee Crocodile (1986), directed by Peter Faiman

Lost in translation (2003), directed by Sofia Coppola

Marie Antoinette (2006), directed by Sofia Coppola

The Fabulous Destiny of Amélie Poulain (2001), directed by Jean-Pierre Jeunet

Moulin Rouge (2001), directed by Baz Luhrmann

10 things I hate about you (1999), directed by Gil Junger

Brokeback Mountain (2005), directed by Ang Lee

Dark Knight (2008), directed by Christopher Nolan

ACKNOWLEDGEMENTS

To all my ancestors for creating the roots I was grounded on. I stand on your shoulders every single day. Thank you for paving my way.

To my parents for welcoming me into this beautiful world. My mother Eliane de Almeida Raschke and my father Edson Riedel (in memory) who did their very best to make me as human as they possibly could during this time on Earth. I see you, I love you (more than you'll ever understand).

To my older brother Walter Riedel Neto for walking side by side with me, without ever stepping on my toes. Respect is the highest form of love. You mean the world to me.

To my younger brother Edson Riedel Jr. and younger sisters Gabriela Riedel and Fernanda Riedel for showing me that half brothers and sisters can be whole. My love for you is real.

To my nephews and nieces for bringing so much love, joy and laughter to my life. I hope you read 'Aunty Carol' when the time is right.

To every person who made it into this book, thank you. I couldn't have imagined better characters.

To all the men I loved in many different ways. Thank you for teaching me that feelings are real and memories can be beautiful.

To all my friends (too many to name) who read and listened to my stories, and encouraged me to widely share them. Thank you for seeing the writer in me before I was ready to see it myself.

To every single employer, business partner and client I ever had, the ones who supported me financially along this crazy, wild, self-funded journey. Thank you, I couldn't have done this without you.

To all the surfers who made the Salomon Masters 2005 an amazing show. Special thanks to the Brazilians Neco Padaratz, Pedro Henrique and Armando Daltro. To Aussie Troy Brooks and Hawaiian Roy Powers. And to the MC for bringing such a high energy to that event.

To all the artists who inspired me with their songs, books, movies, poetry, or any other form of art. All the credits are on the featured songs and movies list in the Bibliography. Your art is medicine to my soul. I couldn't have made it here without your help. I just want to share with the world how much you mean to me and how powerful you all are.

To everyone who sees beauty in humanity and shines a light on it from this subtle subjective perspective of art, I honour you. We need you, more than ever.

My special acknowledgement to James Redfield for his outstanding work in The Celestine Prophecy. I hope to inspire everyone to read (or re-read) your books. They are more relevant than ever. Thank you for being alive and awake at the same time as me. What an honour to watch a wise soul fully expressed through the power of storytelling. Your words changed my life forever.

To Maya Angelou and Elisabeth Gilbert, for showing me how memoirs can change people's lives in very profound ways. Thank you, you made me see writing in a whole new light.

To Brené Brown for helping me to accept how human I am - and being at peace with that. Your courage is truly inspiring. Thank you.

To Sofia Coppola for embodying the creative woman role model. You changed the game for me and so many women.

To nature, for the endless supply of sunrises and sunsets. For the earth who kept holding my ground with all the trees and flowers when everything seemed to be falling apart. To the ocean for reminding me of my own infinity every day.

To all the amazing animals out there who don't require a single word to make their presence felt and powerful. We have so much to learn from you. To all the birds for coming together in flocks to show me that while the flight may be solo, the most beautiful dance happens in the collective.

To every single person on the street. Every image I see and every word I read. To all the diversity out there. Every tiny little thing that ignites my creativity and inspires me to stay alive.

To Leanne Walsh and Louis Kelemen for giving me a home and a family in Melbourne when I needed it most. Thank you for your kindness and generosity. You brought me back to life. Your Brazilian daughter loves you.

To Quinton Li, this bright young writer-editor I met at the Williamstown Literary Festival for accepting the challenge to help a first time writer make her 'dream book' real. Thank you for every word you shared and deleted from my manuscript. You made this story so much better.

Last, but not least, to my spiritual guidance, my higher self and the higher force that orchestrates life as we know it. I believe in it, I live by it. I am here because of it.

To myself, Carolina Luiza Riedel. For never giving up the fight and for always trusting my sweet little voice within despite all external noises.

Thank you life for giving me a chance to make it just in time. It feels good to fully express myself in writing and know that it's enough to be 'just me'.

ABOUT THE AUTHOR

Brazilian born Carolina Luiza Riedel moved to Australia in the early 2000s and spent almost a decade down under. She worked her way up in a very unorthodox career path that led her to becoming officially Australian.

With a degree in Advertising, Carolina held multiple jobs across different industries, until she came to terms that she was not only a multi-passionate creative, but also a risk taker who thrives on the move.

So, when her Brazilian roots called, against all odds, she made her way back and paved a brand new trail where there was nothing left.

After a couple of unfruitful entrepreneurial efforts and attempts to fit back into previous roles, she partnered with a number of designers and delivered a variety of projects as a brand storyteller. This little experiment led to her becoming a full-time partner in a creative studio that blended storytelling and design.

After facing some personal challenges and struggling with grief, Carolina knew it was time to take another risk and step into her real passion: writing.

Now, in her early forties, the Brazilian-Australian storyteller moved back to Melbourne to rewrite her own story.

Her first self-published memoir 'Dream On - and make it happen' is a very raw, honest and human narrative about her first move to Australia and her rollercoaster ride as a creative woman on a mission to create her own life (that she plans on riding for years to come).

www.ingramcontent.com/pod-product-compliance
Lightning Source LLC
Chambersburg PA
CBHW060548080526
44585CB00013B/483